Moreton Morrell Si

Product and Services Management

Product and Services Management

George J. Avlonitis
and
Paulina Papastathopoulou

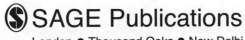

SAGE Publications

London ● Thousand Oaks ● New Delhi

First published 2006

SAGE Publications Ltd
1 Oliver's Yard
55 City Road
London EC1Y 1SP

SAGE Publications Inc.
2455 Teller Road
Thousand Oaks, California 91320

SAGE Publications India Pvt Ltd
B-42, Panchsheel Enclave
Post Box 4109
New Delhi 110 017

British Library Cataloguing in Publication data

A catalogue record for this book is available from the British Library

ISBN-10 1-4129-0864-7   ISBN-13 978-1-4129-0864-1
ISBN-10 1-4129-0865-5   ISBN-13 978-1-4129-0865-8 (pbk)

Library of Congress Control Number: 2005932164

Typeset by C&M Digitals (P) Ltd., Chennai, India
Printed and bound in Great Britain by Athenaeum Press, Gateshead
Printed on paper from sustainable resources

Contents

About the Authors

George J. Avlonitis received his PhD in Marketing from the University of Strathclyde, Scotland, where he lectured for five years. He is Professor of Marketing in the Department of Marketing and Communication at the Athens University of Economics and Business, and Director of both the Athens Laboratory of Research Marketing (A.L.A.R.M.) and the MSc in 'Marketing and Communication with New Technologies' (Executive Programme) of the same department. His primary research, teaching and consulting activities are in the areas of product policy, sales management, industrial marketing, technological innovation and strategic marketing. He has presented various papers in USA, Canada and Europe, and has published more than 90 articles in the proceedings of international conferences, and the most prestigious international scientific journals including *Journal of Marketing, Journal of the Academy of Marketing Science, Industrial Marketing Management, International Journal of Research in Marketing, European Journal of Marketing, Journal of Product Innovation Management*. He is also on the editorial review board of several journals, including *Industrial Marketing Management, Journal of Business Research* and *European Journal of Marketing*.

Paulina Papastathopoulou received her PhD in Marketing from the Department of Management Science and Marketing at the Athens University of Economics and Business in Athens, Greece. She is presently a Lecturer in Marketing at the university. Her work has been published in the proceedings of international conferences and various journals including the *Journal of Product Innovation Management, Industrial Marketing Management, European Journal of Marketing, Journal of Services Marketing* and *Journal of Marketing Management*. Her main research interests pivot on new services development and deletion, adoption and diffusion of new technologies.

Introduction

The **product** is the **raison d'être** of the company and its **sine qua non**. The most important decisions that a company makes and which influence its long-term survival and further development involves the **products provided** and the **markets served**. Only when
these decisions have been made can the company's management decide about a) the
specific product characteristics; b) their price; c) their communication strategy which
will promote the preferred positioning in the selected target-markets; and d) the distribution channels and points of sales which are compatible with the preferred positioning
of the products and the buying behaviour of the selected target-markets.

Any **conscious change** in the company's **product portfolio** as viewed by the buyer
is defined as **product decision**. There is a great variety of possible changes in the company's product portfolio and consequently a great variety of product decisions. At one
extreme there are minor changes such as the modification of a label or colour of the
package, and at the other extreme changes such as diversification into new business
fields either through internal research and development or through mergers and
acquisitions.

In this sense, the evolution of a company's product portfolio is of vital concern to
management because of its strategic implications upon the ability to gain advantage
over competitors, the development and deployment of resources and the achievement
of overall objectives. However, given the rapidly changing technological, competitive,
legal and social environment, the product portfolio must be constantly manipulated to
reflect these changes, if it is to remain in a viable condition. The **manipulation** of the
product portfolio involves the addition of new products, the modification of existing
products and the elimination of products no longer contributing towards the objectives.

Historically, major consideration given to the management of the product portfolio
by practitioners and scholars has focused on the development of new products, under-
estimating, in a sense, equally important product decisions such as the rejuvenation or
deletion of existing products.

The **objective of this book** is to provide a complete and systematic approach to the
examination of product decisions, covering not only the decisions relating to tangible
products, but also to intangible products or services.

The book provides an **holistic approach** to the study of product and services management. We look at the key milestones within a product's or service's life cycle and consider in detail three crucial product/service-related areas; namely, product/service portfolio
evaluation, new product/service development and product/service elimination.

The three most important features of this book are as follows:

1. It combines two topics that have not been addressed jointly or as extensively in any
   other textbook; namely, new product development and product deletion.
2. It is research-based, presenting and discussing the relevant studies, which have been
   conducted mainly in European and North-American countries.
3. It covers the development and elimination of both manufactured products and
   services.

The first four chapters **introduce** the reader to:

- the product as an economic variable, providing a historical overview of the main product-related concepts and taxonomies (Chapter 1);
- the types of product decisions (Chapter 2);
- the product life cycle model and the related marketing strategies (Chapter 3);
- the various approaches which have been proposed in the literature for the evaluation of product portfolios (Chapter 4).

The next four chapters cover the **development and diffusion** of new products and services by providing an extensive presentation of:

- the new product/service development and portfolio models (Chapter 5);
- the pre-development activities of new products and services (Chapter 6);
- the development, testing and launching of new products and services (Chapter 7);
- the successful adoption and diffusion of new products and services (Chapter 8).

The two chapters thereafter deal with the **elimination process**, focusing on:

- the identification and revitalization of weak products and services (Chapter 9);
- the evaluation of weak products/services and elimination strategies (Chapter 10).

Finally, Chapter 11 presents the **organizational arrangements** for developing, managing and eliminating products and services.

The book includes revealing **mini-cases** that will help students make important connections between theory and practice. The **pedagogical features** in each chapter are:

- chapter introduction;
- summary;
- questions;
- further reading.

Additional material for instructors, including **PowerPoint slides** and **indicative answers** to each chapter's questions, can be found at www.sagepub.co.uk/avlonitis.

Product and Services Management is written for **managers** as well as **undergraduate** and **graduate** students of business administration and marketing who are pursuing courses in marketing management, product portfolio management, new product development and product strategy/policy.

This book could not have been realised without the help of various people. We owe our **sincere thanks** to them. First of all, we would like to thank our students in the undergraduate and postgraduate courses at the Athens University of Economics and Business who contributed to the finalization of the book's content with their critical reasoning and constructive comments. Also, special thanks go to the anonymous reviewers who challenged our thinking and provided critiques and fruitful suggestions that improved the book, our colleague Dr Sandra Cohen for preparing Appendix 1, our secretaries Irene Mavromara and Nana Georgiou for their help, and also Delia Martinez Alfonso, Sharika Sharma and Anne Summers from Sage who, with enthusiasm and systematic work, managed the transformation of the book from the manuscript through to its final format.

George J. Avlonitis
Paulina Papastathopoulou

1 The Product as an Economic Variable

Introduction

The product is the raison d'être of every company. In general, every economic activity revolves around products. A product can be either tangible or intangible. In the case of tangible products we refer to goods, whereas intangible products are usually called services.

Every product reflects the efforts of the company to match its resources with the demands of the market. Although the success or failure is the result of various factors, matching resources with market demands is crucial.

The product is the starting point for the majority of the planned marketing activities of a company. It is impossible to decide about pricing, promotion or distribution channels if the nature and the characteristics of the product are not properly defined. In the long run, the strategic and tactical marketing decisions revolve around the product because this is the main source of revenue for the company.

In this chapter, we address the following questions:

- How does the economics and marketing literature treat the product concept?
- Which are the main product-related concepts?
- Which are the various product classification schemes on the basis of tangibility, durability and use?

Historical overview of the product concept

When reviewing the history of economic activity it becomes apparent that the idea that the product itself was a planned variable, while its sales administered by the seller is of quite recent origin.

This idea is rooted to the concept of differential (competitive) advantage which in turn – being the belief of a consumer that one seller's offering possesses more want satisfaction ability than other sellers' offerings – is rooted in the competition and in the varied needs and wants that exist in the market place.

Up to the 1930s, the concept of differential (competitive) advantage in terms of 'product' is absent in the literature of Economics. Until that time, the price is the basis for competition in the economic system and the consumer has no choice preference for different products under the assumption of homogeneity on both demand and supply side, made by the classical and marginalist economists.

These assumptions remained partially valid until the end of the nineteenth century. By virtue of the mass production techniques brought by the industrial revolution, product homogeneity was probably more of a reality in the eighteenth and nineteenth centuries, when producers had to compete on the basis of price, emphasizing quantity rather than quality or choice.

With the advent of the twentieth century these assumptions were no longer valid. The economic system witnessed a number of changes which brought different bases for competition: variety both in materials and in means of production had started to be introduced at an increasing rate; improved forms of transportation has largely eliminated the security of locational monopolies and has broadened market opportunities which would support more sophisticated production systems; improved means of communication with the market disperse information about the sellers' products and also provided strong incentive for the inclusion of the product in the sellers' 'total offering' (marketing plan).

These concurrent revolutions in production, communication and transportation coupled with the fact that industries become oligopolistic (namely, the supply of products was concentrated in the hands of relatively few sellers) brought forward other non-pricing bases of competition. In the beginning of the twentieth century the more percipient economists had recognized that such changes had taken place and that product differentiation was more typically the basis of competition than was price. This view was crystallized by Robinson (1932) and Chamberlin (1933). Abandoning the assumptions of a homogeneous product, both authors developed the theory of 'monopolistic competition' under which the seller's sales are limited and defined by two more variables in addition to price, namely the nature of the product and advertising outlays.

In Chamberlin's monopolistic competition theory the product is defined as a 'bundle of utilities' in which the physical offering is but one element, and becomes the basis on which a seller can differentiate his offering from that of his competitors. Chamberlin (1957) argues that buyers in the market have a real freedom to differentiate, distinguish, or have specific preferences among the competing outputs of the sellers. This view led to the development of the differential advantage concept, one of the most important concepts in the marketing theory.

Alderson (1965) has attempted to provide the link between the concept of differential advantage and the economy as it actually exists. Alderson has noted that differentiation in a product's characteristics gives a seller control over the product with that exact identity and configuration, supporting the view that 'the seller offering a product different from others actually does occupy a monopoly position in that limited sense'. However, product differentiation can be based on product characteristics such as patented features, trademarks, packaging (for example, design, colour, style) (Alderson, 1965).

It is, however, the existence of varied wants and needs in the market place that allows competition through product differentiation and a policy of differential advantage to be pursued. Alderson asserts that, behind the acceptance of differentiation are differences in taste desires, income, location of the buyers, and the uses of commodities. Smith (1956) also notes that the seller pursues a policy of differential advantage in general, and product differentiation in particular, in order to meet both competitive activities and the various needs and wants in the market place. However, the seller can pursue a policy of product differentiation, either by offering the same product throughout the whole market and secure a measure of control over the product's demand by advertising and promoting differences between his/her product and the product's of competing sellers, or by viewing the market as a number of small homogeneous markets (market segments) each having different product differences and adjusting the product and the elements surrounding its sale according to the requirements of each market segment.

The seller who adopts the latter method in pursuing a policy of product differentiation, is actually pursuing a policy of market segmentation.

However, a policy of differential advantage must be dynamic in nature since the seller must continually adjust his/her 'total offering', to match the ever changing competitive activities and customers' 'motivation mixes' in the market place. Naturally, such adjustments alter the seller's cost structure and profitability. The seller therefore must be constantly engaged in creating a 'total offering' from all the elements under his/her control, in a way that will give differential advantage and profitability. This 'axiom' has led to the development of the marketing mix concept.[1]

Despite the fact that the product variable is central in the marketing literature, the competitive theory of the firm based on the theory of microeconomics emphasizes the price as the predominant variable under the seller's control.

Undell (1968) was the first to carry out research to test the hypothesis that non price-related facets of competitive strategy are at least as important as pricing from the seller's point of view. According to his findings, the sales effort or marketing communication including advertising and other promotional programs was perceived first in importance, product effort including product planning, product R&D and the services accompanying the product was perceived second, while pricing ranked third.

In the light of Undell's research results, it could be wise to agree with Wentz, Eyrich and Stevenson (1973) who argue that 'prior to the twentieth century price was the main instrument of competition and the primary weapon for the destruction of competing firms. Today the product play this role ...'.

A different version of the importance of product variable is given by Thompson (1962) who asserts that, 'the two most important factors in Marketing are a) the product and b) the ultimate consumer (people) ... the obvious objective is to get these two in perfect harmony ... if this situation does not exist which of the two major elements is the easiest to change: product or people?' He then proceeds to state that, although companies can rather easily change products, they cannot change people, but simply influence them. It is actually easier to identify 'what people want and to supply it than it is to influence them to want what you make'. The author's conclusive remark is that, the most important controllable factor in marketing is the product.

Main product-related concepts

The recognition of the importance of the 'product' variable in the Marketing literature has driven many marketing scholars in the development of a number product-related concepts as well as various product classifications.

In the remainder of the chapter we turn our attention to these concepts and classifications.

Product levels

Levitt (1980) has proposed that the product can be analysed in five distinct levels:

- *Core benefit* – refers to the main benefit the customer buys (for example, the buyer of a vehicle purchases 'transportation').
- *Basic product* – refers to the basic characteristics or attributes of the product, without which there is no product (for example, tyres of a car).
- *Expected product* – refers to the characteristics of the product that the customer takes for granted (for example, tyres in a good condition).

- *Augmented product* – refers to the product characteristics that surpass the customer's expectations (for example, road assistance).
- *Potential product* – refers to those characteristics that could be added to the product in the future and offer customer delight.

Nowadays, companies are competing at the augmented product level. In other words, they try to differentiate their offerings by providing product characteristics that are beyond the expected functional features. An extensive discussion of the augmented product is provided in Chapter 2.

Product hierarchy

According to Kotler (2003), product hierarchy comprises the following five categories:

- *Need family* – the basic need underlying the existence of a product family (for example, security).
- *Product family* – all the product classes that can satisfy a basic need effectively (for example, savings and income).
- *Product class or category* – a group of products within a product family (for example, investment products).
- *Product line* – a group of products within a product class, which are closely related because they are targeted to the market, through the same distribution channels or are priced within a specific range (for example, investment accounts).
- *Product type* – a group of items within a product line that function in a similar manner (for example, capital guaranteed accounts).
- *Brand* – the name of a product (for example, Dunbar Bank).
- *Item* – a unit within a brand or product line which is distinguished by size, price, or some other characteristic of element (for example, the FTSE 100 index).

Product hierarchy provides the different levels at which a product should be managed. For example, product line management is associated with different decisions compared to brand management. In Chapter 2, we address such product-related issues in more detail.

Product life cycle

One of the most important product-related concepts is the product life cycle (PLC). This concept can be illustrated as a curve in a diagram in which the horizontal axis represents time, while the vertical axis portrays sales/profits of the product. Typically, the product life cycle curve is S – shaped, as presented in Figure 1.1.

This curve is divided into four successive stages namely, introduction, growth, maturity and decline. The PLC model is useful mainly as a framework for developing effective marketing strategies in different stages of the life cycle of both physical goods and services. Some leading experts who view the PLC model as the foundation of marketing strategy have made a number of suggestions regarding the marketing implications that each stage has for marketing action. Their suggestions for each stage can be summarized as follows:

Introduction stage

During the *introduction stage* of the product life cycle the product is relatively unknown, sales volume rises slowly but the expenses involved in communicating the availability

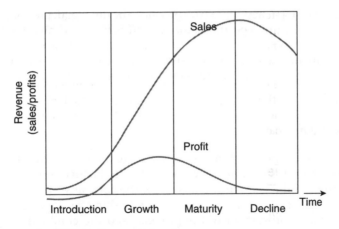

Figure 1.1   **The product life cycle concept**

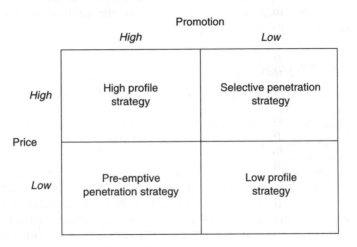

Figure 1.2   **Introductory marketing strategies**

of the product as well as the expenses of establishing channels of distribution are high and consequently little or no profits are realized despite the fact that price is on the high side.

In introducing a new product (line), management should offer a limited number of models with modular design to permit the flexible addition of variants to satisfy new segments as soon as they are identified. Quality and quality control is highly important during this stage. If price and promotion are considered together management has to select between four alternative strategies at this stage (Figure 1.2): first, a high profile strategy which consists of introducing a new product with a high price and a high promotion level, secondly, a low profile strategy which consists of introducing the new product with a low price and low level of promotion, thirdly, a selective penetration strategy which consists of high price and low promotion and fourthly, a pre-emptive penetration strategy which consists of low price and heavy promotion. The basic factors that management has to consider in selecting any of these four strategies are: first, the market size, secondly, the market awareness about the product, thirdly, the degree of price sensitivity in the market, fourthly, the type and nature of competition, fifthly, the company's cost structure.

As far as distribution is concerned it should be intensive and extensive with introductory deals and logistics weighted heavily towards customer service and heavy inventories at all levels.

Growth stage

If the product gains acceptance, it moves into a stage of more rapid sales, known as the *growth stage*, because of the cumulative effect of introductory promotion, distribution and word-of-mouth influence. During this stage, the company's profits increase.

At this stage, management should focus on best selling versions, the addition of few related models, the improvement of the product, and the elimination of unnecessary specifications with little market appeal. As far as pricing is concerned management should focus on the market broadening and promotional pricing opportunities. Promotion should shift the emphasis from building product awareness to nurturing product preference. Distribution should be intensive and extensive with the addition of new distribution channels to gain additional product exposure.

Maturity stage

If the product has achieved the market acceptance associated with the growth stage, it might be expected that competition would enter the market. If price was not crucial at the beginning the advent of competition would lead to a reduction of prices. During the *maturity stage* sales cease to grow exponentially and they tend to stabilize and the gross margin may be reduced.

During this stage, which lasts much longer than previous stages, management is facing the most formidable challenges. Most products are in the maturity stage of the life cycle and most of the product decisions (changes in the product's physical configuration and in the augmented product) discussed in the previous section are made at this stage. Management should try to break out of a stagnant sales picture by initiating changes in the product's tangible and intangible characteristics that will attract new users and/or more usage from the current users. Attention should be paid to possibilities for product improvement and cost reduction through changes in the quality features and style of the product. Proliferation of packages, private brands and product services could also bring positive results for the company at this stage.

Price should be reduced as a way of drawing new segments into the market as well as attracting customers of competitive products. Management should also search for incremental pricing opportunities including private branding contracts. Promotion should maintain consumer and trade loyalty and a search for new and brilliant advertising appeal that wins the consumer's attention and favour should be pursued. Another way to attract the consumer's attention at this stage is through heavy incentives programs and many short-term promotions, deals and contests. Distribution should be intensive and extensive as in the previous stages.

When a high proportion of the potential buyers of the product have purchased it and sales settle at a rate governed by the replacement purchases of satisfied buyers, the market may be said to be saturated. Gross margins tend to decline since prices begin to soften as competitors struggle to obtain market share in a saturated market.

Decline stage

Finally, the product reaches the *stage of decline* during which it ceases to be profitable. This may occur because technologically advanced products become available and/or because of changes in the buyers' economic environment and habits.

As the sales of the product decline at this stage, management should either eliminate the product or in the case that it is offered in a number of versions, sizes and models, should eliminate those items, which are not returning a direct profit. However, there are a number of strategies that management could follow to eliminate the product. For instance, it could adopt a concentration strategy in which case it concentrates its resources only in the strongest markets while phasing out promotional and distribution activities as they become marginal and maintaining profit level pricing with complete disregard of any effect on market share. Alternatively, management could follow a milking strategy in which case it sharply reduces its marketing expenses to increase its current profits, knowing that this will accelerate the rate of sales decline and the ultimate demise of the product. If a hard-core loyalty remains strong enough at this stage the product may be marketed at the old or even a higher price, which means good profits.

Product positioning

The term 'positioning' belongs to two advertising executives Al Ries and Jack Trout (1982) and refers to the development of a destined image/position of the product in the mind of the customer. In other words, it has to do with the perceived personality of the product by the customer. In order to understand better the concept of positioning, just wonder how different is the perception you have about a Ferrari and a Daewoo, or Chanel clothes compared to Zara. Product positioning can be based on various dimensions. The perceived position of a product in the customer's mind can be represented graphically in the so-called perceptual map through a process, which is known as perceptual mapping.

Perceptual maps can be designed with multidimensional scaling techniques using empirical data about customer perceptions. More specifically, the process initiates with the identification of the most important dimensions that differentiate products (or brands) from one another. Usually, the positions of products in a market are depicted in two-dimensional or three-dimensional maps, depending on the number of dimensions used (two or three, respectively).

In Figure 1.3 we present a hypothetical perceptual map from the car market, where Ferrari is perceived as high priced and sporty looking, while Peugeot is medium priced and less sporty looking.

Perceptual mapping has various applications, such as:

1 *Identification of important attributes*: which attributes does the customer use for evaluating a specific product class?
2 *Identification of close substitutes-main competitors*: which brands are positioned relatively closely in the perceptual map? To put it differently, which brands are perceived as similar by the customer?
3 *Identification of differentiated brands*: which brands are positioned in relatively isolated parts of the map? In other words, which brands are perceived as different by the customer?

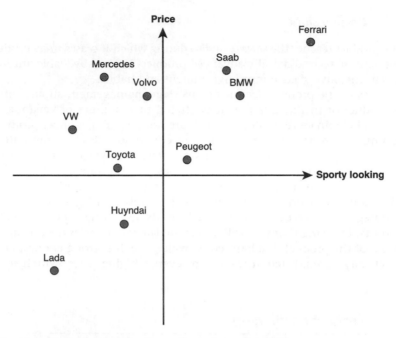

Figure 1.3   **Hypothetical perceptual map from the car market**

4 *Market segmentation*: in a perceptual map different market segments can be illustrated based on the desired combinations of product attributes (for example, car style and performance).
5 *Identification of gaps in the market new product opportunities*: a gap in the market is identified when there is no brand with the desired combination of product attributes. In this case, a company could fill this gap with a new product. It is apparent that perceptual mapping is directly related to the positioning strategy of the company.

The positioning strategies that can be implemented by a company in order to create a distinct product position in the mind of the customer are as follows (Aaker and Shansby, 1982; Wind, 1982):

- Positioning by *attribute*: a specific product characteristic or attribute is emphasized, for example, 'Think small' of the Volkswagen 'Beetle'.
- Positioning by *benefits*: emphasis is given to the benefit provided to the customer, for example, Dentyne Ice: 'Nothing is cooler than ice'.
- Positioning by *price/quality*: the value of money paid by the customer is stressed, for example, 'Good food costs less at Sainsbury's'.
- Positioning by *competitor*: differentiation from competitive offerings is emphasized, for example, 'You have tasted the German beer that's the most popular in America (namely, Lowenbrau). Now taste the German beer that's the most popular in Germany (namely, Beck's)'.
- Positioning by *application*: emphasis is given to the product use, for example, 'Volkswagen announces a bus you really can take anywhere' (for VW Bus Syncro).
- Positioning by *product user*: the profile of the target market is stressed, for example, 'Motrin-for people who don't fool around with pain'.

- Positioning by *product class*: emphasis is given to the creation of a distinct product class, '7UP – The Uncola'.
- *Hybrid* positioning: combination of more than one strategy as long as they act complimentary and they do not create confusion to the customer.

In case a product is totally to the market, without intense competition, the company can more easily choose among the aforementioned positioning strategies. In contrast, when there are other competitive products in the market, the company has to study carefully the positioning of the competition and make sure that it creates a unique position for its product in the mind of the customer.

Despite the efforts of companies to differentiate their products, on many occasions the following mistakes can be made (Kotler, 2003):

- *Underpositioning*: buyers do not understand any difference between the company's brand and competitive brands.
- *Overpositioning*: buyers may have a narrow image of the brand.
- *Confused positioning*: buyers may be confused as to what a brand stands for, usually because of the existence of many different communication messages or the changes of positioning strategies.
- *Doubtful positioning*: buyers may doubt about the claims in view of the product's features, price of distribution, etc.

Sometimes, a company may decide to reposition a product in the market. Repositioning may result from changes in:

- competitors' activities
- customers' needs and wants
- the environment (for example, legislation).

There are two main *repositioning* strategies, namely:

- Repositioning in existing customers, for example, a recent change in the packaging of Pampers, which make them more modern.
- Repositioning in new customers, for example, the classic example of Johnson's baby shampoo for adults who wash their hair on a daily basis or the repositioning of Lucozade which was first positioned as a children's health drink, then it was repositioned as a mid-day 'pick-me-up' drink for mothers and more recently as an energy drink.

Finally, a company may attempt to direct a competitive brand to a worse position. This is called *depositioning*. An increasing number of companies use comparative advertising in order to deposition competitive products. For instance, Tylenol tried to deposition aspirin by running advertisements explaining the negative side effects of aspirin. A more recent example from Greece of such a strategy is provided below.

Ariel v. Skip: the battle of the 'tumblers'

Two major brands of detergents try to deposition one another. The battle started when the advertisement of Skip (a Procter & Gamble detergent) was 'on air' as an answer to an advertisement of Ariel (a Unilever brand).

(Continued)

(Continued)

More specifically, in the Ariel advertisement, the presenter (a popular TV personality) in an attempt to prove that Ariel is superior to competitive products, took two tumblers, filled one with water and a small quantity of Ariel, while the other was filled with water and a competitive product. Next, he added a small piece of cloth, stained with chocolate ice cream in each tumbler and shook both. When the two pieces of cloth were presented on a counter, it became obvious that the stain on the cloth washed in the Ariel mixture had vanished, while the other stain washed with the competitive detergent had not been removed completely.

In attempt to deposition Ariel in the minds of the customers, the Skip advertisement shows a person with a tumbler in his hand saying: 'In the tumbler you can shake whatever you like, but in the washing machine only Skip'. In order to minimize any negative effect, in Ariel's recent advertisement tumblers have been replaced by a washing machine! And the battle goes on.

Product innovativeness

Another important product-related concept refers to the product's degree of innovativeness. Products can be classified in different categories depending on how innovative or new they are. Newness either to the firm and/or to the market can be used, while new product projects may be more or less innovative on a number of dimensions, for example market, technology, managerial practices.

The most popular classification of new products belongs to the consulting firm Booz et al. (1982). Specifically, the following six categories of products have been identified:

- *New-to-the-world products*: products that are first of their kind and they create a new market, for example, Sony Walkman, 3M, post-its.
- *New product lines*: products that are not new to the market, but they are new to the company and they allow it to enter a new market for the first time, for example, the IBM Laserjet printer.
- *Additions to existing product lines*: products that are new to the company, and are added to an existing product line, for example, Coca-Cola Vanilla.
- *Revisions/improvements to existing product lines*: products that replace existing company products, offering better performance or increased perceived value to the customer, for example, Detergents with a 'new and improved' formula.
- *Repositionings*: existing company products that are targeted to a new market; for example, Johnson's Baby Shampoo for adults.
- *Cost reductions*: products that replace existing ones, offering the same benefits at a lower cost.

On the basis of market newness and product newness, Ansoff (1987) identified four different business opportunities that can be pursued using four different types of product development respectively, ranging from new products or markets, through new product lines and product line extensions, to product improvements.

In the early 1990s Wheelwright and Clark (1992) proposed a typology of development projects, or a development map, based on two dimensions first, the degree of change in the product, and secondly, the degree of change in the manufacturing process. Five distinct types have emerged:

1 Breakthrough projects imply fundamental changes to existing products and processes. These projects often incorporate radically new technologies or materials and require revolutionary manufacturing processes.
2 Platform projects refer to the creation of new product lines. They symbolize the degree of product-market differentiation and diversification the company aims at.
3 Derivative projects are characterized by incremental changes, both from a product and a process perspective. They range from cost-reduction versions of existing products to improvements of an existing production process.
4 Research and advanced development projects lie outside the development map, and refer to the creation of know-how and know-why of new materials and technologies that could ultimately be translated into a commercial offering.
5 Alliances and partnership projects are also not included in the development map. They can be formed to pursue any type of project, R&D, breakthrough, platform or derivative.

The authors conclude that all five development categories are very important if the organization is to respond to the market. Each projects plays its role in creating and/or sustaining a competitive advantage. Therefore, companies must create a balanced product portfolio that includes a mixture of these different project types.

Based on the typology of Booz et al. (1982), Cooper and Kleinschmidt (1993) seven classes of new product types can be distinguished, namely:

- True innovations: a totally new product for the world that created an entirely new market.
- Totally new products for the world, but for which there was an existing market.
- Totally new products for the company, but which offered new features vs. competitive products in an existing market.
- New product lines for the company, but which competed against fairly similar products in the market.
- New items in an existing product line for the company which were sold into an existing market.
- Significant modifications of existing company products.
- Fairly minor modifications of existing company products.

Finally, combining the degree to which technology is new to the company or it is applied in a new way and the extent to which the innovation is based on an existing product, Crawford (1997) described three types of innovations, which are first, pioneering, that refers to first-to-market products, secondly, adaptation that is product improvement, and thirdly, imitation or emulation that refer to me-too products.

The categories of innovativeness do not differ considerably in the case of services. More specifically, Gadrey et al. (1995) have observed four types of financial service innovations, namely:

- innovations in service products which refer to totally new-to-the-market services;
- architectural innovations which bundle or un-bundle existing service products;
- innovations which result from the modification of an existing service product, and
- innovations in processes and organization for an existing service product.

Recently, the authors of this book combined fourteen dimensions of innovativeness and constructed a typology of new service innovativeness that consists of six types of financial service innovations (Avlonitis et al. 2001). These six types could be conceptualized as representing a continuum depending on the degree of innovativeness that characterizes each type (Figure 1.4). At the most innovative extreme of the continuum

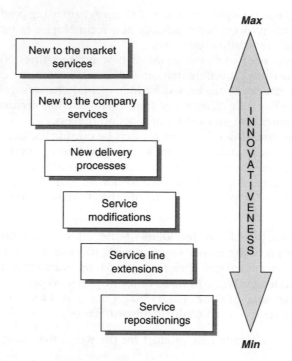

Figure 1.4   **Service innovativeness categories**

the new-to-the-market services are placed; at the least innovative end, the service repositionings can be found. In between, the remaining four types could be classified (starting from the most to the least innovative type) as follows: new-to-the-company services, new delivery processes, service modifications, and service line extensions.

Product classification schemes

The existence of millions of different products in the market has led to various classification schemes, just like biology classifies all living creatures. The classification of products is essential because of the different categories of products aiming at different target markets and the fact that the marketing strategy for each market depends on how the product is classified.

The classification schemes that have been proposed in the literature are based on a number of basic characteristics, such as tangibility (tangible vs. intangible), durability (durable vs. non-durable), and use (consumers vs. industrial).

Product tangibility

Depending on their degree of tangibility/intangibility products are classified as tangible or intangible. Tangible products are also called goods, while intangible products are referred to as services.

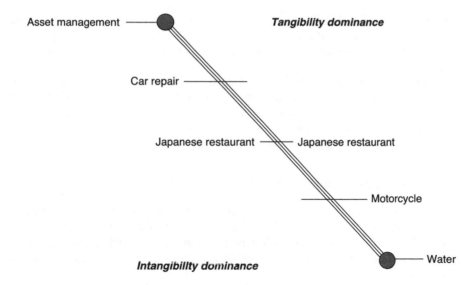

Figure 1.5   **Intangibility versus tangibility dominance**

Apart from intangibility, services as opposed to goods have three more distinct characteristics:

- Inseparability of service: production and consumption. For example, the 'production' of a trip on the train which cannot be separated from its 'consumption' by the customer.
- Heterogeneity of service: for example, room service in a hotel is offered somewhat differently depending on the person providing service.
- Perishability of service: for example, a free seat on a flight from Amsterdam to Glasgow cannot be added to the seats available on the next flight to the same destination. It is lost forever.

It is apparent that the basic characteristic of services is intangibility, while the degree to which the other three characteristics exist stems from intangibility per se. In Figure 1.5 we present examples of products on the basis of tangibility or intangibility dominance. For example, water is highly tangible, whereas asset management is highly intangible.

Product durability

Depending on their durability, products can be classified as durables and non-durables. Durables are products that satisfy a certain need for a long period of time (for example, refrigerators, machine tools). Non-durables or fast moving consumer goods (FMCG) are products that satisfy a need once (for example, refreshments, pasta).

Product use

One of the most common and widely used classification of products is between consumer (B2C) and industrial (B2B). Consumer products are bought from individuals in order to satisfy personal and family needs, while industrial products are bought from companies or organizations in order to be used as an input for the production of other products (for example, raw materials), for company use or sale to other companies.

Certainly, many products can be seen as consumer as well as industrial. Let us take, for example, a car. When a car is bought from an individual for personal or family use, then it is a consumer product. On the contrary, when it is bought as a company car, then it is an industrial product. This is to say that, characterizing a product as consumer or industrial depends on who buys it and for what reason.

Types of consumer products

Historically, one of the most widely accepted classification of products has been proposed by Copeland back in 1923. He proposed a three-fold classification: *convenience goods, shopping goods and specialty goods,* based on consumer buying habits. Although his concern was with consumer goods his scheme may be easily generalized to include industrial goods as well.

Convenience goods are those for which the consumers will not spend much money or time in purchasing them nor does the customer perceive significant levels of risk in making a selection. Examples of consumer goods that fall into the convenience category include fresh produce and grocery staples, umbrellas, chewing-gum and batteries. Supplies and raw materials, which are commodities could be classified as convenience items for industrial buyers.

Shopping goods as the name implies are those for which the buyers are willing to spend a significant amount of time and money in searching for and evaluating these products. Increased levels of risk are also perceived for these high involvement products. Example of shopping goods include vehicles, clothing and furniture for end consumers and equipment and component parts for industrial users.

Specialty goods are 'unique' in some regard and require special effort in terms of both money and time for their acquisition. Comments such as '[I would] wait for weeks' 'not settle for anything else' are good indicators of the time and effort that distinguishes specialty products. Examples of specialty products include rare vintage imported wines, expensive sports cars and paintings by well-known artists. In the industrial sector, installations (buildings) would be specialty products because their location, cost and furnishings require great organizational effort and risk.

Holbrook and Howard (1976) made a major contribution to the study of goods classification by proposing a fourth category, *preference goods,* which involve low shopping effort and low ego involvement, but high brand preference. This four-product category classification was adopted by Murphy and Enis (1986). Building on the works of Copeland and Holbrook and Howard, they developed an integrated product classification scheme consisting of the four aforementioned product categories defined in terms of the effort and risk dimensions of price as perceived by both organizational and ultimate consumers. According to the authors, their proposed product classification scheme provides a managerial road map for strategy development: buyers' perceptions, marketers' objectives and basic strategy and specific strategies for each element of the marketing-mix. Table 1.1 presents certain marketing implications of the scheme proposed by Murphy and Enis.

The product classification schemes suggested in the literature and the one discussed here, indicate that the classification of products, can form the foundation for building a meaningful marketing strategy. However, the managers who attempt to devise a

Table 1.1   Marketing implications examples of Murphy and Enis's product classification

Product category	Buyer behaviour	Marketer's objective	Product strategy	Promotion strategy
		Marketing issue		
Convenience	Impulse or habit	Move to preference, or shopping, or dominate via low cost	Standard grades and quantities, quality control, innovations copied quickly	Point-of purchase, some sales promotion
Preference	Routine	Brand loyalty	Standard grades and quantities, quality control, some R&D	Mass advertising, sales promotion, some personal selling
Shopping	Limited	Source or store loyalty	Standard base, many options, much R&D, warranties	Personal selling, some advertising
Specialty	Extensive	Source and brand loyalty	Custom design, much R&D, warranties, personalised service	Publicity, personal selling, testimony

Source: adapted from Murphy and Enis (1986)

workable marketing strategy as a function of product classification should be aware of certain deficiencies inherent in this approach.

First, neither every product nor every marketing variable fits precisely into the suggested framework since the classification of products in the suggested groups will vary between different individual customers, groups of customers, and even geographical markets. This indicates how important it is to analyse market opportunities and target markets before developing a marketing strategy to appeal to that particular market. Second, the classification of products is, like all marketing, dynamic and, therefore, a product once considered in a particular group may not stay in that group indefinitely. This is because of changes that occur in the buyer's economic environment and habits, in the performance of basic marketing variables, and in other environmental conditions. These changes in turn affect the market demand of the product as well as the composition of the marketing mix that supports it.

The fact that the product's position, and even its concept, can be expected to change over time, led to the development of the product life cycle model as a framework for the selection of meaningful marketing strategies.

Types of industrial products

Depending on how they enter the production process, as well as the cost structure of the buying organization, individual products and services can be classified in various categories.

According to Kotler (1997), industrial products and services can be classified into three distinct groups:

1 *Entering goods*: they comprise raw materials and manufactured materials and parts that enter the manufacturer's product completely. Raw materials can be either farm products (for example, cotton, fruit) or natural products (for example, crude oil). Manufactured materials and parts are further divided into two groups: component

materials (for example, yarn, cement) which are processed further, and component parts (for example, batteries, engines) which enter the finished product with a slight or even no further change in form.

2   *Foundation goods*: they refer to capital items that are long-term investments facilitating the development and management of finished products. There are two types of foundation goods, namely installations and equipment. Installations are major purchases and comprise buildings and large mechanical equipment, while equipment consists of portable factory equipment and tools (for example, lift trucks) and office equipment (for example, notebooks, printers, desks).

3   *Facilitating goods*: they consist of supplies and business services, which are necessary for the smooth operation of every company. Supplies, which are not part of the product, can be further divided into first, operating supplies such as stationery and lubricants, and secondly, maintenance and repair items, like for instance, detergents and nails. Moreover, business services fall into two main classes: maintenance and repair services (for example, photocopier repair), which are usually provided on a contractual basis, and business advisory services (for example, accountancy, legal).

Another useful classification of industrial product is provided by Shapiro (1977), who divides industrial products into the following four types:

- *Proprietary of catalogue products*: these products are offered with certain specifications, are standardized and are produced to satisfy future orders.
- *Custom-built products*: these products are offered as a group of basic units with a large number of extras, which are customized to the buying needs of the customer. For example, a weighting system can have certain standard units (for example, weights) and a number of optional units (for example, electronic indicators), which are custom-made.
- *Custom-designed products*: these products are designed to meet the needs of just one or a limited number of customers. Sometimes, such products are unique, for example a certain type of machine tool or an energy production factory. In other occasions, products are produced in batches, as in the case of aircraft for example, Boeing 757s which were specially designed for Easyjet.
- *Industrial services*: as discussed earlier, these services comprise maintenance, repair, consulting services, and so on.

Summary

- Products are central assets in creating leading enterprises. They can be either tangible or intangible. In the case of tangible products we refer to goods, whereas intangible products are usually called services.
- The product idea is rooted in the concept of differential competitive advantage, which recognizes that customer demand is not homogeneous and thus, price is not the only basis for competition.
- Differentiation in a product's characteristics can take various forms such as functional features, trademarks, packaging, quality, style or product services.
- There exist four important product related concepts, namely levels of product, product hierarchy, product life cycle, product positioning.
- Products can be classified on the basis of tangibility, durability and use.

Questions

1 Give one example for each of the five levels of a product from the fast food market.
2 Select four products that you have used during the last month and try to identify their type of product innovativeness.
3 Think of three brands from the beverages industry and describe their positioning strategy.
4 Select two products, one convenience and one specialty and describe three differences in terms of their product strategy.

Notes

1 The idea can be traced to James Culliton (1948) who described the marketing administrator as a 'decider' or 'artist' – 'a mixer of ingredients'.

References

Aaker, D. and Shansby, G. (1982) 'Positioning your product', *Business Horizons,* May–June: 56–62.
Alderson, W. (1965) *Dynamic Marketing Behavior.* Homewood, IL: R.D. Irwin Inc.
Ansoff, I. (1987) *Corporate Strategy.* Harmondsworth, Middlesex: Penguin.
Avlonitis, G., Papastathopoulou, P. and Gounaris, S. (2001) 'An empirically-based typology of product innovativeness for new financial services: success and failure scenarios', *Journal of Product Innovation Management,* 18, pp. 324–42.
Booz, Allen and Hamilton (1982) *New Products Management for the 1980s.* New York: Booz, Allen and Hamilton.
Chamberlin, E.H. (1933) *The Theory of Monopolistic Competition.* Cambridge, MA: Harvard University Press.
Chamberlin, E.H. (1957) *Towards a More General Theory of Value.* Oxford University Press.
Cooper, R. and Kleinschmidt, E. (1993) 'Major new products: what distinguishes the winners in the chemical industry', *Journal of Product Innovation Management,* 10: 90–111.
Copeland, M. (1923) 'The relations of consumer buying habits to marketing methods', *Harvard Business Review,* 1: 282–9.
Crawford, M. (1997) *New Products Management.* Homewood, IL: Richard D. Irwin, Inc.
Culliton, J.W. (1948) *The Management of Marketing Costs.* Boston: Harvard University.
Gadrey, J., Gallouj, F. and Weinstein, O. (1995), 'New modes of innovation: How services benefit industry', *International Journal of Service Industry Management,* 6(3): 4–16.
Holbrook, M.B. and Howard, J.A. (1976) 'Frequently purchased nondurable goods and services' in Robert Ferber (ed.), *Selected Aspects of Consumer Behaviour.* Washington, DC: National Science Foundation, pp.189–222.
Kotler, P. (1997) *Marketing Management: Analysis, Planning, Implementation and Control,* 9th edition, Englewood Cliffs, NJ: Prentice Hall.
Kotler, P. (2003) *Marketing Management: Analysis, Planning, Implementation and Control,* 11th edition, Englewood Cliffs, NJ: Prentice Hall.
Levitt, T. (1980) 'Marketing success through differentiation – of anything', *Harvard Business Review,* January–February: 83–91.
Murphy, P.E. and Enis, B.M. (1986) 'Classifying products strategically', *Journal of Marketing,* 50(3): 24–43.
Ries, A. and Trout, J. (1982) *Positioning: The Battle for Your Mind.* New York: Warner Books.
Robinson, J. (1932) *The Economics of Imperfect Competition.* London: Macmillan.
Shapiro, B. (1977) *Industrial Product Policy: Managing the Existing Product Line.* Cambridge, MA: Marketing Science Institute.
Smith, W.R. (1956) 'Product differentiation and market segmentation as alternative marketing strategies', *Journal of Marketing,* 21 (July): 4.
Thompson, H.U. (1962) *Product Strategy.* London: Business Publication Ltd.

Undell, J.G. (1968) 'Towards a theory of marketing strategy', *British Journal of Marketing*, (Winter): 298–303.

Wentz, W.B., Eyrich, G.I. and Stevenson, D.K. (1973) 'Marketing of Products' in H. Britt (ed.), *Marketing Manager's Handbook*. Chicago, IL: Dartnell Corporation.

Wheelwright, S. and Clark, K. (1992), *Revolutionizing Product Development*. New York: The Free Press.

Wind, Y. (1982) *Product Policy: Concepts, Methods and Strategies*. Reading, MA: Addison-Wesley.

Further reading

Desmet, S., Van Looy, B. and Van Dierdonck, R. (1998) 'The nature of services', in B. Van Looy, R. Van Dierdonck and P. Gemmel (eds), *Services Management: An Integrated Approach*. London: Financial Times Pitman Publishing.

2 Types of Product Decisions

Introduction

We define product decision as every conscious decision made by a company for a product. There are many different such decisions. At one extreme there are such things as a minor modification of the label or colour of the package. At the other extreme, there are such things as diversification into new business fields, either through internal R&D or mergers and acquisitions.

In Figure 2.1, there is a three-fold classification of product decisions:

- What are the decisions that a company should make about the product types?
- What are the decisions that a company should make about the tangible/physical product?
- What are the decisions that a company should make about the intangible/augmented product?

The chapter is concluded with a special section about the product decisions made by service providers.

Decisions about the product types

The decisions about the product types to be offered represent the most critical decisions in determining the future of a company. The management must first decide what products to offer in the market place before other intelligent product decisions pertaining to the product's physical attributes, packaging branding, and so on, can be made.

There are two distinct levels at which such changes take place, namely:

- the product-mix level and
- the product-line level.

The Committee on Definitions of the American Marketing Association has defined product mix as 'the composite of products offered for sale by a firm or business unit'. The same committee has defined product line as 'a group of products that are closely related either because they satisfy a class of need, are used together, are sold to the same customer groups, are marketed through the same type of outlet or fall within a given price range' (Alexander, 1980).

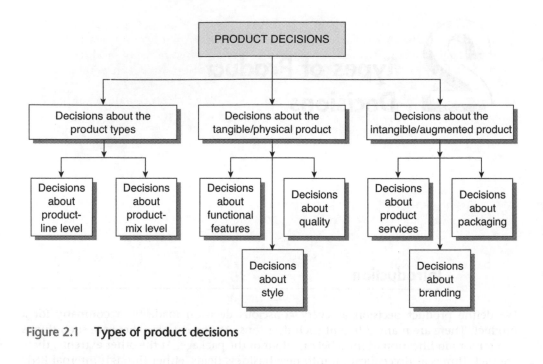

Figure 2.1   **Types of product decisions**

Decisions at a product-mix level

Decisions at the product-mix level represent the highest order decisions made by the company constraining all the subsequent lower order decisions and identifying the business that the company operates.

A company's product mix refers to the total number of products that are offered for sale. The product mix has certain width, length, depth and consistency (Kotler, 2003).

- The *width* of a product mix refers to the total number of different product lines of the company. For example, width = 2 (pasta and pasta sauces).
- The *length* of a product mix refers to the total number of brands in all of the company's product lines. For example, length = 5 (three pasta brands and two brands of pasta sauce).
- The *depth* of a product mix refers to the average number of variants of the company's products. For example, depth = 4 (three pasta brands, each marketed in two sizes: $3 \times 2 = 6$ and 2 pasta sauce brands, each marketed in 1 size: $2 \times 1 = 2$ means $6 + 2 = 8/2 = 4$).
- The *consistency* of a product mix refers to how closely related are the company's product lines in terms of characteristics, production process, distribution channels to name just a few.

Product decisions at the product-mix level tend to determine the *width* of a company's product mix. The basic product-policy/strategy issues at the product-mix level cluster around the following questions:

1 Which product categories should we offer? Will we function primarily as a supplier of materials and components or as a manufacturer of end products?
2 What are the groups and classes of customers for which our products are intended to serve?

3 Do we seek to serve our markets as full-line suppliers or limited line specialists? Closely allied to this is the degree of custom manufacturing to meet the needs of individual buyers versus quantity production of a limited range of product types.
4 Will we attempt to take a position of technical leadership or will we achieve greater success as a follower?
5 What are the business characteristics (criteria) such as target rate of profit, payback period on investment, minimum sales volume, etc., that each product line must meet in order to be included in the product mix (portfolio)?

The answers to the foregoing questions tend to form the company's general product policy, which will guide management in making decisions pertaining to the *addition or elimination of product lines* from the company's product mix. In adding new product lines management has to decide about the type and the nature of the product lines as well as the ways that these lines should be added to the mix. The decision to add new product lines to the mix is ordinarily described as *diversification* and it can be materialized through internal R&D, licensing, merger and acquisitions, joint ventures or alliances.

We may distinguish between related and unrelated diversification (Aaker, 1992). Related diversification provides the potential to obtain synergies by the exchange or sharing of skills or resources associated with any functional area such as marketing, production or R&D. Delta, a large Greek dairy products company, successfully introduced a new line of beverages exploiting synergies in distribution, marketing, brand name recognition and image.

Unrelated diversification lacks commonality in markets, distribution channels, production technology or R&D. The objectives are therefore mainly financial, to manage and allocate cash flow, to generate profit streams that are either larger, less uncertain or more stable than they would otherwise be. For example, tobacco firms like Philip Morris and Reynolds have used their cash flows to buy firms like General Foods, Nabisco and Del Monte, in order to provide alternative core earning areas in case the tobacco industry is crippled by effective anti-smoking programmes.

However, companies are also involved in contracting their product mixes through the elimination of product lines. Decisions are made about identifying, evaluating and specifying which product lines are to be removed from the market. If a company continues to devote time, money and effort to a product line that no longer satisfies customers, then the productive operations of marketing are not as efficient and effective as they should be. The procedure of eliminating product lines from the company's product mix is called *divestment* or *divestiture* and unlike the addition of product lines (diversification) is final with no alternatives.

However, there are various ways that a product line can be eliminated. For instance, a company may decide to harvest the product line by cutting back all support costs to the minimum level that will optimize the product-line performance over its foreseeable limited life, or it may decide to continue manufacturing the product line, but agree with other companies to market it or the company may sell or license the product line to someone else or it may abandon it completely. An extensive discussion of these strategies are provided towards the end of Chapter 3.

Decisions at a product-line level

Important and complex decisions are also made at the product line level, which tend to determine the length of a company's product mix. The basic product policy/strategy issues at the product-line level cluster around the following questions:

1 What is the limit beyond which no product should be added?
2 What is the number of different products to be offered in the line and to what extent should they be differentiated?
3 What is the number of different versions (models) to be offered for each product in the line?
4 What are the business criteria (for example, minimum profitability, minimum sales volume) that each product must meet in order to be included in the line?
5 In how many segments should we compete in order to maintain a secure overall cost and market position vis-à-vis competitors?
6 Should we keep in the line unprofitable products in order to keep a customer happy or should we let the competitors have them?

In close relation to the company's product-line policy is the company's design policy. The formulation of a design policy may aim at:

1 Giving attention to innovation, high quality and reliable performance, to allow each product in the line to be differentiated from its competitors.
2 Making the products compatible with the needs, emotional and rational, of the customer.
3 Achieving variety reduction of the range of product types in the line, and a simplification of the design and construction, to secure reduction in overheads and inventories.
4 Replacing expensive materials and those production processes requiring skilled labour to bring about savings in production costs.

The number and the types of products, which comprise a product line, are the result of decisions at this particular level. Decisions at the product-line level imply either the extension of the line through the addition of new products (for example, Coca-Cola with lemon, Baileys with coffee), or the contraction of the line through the elimination of products, or the replacement of existing products with new and improved ones. The products that are added, eliminated or replaced in the product line might be either versions of existing products, models, sizes and the like – or product types that make up the product line.

In particular, product line extension can be made in two forms (Kotler, 2003):

- *Line stretching* occurs when the company stretches its product line beyond its current range. In this respect, when a company serves the upper market, it can stretch its line *downward* by offering a new product in a lower price/quality (for example, Mercedes Benz in cooperation with Swatch launched Smart). By contrast, companies that serve the lower end of the market can make an *upward* stretch of their line by offering a new product in a higher price/quality (for example, Toyota introduced Lexus). Alternatively, when a company targets its products in the middle market, it can stretch its line both ways.
- *Line filling* occurs when new products are added to a company's present line for reasons like establishing an image of a full-line company, taking advantage of excess capacity, filling gaps in the market and discouraging competitive actions. For instance, there are various Kinder chocolate products in the market, such as Kinder Milk Chocolate, Kinder Bueno, Kinder Delice, Kinder Chocolate Eggs and Kinder Happy Hippo. Keeping both products in the company's portfolio can be quite successful, as long as they are targeted to different segments and do not result in customer confusion and product cannibalization.

Product cannibalization can be caused when a new product introduced by a company in the market takes sales out of an existing company product. According to McGrath (2001), cannibalization is unfavourable, particularly for market leaders, when, first the new product will contribute less to profits, secondly, the economics of the new product might be unfavorable, thirdly, the new product will require significant retooling, fourthly the new product has greater technical risks.

Despite the aforementioned negative aspects of cannibalization, it can well be a planned action as part of an attacker's product strategy. Deliberate cannibalization can be implemented using two main strategies:

1 Cannibalizing an existing market to attack the market leader: This strategy is suitable for attacking an entrenched market leader. In this case, the attacker can introduce its product using a different distribution channel (for example, offer a new bank loan through the Internet, instead of the traditional bank branch). Although the attacker cannibalizes its own product, it also erodes the position of the dominant company. Since the attacker has less to lose than the leader, it hopes to compensate for its losses with increased market share in the redefined market.
2 Introducing a new technology first: this strategy is common in high-technology industries where the market leader has an increased interest in maintaining the existing technology as long as possible. Using this strategy, the attacker can leapfrog the market leader by motivating the existing customers to replace their brand with a superior brand (namely, new technology).

Decisions about the tangible/physical product

The decisions about the product types offered at the product-mix and product-line levels imply mainly the addition or elimination of products, and represent as we have already seen, the extreme and most complex types of product decisions.

However, companies are also engaged in relatively less complex decisions, which imply the addition, elimination and modification of the products' specifications and physical attributes.

Since products have a multitude of specifications and physical attributes there is almost an unlimited number of ways that products can be changed. Nevertheless, *quality, functional features*, and *style*, are the typical dimensions along which decisions are made. These types of product decisions may result in new and improved products, which are either added to the product line, or replace existing products in the line and consequently they are intimately tied up with the product-line decisions.

Product quality

In formulating a product quality policy, management must answer the following questions:

1 What level of quality should the company offer compared with what is offered by the competitors?
2 How wide a range of quality should be represented by the company's offerings?
3 How frequently and under what circumstances should the quality of a product (line) be altered?
4 How much emphasis should the company place on the quality in its sales promotion?
5 How much risk of product failure should the company take in order to be first with some basic improvements in product quality?

Quality stems from manufacture, design or processing, and its basic dimensions are reliability and durability. Altering the materials from which the product is made and/or changing the way the materials are configured can vary both reliability and durability. A company may realize that it can make a real gain from its competitor by increasing the quality of its product and launching the new and improved product. Decisions of offering products with a higher quality may also be linked to a policy of trading up.

However, an increase in the quality usually means higher costs and although the relationship between level of quality and cost can usually be reflected in the company's cost function, the explicit relationship between demand and quality is far more elusive. The estimation of the elasticity of demand with respect to quality is a difficult exercise. In addition, the more durable the product is, the longer the time before it must be replaced.

The importance of the replacement market has suggested to some companies the intentional design and manufacture of less durable products. In this instance, a company decreases the quality of the product so it will wear out physically (physical obsolescence) within a reasonably short period of time. It follows, therefore, that a company's product quality policy is clearly related to its design and induced obsolescence policies.

The functional features of a product

Another set of decisions revolves around the functional characteristics of the product. The selection of functional features depends very much on the company's design policy, which should give answers to the following questions:

1 What specific product features should be developed and made ready for the next product change?
2 Which of our competitors' product changes should we copy?
3 Should we hold back certain new product features – and which ones – for possible slowdown in sales?
4 What product features should our company emphasize?

Functional features can make the product more attractive to customers. Functional features modification has several competitive advantages and may assist the company, among other things, to find new applications for its product. The rate at which new functional features are adopted depends on the ability of the customer to discern differences in performance as well as on the company's induced obsolescence policy. Significant improvements as measured by technical standards create functional or technological obsolescence.

The style of the product

Finally, another set of decisions relating to a product's physical configuration involves style decisions, which aim at improving the aesthetic appeal of the product rather than its functional performance. Decisions about style may render a product 'different' in terms of its functional capacity and quality level. Style decisions again depend on the company's design and induced obsolescence policies. For example, frequent changes in style can make a product out of date and thus increase the replacement market. This is called style or psychological obsolescence and intends to make a person feel out of date if he/she continues to use it. However, despite the fact that style changes can be extremely effective for a company, they contain a significant element of risk. To start with, style decisions are usually thoroughgoing; companies tend to eliminate the old style by introducing the new one and therefore they risk losing some of the customers who liked the old style in the hope of gaining a large number of customers who like the new one. Moreover, styling is usually not as flexible as functional features. Style can be adopted or dropped quickly but it usually cannot be made optional as easily as functional features. With functional features it is often possible to fit features to satisfy the requirements of specific market segments; with styling it is usually more difficult to predict what kind of people will prefer the new style.

Decisions about the intangible/augmented product

Customers usually seek more from a product than the performance of some specific tangible function. The tendency to attach a lot of emphasis to the physical product as a basis for customer appeal might have severe consequences for the manufacturer. Management has become more cognizant in recent years of the fact that distinction between the physical characteristics of competing products and their performance efficiency has diminished, and the period of exclusive advantage in the product's physical qualities has been shortened, and as such seeks to develop innovations in areas external to the physical product. The recognition of the fact that characteristics other than the physical ones assist a company to gain a comparative advantage led to the development of the 'augmented product' concept. *Augmented product* is the physical product along with the whole cluster of services that accompany it. Put another way, it is the totality of benefits that the buyer receives or experiences in obtaining the physical product. It is more the development of the right augmented product rather than the development of the right physical product that distinguish a company's product from those of competitors. According to Levitt (1969) the competition of product augmentation is not competition between what companies produce in their factories but between what they add to their factory output in the form of packaging, services, advertising, customer advice, finance, delivery arrangements, and other things that people value.

In the same context, Blois (1990) argues that 'in an attempt to ensure that their product is not regarded as a "commodity" undifferentiated from their competitors' products, firms will seek ways of augmenting their product – that is adding goods or services to the product over and above what the customer had come to expect'.

As far as the product variable is concerned, the key characteristics external to the physical product that offer a company means of achieving a competitive plus are:

1 branding,
2 packaging and
3 product services.

Branding

A brand is a name, sign, symbol or design or a combination of them which is intended to identify the goods or services of one manufacturer or group of manufacturers and to differentiate them from those of competitors.

Branding has its roots in ancient times. According to Nilson (2000) the first example of branding is found in the manufacture of oil lamps on the Greek islands thousands of years ago. Apparently it was impossible to distinguish between a good and a bad lamp at the time of purchase. However, craftsmen on one Greek island produced a better, more long-lasting lamp as they were either more efficient, or had better clay. So, they started to mark their lamps with a special symbol to differentiate it from competitive oil lamps. However, 'brand' as a term is originated in the Old Norse word *brandr*, which means 'to burn'; this was how owners of livestock marked their animals to identify them (Vaid, 2003).

The more the products in the market have reached a plateau of similarity, the greater is the need for branding to achieve distinction; this applies equally to both industrial and consumer goods. Branding decisions can be either strategic or tactical.

Strategic branding decisions

Management should make some more fundamental policy or strategic decisions pertaining to branding. Some of the questions to be answered in formulating a branding strategy include the following:

First, should we establish our own brand names or should we engage exclusively in reseller brands (private labels or own label brands)?

This question is considered highly by medium-sized companies, which due to limited resources and specialized knowledge, prefer in many cases to sell their products without their own brand. However, it is important to bear in mind, that notwithstanding the increased resources needed for establishing a brand in the market, there are also considerable benefits such as (Kotler, 2003):

- Branding gives the seller the opportunity to attract a loyal and profitable set of customers. Brand loyalty gives sellers some protection from competition and greater control in planning their marketing programme.
- Strong brands help build the corporate image, making it easier to launch new brands and gain acceptance by distributors and consumers.
- Branding helps the seller to segment markets. Instead of Lever Brothers selling a simple detergent, it offers many detergent brands, each formulated differently and aimed at specific benefit-seeking segments.
- The seller's brand name and trade mark provide legal protection of unique product features, which competitors are otherwise likely to copy.
- The brand name makes it easier for the seller to process orders and track down problems.

Ideally, a successful brand name becomes identified with the product category, like for instance Aspirin headache reliever, Post-It notes, Jeep vehicles and Tefal pans. However, this is not desirable when the customer refers to this specific brand but s/he prefers a competitive one (for example, s/he wants to buy a Jeep-type of car, but at the end of the day s/he chooses a Land Rover).

A concept, which is quite important in evaluating a brand's success, is the so-called brand equity (Aaker, 1991). This concept is related to a brand's strength in the market, that is, its acceptability, preference and loyalty.

In the 2005 *Business Week/Interbrand's* annual ranking of the 100 most valuable global brands, Coca-Cola is at the top of the list with a brand equity of $67.5 billion, followed by Microsoft ($59.9 billion) and IBM ($53.4 billion). It is worth noting that US brands claimed eight out the top ten spots, with the exception of Finnish Nokia and Japanese Toyota.

The Interbrand method in which the aforementioned ranking is based, is considered as one of the most established methods of evaluating the equity of a brand. It uses various information including market leadership, stability, global reach and profitability.

Secondly, should we make products for reseller brands similar to those bearing our own brand?

For many years now, various stores, especially supermarket chains worldwide offer products with their own label, also called store brands or private label products (for example, Tesco, Sainsbury, Carrefour). Most store brands are not produced from the retailer. In many cases, they are produced from manufacturers of branded goods. For instance, Heinz has been a major producer of private-label baby food (Quelch and Harding, 1996). Also, Unilever and Nestlé do so on a selective basis.

A recent A.C. Nielsen survey in thirty-six countries revealed that own labels have an average share of 15 per cent, while their growth rate is comparable to that of national brands. More specifically, in Europe the store brands' market share is 22 per cent and their annual growth rate is 6 per cent. In Switzerland, these products have the highest market share (38 per cent), followed by Great Britain (31 per cent), whereas in Sweden, store brands present the highest annual growth rate (25 per cent). At the other side of the Atlantic, their market share reaches 16 per cent, while their sales remain stable. Finally, in Asia and the Pacific Rim and Latin America, although their market share remains relatively low (1 per cent), their growth rate increases rapidly.

At an international level, the highest market shares of store brands are reported in paper products, aluminium foil, plastic wrap and rubbish bags. However, two-thirds of the first twenty product categories with the highest market shares are food-related categories.

The same survey found that store brands are less expensive compared to national brands. The average price difference is 31 per cent. The maximum difference is reported to personal care products (45 per cent), while the minimum price difference appears in frozen food products (18 per cent).

There are many arguments as to the advantages of producing store brands by manufacturing companies (Baltas, 1999). More specifically, manufacturing store brands can create economies of scale in production and distribution, as they are usually related to increases in the production volume. In addition, it can achieve utilization of excess production capacity or simply increase sales without bearing any marketing costs. Further, if the producer already has its own brand in the same product category, producing own label products can be viewed as well as price discrimination because of image differentiation between branded and private-label products. Furthermore, production of store brands can exploit the heterogeneity in consumer demand and offer an opportunity to compete on price against other branded products. In this respect, the consumers who prefer the national brands usually pay a higher price, while the rest of the market prefers the store brands. Private-label contracts may also allow manufacturers to keep overall production costs low enough on their national brands to compete more vigorously with retailers on price. Moreover, retailer products help to increase the category's share of shelf space, which in turn increases the product category's salience and motivates impulse purchases. Finally, store brands' production helps build up and maintain a good relationship with retailers who have control over distribution.

However, there are also certain negative aspects in producing store brands (Baltas, 1999). First, the producer is given tight product specifications from the retailer, without being able to make alterations. Consequently, the producer's effort focuses on cost minimization and production efficiency. Market share growth through supply of private label may come at the expense of profitability as price sensitivity rises. In fact, the additional profits from store brands may not compensate for the declining sales, lower unit prices and reduced margins in the branded business. Disclosing information about production costs and know-how, can give retailers considerable advantage in negotiations. Furthermore, production store brands may be inconsistent with the producer's corporate image and give consumers the impression that the producer's brand and the store brand are comparable, since they are produced from the same company. Hence, it becomes really difficult to account for price premiums over competing store brands. This is a major reason why leading manufacturers such as Kellogg's, Colgate, and Coca-Cola, do not supply store brands and often state this policy on product packages and advertisements. For instance, Colgate uses the logo 'We don't make toothpaste for anybody else'. Finally, when a company produces store brands, while marketing its national brand in the same product category, it must manage a quite complex manufacturing and distribution process.

All in all, the decision to produce store brands in a product category where the manufacturer already has branded products depends on many company as well as market-related factors. According to Baltas (1999), firms that are quite strong in production may favour the store brand production, while firms with a marketing and distribution advantage may prefer to market under their own brand name. At the same time, the very existence of store brands represents a merging of the retailing and branding functions and, to a certain degree, a disconnection of the manufacturing and branding at the level of the firm. It can be assumed that the own labels serve a corrective role, in that they help the market to adjust by sorting out firms that are not efficient in marketing or innovating products, and assigning to them the task of producing tightly specified goods whose distribution and marketing is left to retailers.

Thirdly, should we establish a 'family' brand (multiproduct brand) over all types of products offered or should we create a special brand for each type of product (multibrand product)?

A 'family' or 'umbrella' brand can take the following three forms:

- Corporate/house trade name (for example, United Colors of Benetton).
- A combination of a corporate/house trade name with individual product names; these are brand names with strong company endorsement (for example, Vodafone 60 Promo, Vodafone SMS 150).
- A combination of a common trade name with individual product names (for example, Nescafé Classic, Nescafé Select, Nescafé Gold Blend from Nestlé).

An alternative branding strategy is the development of individual brand names (for example, Ariel, Bold, Tide) for a specific product (Procter & Gamble's detergents). These are brand names with no company endorsement whatsoever.

Deciding the appropriate branding strategy depends on the company's resources, how strong the brand is and how related the products are to one another or to put it differently whether they belong to the same product category (for example, foodstuff, electronics).

Fourthly, should we use our existing brand name to introduce additional items in the same product category?

Companies usually decide to use an existing brand name to launch additional items in the same product category. For example, a sugar confectionery brand (for example, Halls) can be further extended into new flavours (for example, Halls Cherry, Halls Fruit Breezers).

The prerequisites of introducing successfully additional items in the same product category with the same brand are as follows: first, the company has a strong brand name in the category, which can be further exploited by entering a new market segment, secondly, the company follows a full-line policy.

Fifthly, should we use a new brand name for launching products in a new category?

The use of an existing brand name for entering a new product category is called *brand extension*. This strategy has gained much attention by the research community in the last decade.

Whirlpool launches Pret-à-Porter 'dry-cleaning' cubicle

Whirlpool, the white goods brand, has been extended to a new product category, namely fabric-freshening. More specifically, the company has developed a new laundry product in the form of a cubicle called the Whirlpool Pret-à-Porter that helps to remove creases, wrinkles and odours from clothes. The company's brand extension works on a number of fabrics including silks, wool, synthetics and dry-clean only garments.

The brand extension decision is particularly important for medium-sized companies that do not have the necessary resources to support many different brands. Thus, it is worth reviewing the major results of the relevant studies, which have appeared in the literature from early 1990s onwards[1]. More specifically:

1 Brand extensions:

   (a) have lower start up and maintenance advertising costs compared to brands introduced with a new name, although they usually enter more competitive markets.
   (b) achieve higher sales.
   (c) have higher chances of surviving in the market, as only 30 per cent of new brands was found to survive more than four years, while this percentage rises to more than 50 per cent for brand extensions.

2 The above results refer mainly to 'experience' goods (Nelson, 1974), whose quality cannot be visually inspected, as well as products that are introduced after the early stage of the product category's life cycle (among others Smith and Park, 1992; Sullivan, 1992). These positive results for brand extensions can be attributed to the following facts. First of all, there is higher probability of trial, systematic use and loyalty by consumers, when the product's name brings to mind an existing brand name. Further, the retailers will provide more shelf space to a known brand compared to a new one.

3 The evaluation of brand extensions by consumers is influenced mainly from the quality of the parent brand and the fit between this brand and its extensions. Fit refers to the perceived applicability of the skills and assets of a competent manufacturer in the original product class for making the product extension, the perceived product class complementarity, and the perceived product class substitutability. These dimensions of fit are very important. Actually, the first two are more important than the third one. Thus, a fit on either transfer of skills or complementarity may be adequate. A good fit on both is not necessary.

4 The harder the brand extension is, the more positive is its evaluation.

5 The positive perceptions are usually related to brand extensions that do not refer so much to functional attributes, for example, taste, but more to 'abstract' – 'symbolic' attributes, for example, style, quality.

6 The positive reactions of consumers take place when there is consistency with the brand idea and high similarity as far as product attributes are concerned. Certainly, brands that are prestige oriented have higher possibilities of being extended to products with lower similarities, than brands that are function oriented.

7 Previous successful brand extensions enhance the positive evaluations of a proposed brand extension.

8 There is high risk of hurting a well-established brand name by extensions that contain attributes that are incompatible with the perceptions that hold for the original brand. This risk is reduced when:

- brand extensions are perceived to be different from products offered under the family brand name.
- the perceptions refer to more global and less distinctive attributes (for example, quality) than very specific and distinctive attributes (for example, taste).

In order to avoid running this risk, the company can place more 'distance' between the extension and the parent brand through packaging, or decrease joint promotion campaigns, or alternatively, supporting the parent brand or the corporate image.

9 When consumer knowledge of the brands is high, the attributes and benefits of a brand that differentiate it from competing brands (for example, Apple = user friendliness) are more important compared to brand affect and product category similarity.

10 The number of products affiliated with a brand per se does not harm it, and it may even strengthen it as long as there is no quality variance between these brands, which can very well belong to different product categories.

11 A sub-branding strategy (namely, a new name in conjunction with a family brand name) may mitigate the negative effects of brand extension and improve consumer evaluations of extensions belonging to dissimilar product categories. This strategy creates a distance (differentation), which diminishes any negative evaluations.

12 The existence of consistency between the positioning of existing brands and its extensions influence the evaluations of these extensions. In particular, if the extension is risky in terms of brand category fit, product quality, or end-user acceptance a different positioning strategy can be followed for the extension. This, of course, leads to a mediocre increase in the influence of both the brand and the product category.

13 The risks associated with brand extensions are much lower than those associated with line extensions, especially in the case of flagship products. For instance, any extension of Johnson & Johnson's flagship brand, Johnson's Baby Shampoo, in other product categories, like mouth wash (brand extension), may not influence it, but Johnson's Baby Shampoo with Wheat and Vitamin E (line extension) can have a negative influence on the brand, when there is no compatible information for this extension.

14 Brand extension is more accepted in the market, when it is perceived by consumers as being associated with the parent brand relatively to attributes or image.

15 Unsuccessful brand extensions have a negative impact on the parent brand. The degree of this impact depends on the equity of the parent brand. The higher the brand equity, the higher the consequences, irrespective of how close the brand extension is to the parent brand.

Sixthly, should we follow a co-branding strategy in cooperation with other enterprises/ organizations?

A co-branding strategy is followed when a product's brand bears two or more well-known brand names. This strategy is increasingly popular in the packaged consumer goods industry (for example, Ruffles chips with Heinz ketchup), while it is quite common for credit cards. An example of a co-branded credit card is the Citi/AAdvantage® Visa gold card which was created with the cooperation of Citibank and American Airlines, and particularly the bank's Visa gold card with one of the most popular travel reward programmes in the world – the American Airlines AAdvantage® programme. When a company is engaged in co-branding, it aims at taking advantage of the strong image of the cooperating company in a specific market. The benefits sought include an increase in market share and improvement in the company's corporate image. The latter is particularly true for profit-seeking companies, which co-brand their products in cooperation with a non-profit organization. This alternative strategy is called *cause-branding*. A specific 'cause' is supported by the profit-seeking company, usually by offering a percentage of the product's sales to the non-profit company. Cause-branding is also common in credit cards.

WWF Eurobank Visa: a successful cause branded credit card

WWF Eurobank Visa is co-sponsored by the World Wild Fund and EFG Eurobank Ergasias – a leading Greek bank. Apart from offering considerable benefits to its holders, EFG Eurobank Ergasias offers 1.5 euros for every annual subscription, while 3 euros are donated to WWF Hellas for every transaction made with the card.

Tactical branding decisions

Tactical issues to be considered by management about brands include selecting the brand name, selecting the brand symbol/logo, registering a trademark and finally monitoring brand acceptance. We will take a closer look at these tactical issues in the following paragraphs.

Selecting a brand name   Creating a successful brand seems to depend heavily on the selection of the appropriate brand name or mark.
   Further down, we provide a list of guidelines associated with brand name success:

- Use many vowels that makes its pronunciation easier (for example, Ikea).
- Brand names must be preferably short (for example, Fiat).
- Brand names should not carry negative or offensive meanings (for example, Seat's Málaga series could not be used in the Greek market because it sounds very much like an offensive Greek word).
- Artificial brand names ensure that they are not used by another company (for example, Kodak).
- Brand names may describe certain product characteristics or uses (for example, Everyday).
- Brand names may suggest the impact they have on people (for example, EasyJet).
- Brand names should not be similar to competitive brands for avoiding customer confusion (for example, B.F. Goodrich and Goodyear tyre manufacturers usually cause confusion).

   The brand name must fully support the product's positioning, otherwise inconsistencies may create confusion in the customer's mind.

Creative branding: Matching brand name with product positioning

Compact Disc Club is the leader in the market of music products through direct sales. Its activity in the Greek market started in 1992 and during the last three years the company has entered the Cyprian, as well as the US and Canadian markets, targeting the Greek communities.

Compact Disc Club's products cannot be found on the shelves of any record store. They are only available directly to the final consumer through the corporate e-shop and call centre.

The company's music compilations are more than 75. They all include four cds in a special case with inset printed informational material. These compilations fall into three major categories: a) Artists' Portraits (Carlos Santana-The Very Best, Maria Callas, etc.), b) Thematic (Blue Café, Electric Dreams, etc.), c) Special Editions (Children's Fairytales, etc.)

The positioning strategy of direct sales companies in the music market is usually built on low price and average quality. By contrast, Compact Disc Club's strategy is based on unique compilations at premium prices.

In order to support this positioning, the company has chosen to differentiate itself from competition in terms of product and supporting services standards. As far as the product is concerned, Compact Disc Club is very careful in the selections for the repertory, branding and packaging to ensure that it is the best possible. In terms of services the company aims to provide the highest standards of service, through its call centre and all other customer contact channels, continuous stock availability, swift courier delivery, efficient resolving of complaints and problems, etc.

Branding varies in every new compilation release. Major elements are its title and artwork. The aim is to support corporate positioning in order to differentiate its offerings from competition. Here are some interesting examples:

1 Compact Disc Club recently put together a compilation of opera music. One would expect – according to the mainstream practice – a slide of an opera house for the cover artwork and a title such as 'THE BEST OPERAS EVER'. In its attempt though to reach a wider audience than the opera music fans, the company selected a concept based on the mental images created while listening to this music genre. The compilation title selected was 'VOICES OF HARMONY' and the artwork was based on a slide of an imaginary landscape with floating nautili shells in harmonious motion.
2 In another case, where the repertory in question contained Cuban and Latin tracks, the chosen title was 'MOJITO'. The Mojito is currently among the most favourite drinks originated from Cuba. This name served the purpose of attributing freshness and trendiness to the product.
3 In the case of a pop-lounge-chill out compilation, 'YACHTING' was selected as the title and a slide of a luxurious yacht for the cover with the promise that this music takes one on a journey. The concept for this compilation was ideal music for a glamorous ambience.

For all compilations developed by the Compact Disc Club, the decision on a concept comes first the search for repertory revolves around it. All decisions regarding product branding orginate from the selected concept of every compilation.

Selecting a brand symbol/logo   A symbol/logo is a visual expression of a brand. Choosing a brand symbol/logo is extremely important in establishing a brand in the market, especially when there exist many different competitive brands. A brand's symbol is an appropriate vehicle for differentiation, brand awareness and loyalty. Brand symbols can be classified in three groups (Murphy, 1990):

- Corporate names or trade names rendered in a distinctive typographic form (for example, Coca-Cola, Mars).
- Visual devices divorced from the corporate name, but with a close and obvious association with the name or the activities of the business (for example, the 'dough boy' of Pillsbury).
- Abstract logos that have no obvious relation to the corporate or product name (for example, the Peugeot lion). Instead, such logos reflect the brand's values (namely, Peugeot vehicles have the strength of a lion).

Registering a trade mark   A **trade mark** is a word, phrase, symbol or design, or a combination of them, that identifies and distinguishes the source of the goods of one party from those of others. Similarly, a **service mark** is the same as a trade mark, except that it identifies and distinguishes the source of a service rather than a product.[2]

A company must decide whether to register a trademark for a brand or not. Registering a trademark is not compulsory by law, with the exception of medicines. In this respect, a company can register a trademark in order to avoid certain commercial or legal risks.

Commercial risks occur when a company uses an un-registered mark and another product in the same or different product category appears in the market under the same brand. This can cause customer confusion, which, most probably, will lead to reduced sales. In this case, the company that used the brand name first can do nothing to prevent the other company from using it too.

Legal risks arise when a company chooses, intentionally or not, to use a brand name, which is already registered as a trade mark by another company. In such an occasion, the company can be sued for infringement under trade mark law, with no chances of winning the case, thus, wasting significant resources, valuable time, and jeopardizing business and goodwill.

By and large, registered trade marks are followed by the symbol ™('trade mark'), or ˢᴹ('service mark'). These signs can be used even if the trade marks are not registered, with the purpose of alerting the public to the company's claim, regardless of whether it have filed an application with the Trade Marks Office. The sign® ('registered') can only be used only after the mark is actually registered, and not while an application is pending. Also, the registration symbol can be used only on or in connection with the goods and/or services listed in the trade mark registration.

All in all, companies can register:

- A national trade mark: the standard procedure involves filing an application to the Ministry of Commerce or Trade.
- A European trade mark: an application should be submitted to the Office for Harmonization in Internal Market (OHIM), which is based in Alicante, Spain.
- An international trade mark: an application should be filed to the World Intellectual Property Organization (WIPO) based in Geneva, Switzerland. This registered trade mark is valid in more than 150 member states, except the USA which requires a different application.

Apart from brand names of products and services, also domain names can be registered. A domain name works like a company name and is a name by which a company or organization is known on the Internet. There are many registrars accredited to register domain names. Each country has a central registry to store unique names and addresses on the Internet. To register a domain name one must apply to an accredited registrar.

Monitoring brand acceptance   The ultimate level of brand acceptance is usually referred to as brand loyalty, that is a repetitive selection of a specific brand over competitive brands. In the last decade, a rising number of studies have examined brand loyalty (for example, Dick and Basu, 1994; Dekimpe et al., 1997; Yim and Kannan, 1999; Oliver, 1999; Thiele and Mackay, 2001; Gounaris and Stathakopoulos, 2004).

Brand loyalty can be monitored in various ways. First, it can be examined through *brand switching sequence* in the product category. For instance, in a product category with three competitive brands (A, B and C), we can observe the following brand switching sequences (Mowen and Minor, 1998):

- Perfect single-brand loyalty   AAAAAAAAAAAA
- Single brand loyalty with occasional switching   AAAAABBBBCCC
- Divided loyalty   ABCABCABCABC
- Indifference   ABACBCACBCBA

Additional ways for monitoring brand loyalty, and through this brand acceptance, include:

1 Consumers' spending for purchasing the brand as a percentage of the total spending in the product category.
2 Consumers' repurchases of the brand as a percentage of the total number of repurchases.
3 Consumers' future attitude towards the brand by replying to the following scaled questions (usually 1–5, where 1 = totally unlikely, 5 = absolutely certain):

- How likely would you say it is to purchase the brand again?
- How likely would you suggest the brand to a friend/acquaintance?
- How likely would you purchase another product under the same brand?

It is vital for companies to monitor the degree of their brands' loyalty, so that they trace customer migration soon enough and take all the necessary action to avoid losing market share.

Packaging

Packaging is often the key element in assisting mainly consumer goods companies to achieve a comparative advantage.

The critical decisions that must be made on the package are concerned with the functions the product pack will perform as well as with the mix of packaging components best able to perform in different degrees, the particular functions of the packaging. The functions of packaging can be grouped into six categories:

1 *Containment and protection*, concerns the state of goods on arrival to the customer.
2 *Transportation and distribution* is concerned with efficiency in handling at all stages in the marketing channel and covers utilization and pack-size.
3 *Management* refers to efficiency in stock-listing, pricing and ordering and covers some aspects of labelling (for example, bar-codes).
4 *Sale* covers the aesthetic value and sales power to the consumer as well as labelling for recognition, information and product description.

5 Use concerns transportation, storage, opening and possible re-shutting by the customer as well as unit size.
6 Disposal refers to the positive or negative rest-value of the packaging after its content has been used.

It is obvious that management expects a package to perform different functions and meet diverse requirements. Whenever a single element has so many functions to perform and demands to meet, the possibility of conflict emerges. However, the conflict that emerges in packaging becomes obvious at the time management has to decide about the packaging components that perform the packaging functions. The packaging components for which management must take a decision are the following:

1 packaging materials,
2 package size,
3 package shape,
4 package colour, texture and graphic art, and
5 other packaging components such as 'ease of opening', 'ease of use', 're-usability', and so on which are incorporated into the package design.

One of the most important decisions pertaining to packaging components is the package-size decision, which is ultimately tied up with the product-line decisions. Changes in the size of the package may create an illusion of a new product. Companies tend to add to their lines either 'king' or 'giant economy' package sizes or 'small' package sizes. The packaging size decision evolves from appraisals of several factors, but the most important are the consuming unit and the rate of consumption. So important is the package-size/consumption-rate relationship that a major base for market segmentation is that of product usage which, of course, has special meaning for package size. For instance, companies tend to segment markets on the basis of heavy, moderate and light user characteristics, and to develop package sizes accordingly.

Similarly, the shape of the package can be used for segmentation purposes. For instance, Hellman's has recently launched 'Mayonito', which contains the same type of mayonnaise with its classical product. The difference is in the shape of the package, which looks like a little man called 'the tasty man' for children to spread in their sandwiches.

Generally, packaging can be a powerful competitive tool as well as a major component of a marketing strategy. A better box or wrapper, a secondary use package, a unique closure or a more convenient container size, may give a company a competitive advantage. The following example is quite indicative of how companies can take advantage of an innovative packaging to gain a differential advantage over competitors.

3-D Packaging for Fruit by the Foot®

In early 2005, General Mills created a 3-D packaging in the USA for its fruit snacks brand Fruit by the Foot. The 3-D promotion features glasses designed into the package itself, as well as newly created backing paper on the product that features 3-D images.

Designed to drive baseline growth, the promotion grew out of earlier work looking at putting 3-D glasses inside a package.

(Continued)

(Continued)

General Mills' objective was to provide an extra dimension that would help the packaging stand out from others on the shelf. Through the glasses on the box, the consumer can see the Fruit by the Foot pouches inside.

Further, the content of the backing paper is linked to movement, such as following a skydiver jumping and landing, and kayakers on a river. The goal was to bring the consumer into the brand experience and lead them through the various dimensions.

Source: General Mills

However, companies in designing their packaging should also pay attention to the growing environmental and safety concerns. Yet, while some companies, which practise green marketing, design packages that are more friendly to the environment, the responses on the part of the consumers are not always positive. It appears that for some consumers, the lack of convenience could well be a barrier in actually purchasing an environmentally friendly packaged product.

Product services

Finally, one more intangible characteristic through which a company may achieve a comparative advantage is product services. Product services tend to expand a product's utility and the buyers associate them with the physical product when considering alternative offers. For many industrial products, service policies are indispensable; for some consumer products, they are important elements in marketing programmes. However, companies do, and can, offer an almost infinite range of services. However, the product-connected services are rather limited and can be classified, using the type of value they add to the product as a basis for classification, into:

1 product performance enhancing services,
2 product life prolonging services and
3 product risk reducing services.

The *product performance enhancing services* are more important for industrial goods and include installation, application engineering and the training of operators.

The *product life prolonging services* are equally important for both consumer and industrial products and intend to keep the product operating satisfactorily for a long period of time, and therefore, increase the customer's satisfaction. These services are primarily concerned with maintenance and repair.

The *product risk reducing services* intend to reduce the risk associated with the uncertainty about a product and include product warranties. A warranty whether expressed or implied represents a seller's obligation for certain services such as free repair, full and partial refund of the purchase price, or replacement of the product.

However, since every type of service is associated with different cost structures and customer perception, a company should combine services into a total 'service offering' in such a way as to minimize cost on the one hand and maximize favourable customer responses on the other. This means that each time a company changes its product service policies, such change (product decision) should lead towards an 'optimum' product service offering. This, of course, presupposes that the company knows very well the services that customers value most and their relative importance.

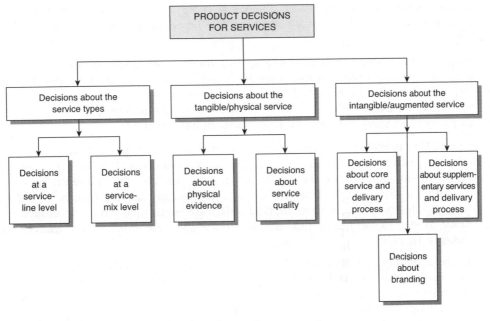

Figure 2.2   **Types of product decisions for service companies**

Product decisions for services

The types of product decisions, which were described in the previous sections, require certain adjustments for service companies (see Figure 2.2). In particular, while the decisions for the products to be offered at the product-mix and the product-line levels remain the same, there are significant differences as to the decisions for the tangible/physical and intangible/augmented product of the service providers (for example, packaging or style have no meaning). In the remainder of this chapter, we are going to take a closer look at these service-specific decisions.

Decisions about the tangible/physical service

Given the intangible nature of services, the decisions regarding the tangible/physical service aim at reducing this inherent intangibility of services, and thus, helping customers perceive the service more easily. In general, this effort is assigned to marketers and it is considered so critical that it is recognised as the fifth p of the marketing mix (namely, physical evidence), along with product, price, place and promotion. Physical evidence includes the following elements (Hoffman and Bateson, 1997):

- facility exterior (for example, car park, signing);
- facility interior (for example, lighting, temperature, interior design);
- tangibles (for example, brochures, business documents, personnel uniforms).

The pertinent decisions a service company has to make include:

1 How tangible should the service be?
2 What elements should they be used to make a service more tangible?

What is more, service providers should have to make decisions relating to service quality.

For measuring service quality, Parasuraman et al. (1985) have developed a survey research instrument called SERVQUAL, which identifies five broad dimensions of service quality, namely:

- tangibles (for example, modern-looking equipment, visually appealing);
- reliability (for example, showing a sincere interest in solving customers' problems);
- responsiveness (for example, willingness to help customers);
- assurance (for example, knowledge to answer customer questions);
- empathy (for example, to give customers individual attention).

The SERVQUAL model is based on the comparison of customers' perceptions of a service and their respective expectations. Despite the serious concerns that have been raised regarding the suitability of the SERVQUAL instrument,[3] its value lies in identifying some key underlying dimensions of service quality. To measure service quality in a B2B context, building on previous research, Gounaris and Venetis (2002) have developed the INDSERV model. According to this model, service quality comprises four underlying dimensions, namely:

- potential quality (for example, offers full service, has required facilities);
- hard process quality (for example, keeps time schedules, honours, looks at details);
- soft process quality accepted enthusiastically (for example, listening to our problems, open to suggestions/ideas, argue if necessary);
- output quality (for example, reaches objectives, contributes to our sales/image).

Potential quality relates to the search attributes that customers use in order to evaluate the provider's ability to perform the service before the relation has actually begun (Bochove, 1994).

Hard quality pertains to what is being performed during the service process, while soft quality pertains to how the service is performed during the service process (Szmigin,1993). Both dimensions describe the service process itself with the former referring to the service blueprint the provider uses, the accuracy with which the service is delivered and so on. The latter pertains to the front-line personnel and the interaction they develop with the client's employees. Output quality refers to the client's evaluation of the end-results of the hard and soft parameters (Szmigin, 1993).

All in all, service companies must make the following decisions in relation to service quality:

1 Which service quality dimensions should the company focus on?
2 How often and under which conditions should the company change the quality of its services?
3 How much emphasis should the company give to service quality during sales promotion?

Decisions about the intangible/augmented service

Decisions about the intangible/augmented service refer to the core service/delivery process, the supplementary services/delivery process and branding. The core service refers to the basic functional characteristics or to put it differently, to the core benefit delivered to the customer (for example, transportation, car repair).[4] Due to its inherent intangibility, a service can be viewed as an 'experience' that the customer lives through a specific delivery process. Designing the appropriate delivery process is an essential decision, which includes how and when the service is going to be offered, as well as the degree of involvement and

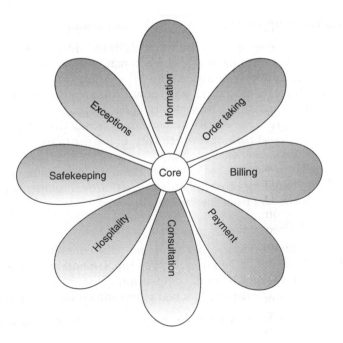

Figure 2.3   **The flower of services**

Source: adapted from Lovelock (1992)

interaction of frontline personnel and customers. For designing a service delivery process better, a 'service blueprint' is used, which represents graphically the whole delivery system.[5] In total, a service company must decide:

1   Which are the basic functional characteristics of its services.
2   Which functional characteristics must be emphasized.
3   How differentiated should these characteristics be from competition.
4   Which processes should be designed for delivering its services.

Furthermore, the supplementary services (and their pertinent delivery process) can be classified into eight clusters, which are listed as either facilitating, or enhancing supplementary services (Lovelock, 1992). These eight clusters are represented as petals of the so-called 'flower of service'.

Facilitating supplementary services ensure the smooth delivery of the core service. These include:

- Information about service details such as service characteristics, delivery time, delivery points, price list, and so on: information should be fast, accurate and complete, and it can be provided by the customer-contact personnel, as well as through brochures, call centres and the Internet.
- Order taking such as applications or reservations: the process of order taking must be as fast, polite and reliable as possible.
- Billing: when a service is not free of charge, bills should be correct, clear and complete without 'hidden' charges and a detailed analysis of the services offered and their prices.
- Payment: when a price is charged to a service, payment can be made using a variety of alternative methods (for example, cash, credit and debit cards, cheques).

Enhancing supplementary services increases value for customers. These include:

- Consultation, which goes beyond mere information and provides customers with advice regarding the optimum use of the company's services (for example, which banking services fit customer needs better).
- Hospitality, which makes customers' stay (or wait) more pleasant (for example, comfortable lobby areas, magazines, newspapers, coffee/water/refreshments).
- Safekeeping, which provides security for customers during their stay in the company (for example, convenient parking for their cars) or the use of its services (safekeeping services in hotels for valuable belongings).
- Exceptions, including special requests (for example, non-smoking hotel rooms), problem solving, handling of complaints/suggestions/compliments and restitution in case of low satisfaction from the service offered.

A service company must decide:

1 Which supplementary services would accompany the core service.
2 How much emphasis should be given to these supplementary services.
3 How differentiated will they be from competition.
4 Which processes should be designed for better delivering these supplementary services.

Finally, the branding decisions of a service company are similar to those of a manufacturing company.

Summary

- The types of product decisions that a manufacturing company has to take differ from those of a service company.
- The product related decisions of a manufacturing company include: first, decisions about the product types to be offered, secondly, decisions about the physical/tangible product, and thirdly, decisions about the intangible/augmented product.
- The decisions about the product types to be offered are taken on a product-mix and a product-line level.
- The decisions pertaining the tangible/physical product refer to functional characteristics, quality, and style.
- Intangible/augmented product-related decisions comprise branding, packaging and product services.
- Product decisions are the same for manufacturing and service companies as far as the types of products/services to be offered, but they differ considerably as to the tangible and intangible service.
- Decisions about the tangible/physical service refer to physical evidence and service quality, whereas decisions for the intangible/augmented service comprise the core and supplementary services and their delivery processes.

Questions

1 Select a fast moving consumer goods company by surfing the Internet, and describe its product mix in terms of width, length and depth.
2 What could be the most desirable results from the introduction of a new mobile phone, although it might cannibalize an existing company product?

3 Give examples of various types of family brands in the services industry and try to guess the rationale behind their selection.
4 If you were to decide whether to use brand extension for a convenience product, what information is required?

Notes

1 See for example, Aaker and Keller (1990); Park et al., (1991); Sullivan (1992); Keller and Aaker (1992); Sunde and Brodie (1993); Barwise (1993); Loken and Roedder (1993); Broniarcyk and Alba (1994); Dacin and Smith (1994); Milberg et al. (1997); Ambler and Styles (1997); Sheinin (1998); Roedder et al. (1998); Kapferer (1998); Serra et al. (1999); Chen and Chen (2000); Bottomley and Holdren (2001).
2 In the remainder of the book, the words 'trade mark' also imply a service mark.
3 See, among others, Buttle (1996); Mels et al. (1997); Lam and Woo (1997).
4 For a presentation of product levels, see Product levels, p. 3.
5 A more detailed discussion of blueprinting is provided in Chapter 7.

References

Aaker, D. (1991) *Managing Brand Equity*. New York: Free Press.
Aaker, D. (1992) *Strategic Market Management*. John Wiley & Sons.
Aaker, D.A. and Keller, K.L. (1990) 'Consumer evaluations of brand extensions', *Journal of Marketing*, 54: 27–41.
Alexander, R.S. (1980) *Marketing Definitions: A Glossary of Marketing Terms*. Chicago: American Marketing Association.
Ambler, T. and Styles, C. (1997) 'Brand development versus new product development: toward a process model of extension decisions', *Journal of Product and Brand Management*, 6 (4) 222–34.
Baltas, G. (1999) 'Understanding and managing store brands', *Journal of Brand Management*, 6: 175–87.
Barwise, P. (1993) 'Brand equity: snark or boojum?', *International Journal of Research in Marketing*, 10: 93–104.
Blois, K. (1990) 'Product augmentation and competitive advantage' in H. Muhlbacher and C. Jochum (eds), *Advanced Research in Marketing*. Proceedings of the 19th Annual Conference of the European Marketing Academy. Innsbruck, Austria.
Bochove J. (1994) 'Bureaus scoren slecht op de belangrijkste succesfactoren', *Nieuwstribune*: 27–36.
Bottomley, P.A. and Holdren, S.J.S. (2001) 'Do we really know how consumers evaluate brand extensions? Empirical generalizations based on secondary analysis of eight studies', *Journal of Marketing Research*, 38: 494–500.
Broniarcyk, S.M. and Alba, J.S. (1994) 'The importance of the brand in brand extension', *Journal of Marketing Research*: 214–28.
Buttle, F. (1996) 'SERVQUAL: review, critique, research agenda', *European Journal of Marketing*, 30(1): 8–32.
Chen, A.C.H. and Chen, S.K. (2000) 'Brand dilution effect of extension failure – a Taiwan study', *Journal of Product and Brand Management*, 9(4): 243–54.
Dacin, P.A. and Smith, D.C. (1994) 'The effect of brand portfolio characteristics on consumer evaluations of brand extensions', *Journal of Marketing Research*, 229–42.
Dekimpe, M., Steenkamp, J., Mellens, M., and Abeele, P. (1997) 'Decline and variability in brand loyalty', *International Journal of Research in Marketing*, 5(14): 405–20.
Dick, A. and Basu, K. (1994) 'Customer loyalty: towards an integrated conceptual framework', *Journal of Academy of Marketing Science*, 22(2): 99–113.
Gounaris, S. and Stathakopoulos, V. (2004) 'Antecedents and consequences of brand loyalty: an empirical study', *Journal of Brand Management*, 11(4): 283–306.
Gounaris, S. and Venetis, K. (2002) 'Antecedents of trust in industrial service relationships and the moderating effect of the duration of the relationship', *Journal of Services Marketing*, 16(7): 636–55.
Hoffman, D. and Bateson, J. (1997) *Essentials of Services Marketing*. London: The Dryden Press.

Kapferer, J.N. (1998) *Strategic Brand Management*. Kogan Page. London.

Keller, K.N. and Aaker, D.A. (1992) 'The effects of sequential introduction of brand extensions', *Journal of Marketing Research*, XXIX: 35–50.

Kotler, P. (2003) *Marketing Management: Analysis, Planning, Implementation and Control*. 11th edition. Englewood Cliffs, NJ: Prentice Hall.

Lam, S. and Woo, K. (1997) 'Measuring service quality: a test-retest reliability investigation of SERVQUAL', *Journal of Market Research Society*, 39: 381–93.

Levitt, T. (1969) *The Marketing Mode*. New York: McGraw Hill.

Loken, B. and Roedder, D.J. (1993) Diluting brand beliefs: when do brand extensions have a negative impact?', *Journal of Marketing*, 57: 71–84.

Lovelock, C. (1992) 'Cultivating the flower of service: new ways of looking at core and supplementary services' in R. Eiglier and E. Langeard (eds), *Marketing, Operations and Human Resources: Insights into Services*, III, Université d'Aix-Marseille Aix-en-Provence: pp. 296–316.

McGrath, M. (2001) *Product Strategy for High Technology Companies*. 2nd edition. New York: McGraw-Hill.

Mels, G., Boshoff, C. and Nel, D. (1997) 'The dimensions of service quality: the original European perspective revisited', *The Service Industries Journal*, 17: 173–89.

Milberg, S.J., Park, C.W. and McCarthy, M.S. (1997) 'Managing negative feedback effects associated with brand extensions: the impact of alternative branding strategies', *Journal of Consumer Psychology*, 6(2): 119–40.

Mowen, J.C. and Minor, M. (1998) *Consumer Behavior*. 5th edition. Englewood Cliffs: NJ: Prentice Hall.

Murphy, J. (1990) *Brand Strategy*. Englewood Cliffs, NJ: Prentice Hall.

Nelson, P. (1974) 'Advertising as information', *Journal of Political Economy*, 82: 729–54.

Nilson, T. (2000) *Competitive Branding: Winning in the Market Place with Value Added Brands*. West Sussex: Wiley.

Oliver L.R. (1999) 'Whence consumer loyalty?' *Journal of Marketing*, 63 (special issue): 33–44.

Parasuraman, A., Zeithaml, V. and Berry, L. (1985) 'A conceptual model of service quality and its implication for future research', *Journal of Marketing*, 49(4): 41–50.

Park, C.W., Milberg, S. and Lawson, R. (1991) 'Evaluation of brand extensions: the role of product feature similarity and brand concept consistency', *Journal of Consumer Research*, 18: 185–93.

Quelch, J. A. and Harding, D. (1996). 'Brands versus store brands: fighting to win', *Harvard Business Review* 74: 99–109.

Roedder, D.J., Loken, B. and Joiner, C. (1998) 'The negative impact of extensions: can flagship products be diluted?', *Journal of Marketing*, 62: 19–32.

Serra, E.D.M., Vieira, J.M.C., and Gonzalez, J.A.V. (1999) 'Brand extensions effects on attitudes and brand beliefs', *EMAC Conference Proceedings*, Berlin.

Sheinin, D.A. (1998) 'Positioning brand extensions: implications for beliefs and attitudes', *Journal of Product and Brand Management*, 7(2): 137–49.

Smith, D.C. and Park, C.W. (1992) 'The effects of brand extensions on market share and advertising efficiency', *Journal of Advertising Research*, 29: 296–313.

Sullivan, M.W. (1992) 'Brand extensions: when to use them', *Management Science*, 38(6): 793–806.

Sunde, L. and Brodie, R.J. (1993) 'Consumer evaluations of brand extensions: further empirical results', *International Journal of Research in Marketing*, 10: 47–53.

Szmigin, I. (1993) 'Managing quality in business-to-business services', *European Journal of Marketing*, 27(1): 5–21.

Thiele, S. and Mackay, M. (2001) 'A brand for all seasons? A discussion of brand loyalty approaches and their applicability for different markets', *Journal of Product and Brand Management*, 10(1): 25–37.

Vaid, H. (2003) *Branding*. London: Cassell.

Yim, C.K. and Kannan, P.K. (1999) 'Consumer behavioral loyalty: a segmentation model and analysis,' *Journal of Business Research*, 44: 75–92.

Further reading

Aaker, D. (1996) *Building Strong Brands*. New York: The Free Press.

de Chernatony, L. and McDonald, M. (1998) *Creating Powerful Brands in Consumer Service and Industrial Markets*. London: Butterworth Heinemann.

3 Product Life Cycle and Marketing Strategy

Introduction

The product life cycle, as already mentioned in Chapter 1, is one of the most important marketing concepts. Many authors have associated this concept with the marketing strategies, which have to be followed in the various stages of a product's life in the market.

However, the product life cycle analysis presupposes a clear definition of the product concept. Basically, we can distinguish three product levels and respective life cycles: first product-class, for example, automotive, secondly, product-form for example, convertible, thirdly, product-brand, for example, Peugeot 206 cc.

On the one hand, the product-class life cycle reflects changes in total market demand (for example, number of automobiles in the market), and lasts much longer than the product-form or product-brand life cycles of a particular company and this is because the duration of the maturity stage can be characterized as 'indefinite'. On the other hand, the product-form and product-brand life cycles tend to reflect the competitive strengths of the company, and consequently, it follows more or less the classic model of product life cycle than the product-class life cycle.

In this chapter, the following issues will be discussed:

- criticism of the product life cycle concept;
- marketing strategies at the introduction stage;
- marketing strategies at the growth stage;
- marketing strategies at the maturity stage;
- marketing strategies at the decline stage.

Criticism of the product life cycle concept

From the mid 1970s, the model of the product life cycle (PLC) has been extensively criticized by various authors such as Flides and Lofthouse (1975), Dhalla and Yuspeh (1976), Doyle (1976) among others. This criticism is focused on the following issues:

1 There are many products whose life cycle does not represent the classic four-stage form: introduction, growth, maturity, decline, as featured in Figure 1.1 of Chapter 1. For example, Cox (1967) conducted a study of 258 pharmaceutical products and found six different product life cycle types. In a similar vein, Rink and Swan (1979)

and Swan and Rink (1982) identified eleven different product life cycle forms, while Kotler (2003) describes eight different PLC shapes. All in all, these authors postulate that product sales in a given time frame (for example, a year) do not necessarily follow an S curve, but can, for instance, go up and down quite sharply (for example, fad products), or follow a scalloped pattern, when sales pass through a success of life cycles based on discovery of new product characteristics, users or uses (for example, new uses have been added to 3G Cellular phones).

2   The changes in the company's external environment as well as the demand of the product from one year to the other make it difficult for a company to predict when the next stage in the product life cycle will appear, how long it will last and what the levels of sales will be.

3   One cannot often judge with accuracy in which stage of the life cycle the product is.

4   The major stages do not divide themselves into clear-cut compartments. At certain points a product may appear to have attained maturity when actually it has only reached a temporary plateau in the growth stage prior to its next big upsurge.

5   The time-dependent PLC model is insufficient for two reasons: first, the PLC is partly endogenous – the long term pattern of sales is determined by the strategic decisions of management. Secondly, exogenous factors are not adequately modelled as random error around the time dependent PLC.

Despite extensive criticism levelled at the product life cycle model, it remains a useful tool for planning the launching of new products, establishing price policies, planning the timed use of the marketing mix and undertaking cash flow and financial investment appraisal.

In the remainder of this chapter, there is a detailed presentation of the alternative marketing strategies, which can be used for products and services at the various stages of their life cycle.

Marketing strategies at the introduction stage

When a company launches a totally new product/service on the market, it may select one of the following marketing strategies (Walker et al., 1999):

- mass-market penetration;
- niche penetration;
- skimming and early withdrawal.

Mass-market penetration

This strategy aims at persuading as many potential customers as possible to adopt the new product/service in order to achieve a decrease in the unit cost and to create a large base of loyal customers before competitors enter the market. The ultimate objective of mass-market penetration is to capture and maintain a large market share for the new offering.

Very often mass-market penetration can take the form of either slow penetration or rapid penetration strategy depending on the price set and promotion expenses made (Kotler, 2003):

- *Slow penetration strategy*: the product/service enters the market at a low price and limited promotion expenses. The implementation of this strategy requires the existence of a large potential market which is highly aware of the product/service, that is price sensitive and further, there is some potential competition.

- *Rapid penetration strategy*: the product/service enters the market at a low price, despite high promotion expenses. In order to implement this strategy, a large potential market should be unaware of the product/service. Most potential customers should be price sensitive and there should be strong potential competition, while considerable economies of scale can be achieved with increases in production.

In order for a company to use a mass-market penetration strategy, the following conditions must be present:

1   There is large potential demand.
2   Potential customers are price sensitive, therefore a low price can lead to market development.
3   There exist economies of scale.
4   Low pricing can discourage existing and potential competition.
5   The product/service life cycle is long.
6   There are product/service substitutes.
7   Barriers to market entry are practically non-existent.
8   Product technology is easily copied.
9   There are many potential competitors.
10 There are many sources of raw materials and components supply.
11 Product process is rather simple.
12 Potential competitors have rather limited resources or skills.
13 The company has extensive marketing, financial, product engineering skills and resources.

A mass penetration strategy can be implemented using the following marketing mix tools:

- rapid product line extensions to appeal to multiple segments;
- low pricing or alternatively high pricing followed by lower-priced versions for facing potential competitors;
- trade promotions and extended trade terms to encourage initial purchases and gain extensive distribution coverage;
- sales promotions in the form of couponing, sampling and quantity discounts to generate initial retail purchases.

Niche penetration

When the company has limited resources it can strive to gain a leading position in a specific market segment. In other words, the company can aim at maximizing the number of customers that try and adopt the product/service, focusing its efforts in a particular niche market, instead of trying to gain and maintain a leader's position in the total market. This strategy can help pioneering companies to make a more efficient use of their limited resources and avoid direct confrontation with larger competitors.

As far as implementation is concerned, niche penetration requires similar tactics as the mass-market penetration strategy. The only difference is that, instead of extending the product/service line, the company must modify and improve its product/service in order to increase its attractiveness in the target market.

According to Walker et al. (1999), the situations favouring a niche penetration strategy are as follows:

- large potential demand;
- fragmented market;
- short adoption process;
- product technology offers little patent protection;
- many sources of raw materials and components;
- relative simple production process;
- many potential competitors;
- some potential competitors have substantial resources and competences;
- limited marketing, financial and product engineering skills and resources.

Skimming and early withdrawal

The skimming and early withdrawal strategy aims at attracting as many customers as possible and maintaining high profit margins. This can be achieved by setting high prices for recovering the product's development and launching costs as quickly as possible in order to maximize ROI and then to exit the market as increasing competition push margins down.

Depending on how high the price is set and the promotion expenses made this strategy can take one of the following forms (Kotler, 2003):

- *Rapid-skimming strategy*: the product/service enters the market at a high price and with high promotion expenses. In order to select the rapid-skimming strategy there must be a small potential market, which is unaware of the product, not price sensitive and further the company faces potential competition and wants to create strong brand preference.
- *Slow-skimming strategy*: the product/service is introduced at a high price, while promotion expenses remain at a low level. The implementation of this strategy requires the existence of a small potential market which is aware of the product/service, also buyers that are not price sensitive, and potential competition is not imminent.

The conditions favouring the implementation of skimming and early withdrawal strategy are as follows:

- There is limited potential demand.
- The new product/service is targeted to innovators who wish to buy it just because it is new, without considering its price.
- It is easier to lower the product's/service's price in the future than setting it higher.
- The product's/service's high price, even with low sales, brings profit to the company which is necessary for covering its high R&D and marketing costs.
- The production of the new product/service cannot increase immediately because one or more production resources are scarce (for example, specialized workforce).
- The cost of a low volume production is high as to weaken the advantage of high price.
- The initial high price does not attract more competitors in the market.
- The high price promotes the message of a unique and superior product/service.
- There are few potential competitors.
- The product technology is patentable or difficult to copy.
- There is a relatively complex production process.
- There are limited sources of raw materials and components supply.
- Some potential competitors should have considerable resources and skills.
- The company possesses strong basic R&D and product development capabilities, as well as sales and promotion skills, but limited financial resources.

Marketing strategies in the introduction stage of PLC: the case of the mobile telephony market in Greece

Telestet (now TIM) and Panafon (now Vodafone) are the two pioneering companies in the Greek mobile phone market. They started their operation almost simultaneously in the summer of 1993. Telestet was a subsidiary of the STET telecommunications group of companies with an international presence in the provision of information and telematics services. Panafon used to be a subsidiary of British Vodafone and France Telecom.

The mobile phone services are technologically advanced services, which require considerable resources for telecommunications infrastructure and high specialization. For survival in this highly competitive market it is imperative for every company to upgrade its network on a continuous basis in order to operate efficiently and to provide high quality services to its clientele.

There are certain market segments where demand is price inelastic (namely, innovators and early adopters). The legal framework of operation does not allow companies to compete in the same technology.

The main potential competitor is the state-owned OTE, which is not allowed yet by law to enter the market.

Both Telestet and Panafon possess adequate financial resources for expanding the telecommunications network and at the same time skills and experience in marketing, ensuring synergies with their parent companies. Further, they aim at maximizing their return on investment (ROI).

Telestet, as well as Panafon adopt a rapid skimming strategy. In particular, they change premium prices in order to finance high investments in infrastructure nationwide, taking advantage of the oligopolistic conditions in the market.

Premium pricing conveys the message of a unique and superior service, which adds prestige to the customer. It must be noted that during this period both companies forecasted a market growth, which was less than the actual ones.

Moreover, they invest considerable amounts in advertising for service awareness, accelerating diffusion in market segment that are not sensitive to price, and to prepare the way for mass adoption. During this phase, both companies are not engaged in extensive promotion.

Both Telestet and Panafon focus their efforts in expanding their network, and improving their quality of communication. Gradually, they develop some value added core services based on GSM technology.

The marketing strategy of Panafon can be viewed as highly successful and efficient and, in a short time, it takes precedence over competition. Panafon's strategy is differentiated from Telestet as follows:

- It is the first to develop a client service, from the first day of its operation, ensuring a competitive advantage. This service is operated in a pioneering way for Greek standards, and it is real evidence of the priority the company gives to complete customer support.
- Panafon adopts a quite efficient distribution strategy following on the suggestion of its parent company Vodafone.

It built up its distribution channel through seven trade partners, with whom it signed contracts of exclusive distribution. These trade partners sell, support, price as well as collect

(Continued)

(Continued)

bills. These partners are Citicom, Panavox, Radio Korasidis, Telecom, Q-Phone, Palmaphone, and Viafon. This strategy reduced bad debts and contributed to the reduction of operational costs. The sales force of trade partners made considerable efforts, which focused on innovators and early adopters.

By contrast, Telestet signed an exclusive sales contract with Mobitel, which developed a nationwide sales network which was targeted to corporate clients and at the same time it developed a distribution network through Cooperation with dealers. Telestet reconsidered this strategy several years later, in 1997, having already lost a significant market share. Moreover, with considerable delay, it created a client service, in 1995.

Source: Avlonitis and Nikiforaki (2000)

Marketing strategies in the growth stage

The marketing strategies for products/services in growing markets depend on whether the company is the market leader or market follower.

Strategies for market leaders

The basic marketing objective of a market leader is to maintain its market share. This means that the leading firm must first, avoid losing share from its current customers, and secondly, capture the largest part of sales made by new customers in the market.

Data from the PIMS database, an acronym for a large scientific Profit Impact of Marketing Strategy project of Harvard Business School (Buzell and Gale, 1987), revealed that a large percentage of leaders face decreases in their market share. In fact, 45 per cent of leaders having market share over 50 per cent experienced losses in relative share.

The company can follow various marketing activities, which have been proved to help a firm maintain its leading position. These activities can be grouped in five different strategies that the market leader may implement individually or in combination (Kotler and Singh, 1981).

More specifically, these strategies are as follows:

First, *fortress or position defence strategy*: The objective of this strategy is to increase satisfaction, loyalty and re-purchases of current customers by building on existing company strengths. Also, another objective is to attract those customers that have not adopted the product yet.

The fortress or position defence strategy is more applicable when the following conditions are satisfied:

1 The market is relatively homogeneous.
2 The leading firm enjoys increased awareness and preference among existing and potential customers.
3 The leading firm has competencies and skills in crucial business functions like marketing, for building awareness, preference and satisfaction.
4 Competitors do not possess 2 and 3.

Examples of marketing actions for implementing a fortress or position defence strategy include: emphasis on quality and product enhancement; positioning strategy that stresses uniqueness and superiority of product features; reminder advertising; improving after sales service; emphasis on key account management; improving logistics.

Secondly, *flanker strategy*: The objective of this strategy is to defend an exposed flank, which, in business terms, is translated into a weakness in the leader's offering. More specifically, a follower may try to capture a leading share in a market segment with a differentiated product in a territory where the leader is not strong. In this case, the leader may develop a second brand, usually called flanker brand.

The leader may develop a higher quality, higher-price brand (trading up strategy) or a lower quality, lower price brand (trading down strategy). An example of trading up strategy is Lexus of Toyota, while Mercedes used a trading down strategy with the introduction of A Class series.

Thirdly, *confrontation strategy*: The leader confronts competitive offerings by improving its product, increasing its promotional efforts or lowering its prices. It must be noted, though, that a simple price decrease may actually result in shrinking margins, which does not help re-establishing a sustainable competitive advantage for the leader. Therefore, such a tactic must be well planned and combined with other marketing tactics as well.

In general, the leader must invest heavily in improving its production facilities for putting down unit costs, and developing new products with superior features which represent better value for money.

Fourthly, *market expansion or mobile strategy*: The leader defends its market share versus competitors by establishing strong market positions in different market segments.

The conditions favouring the use of this strategy are as follows: fragmented markets with heterogeneous needs and wants, necessary company resources and expertise in product development and marketing.

In order to implement a market expansion or mobile strategy the company must:

- develop line extensions, new brands, or alternative product forms utilizing similar technology to appeal to multiple segments;
- build specialized distribution networks for the more efficient access to specific users;
- design multiple promotion campaigns for different segments (Walker et al., 1999).

Fifthly, *contraction or strategic withdrawal strategy*: The leader may find it difficult to defend its market position in different segments, especially when the market is fragmented. In this case, the leading firm may either reduce or even stop its marketing efforts in some segments and focus on the most promising segments where it has or can create a sustainable relative advantage.

Followers' strategies

A company that is characterized, as a follower in a market should aim at building a market share by increasing acquisition of some of the competitor's customers as well as new customers.

Data drawn from the PIMS database suggest that followers that increased their share compared to those that lost market share (Buzzell and Gale, 1987):

- did not have significant differences in their prices;
- increased the quality of their products relative to competition;
- developed more new products, product-line extension or product modifications;
- increased their marketing expenses faster than the market growth rate.

Kotler and Singh (1981) suggest five strategies for followers in growing markets. We shall now look at them in more detail.

Frontal attack strategy is often characterized by an all-out attack on the opponent's territory (Hooley et al., 2004). In this sense, the aggressor attacks the opponent's strengths. The frontal attack is applicable when:

- the market is relatively homogeneous with few underserved segments;
- there is one well-entrenched competitor;
- existing customers do not have a strong brand preference; and
- the company has more resources and capabilities than its main competitor.

The marketing tools which can be used as part of a frontal attack strategy include development of superior products, more promotion and distribution expenditure than competitors, and better customer service to name a few.

Flanking attack strategy aims to catch the defender off guard, as the aggressor attacks the opponent's weaknesses. This strategy is applicable when:

- the market leader or/and other major competitors hold a strong position in the primary segment;
- the aggressor has less resources than the opponent;
- no existing brand fully satisfies the needs of customers in at least one other segment.

The marketing tools that can be used for implementing a flanking attack strategy include: developing a unique and superior product which satisfies the unmet customer needs by existing offerings; designing promotional campaigns to stimulate demand in an underserved segment; building appropriate distribution networks for accessing this segment.

Encirclement strategy aims at launching a large-scale attack of the opponent on several fronts. Hooley et al. (2004) suggest two approaches to the encirclement attack: first, to attempt to cut off the competitor from its main suppliers and/or customers; secondly, to offer a unique and superior product or service compared to competitive offerings in the market.

The necessary condition for implementing an encirclement strategy is that the market can be broken down in many smaller regional or applications market segments.

In order to implement an encirclement strategy, a follower can use the following tools: developing product line extensions appealing to the needs and wants of customers in the underdeveloped segments; designing promotional campaigns to stimulate demand in the underdeveloped segments; building appropriate distribution networks for accessing the underdeveloped segments.

Bypass or leapfrog strategy aims at avoiding the competitor's main market and concentrating on new markets. According to Kotler (2003), there are three alternative approaches of a bypass strategy: first, diversifying into unrelated products; secondly, diversifying into new geographical markets; thirdly, surpassing existing products with new technologically advanced products (the so-called technological leapfrogging).

The necessary conditions for implementing a bypass or leapfrog strategy are as follows (Walker et al., 1999):

- the company has technological superiority relative to competitors;
- the company can use this technology for developing an appealing product;
- the company has the necessary marketing resources for promoting the product and persuading customers already committed to the specific technology that the increased benefits of the new product justify their decision to replace their current brand with the new one;
- the company must operate in markets where replacement purchases are rather frequent.

In order to implement a bypass or leapfrog strategy, a follower can use the following tools: develop a new generation of products with unique features which appeal to existing and potential customers; sales promotion and comparative advertising to stimulate initial trial; product demonstrations from well-trained sales people.

Guerrilla attack strategy aims at harassing the market leader by disrupting its plans and diverting some of its resources and attention. Guerrilla attacks are sudden and sporadic. This strategy is particularly effective when:

1 the market segment is rather small and weakly defended;
2 aggressor has limited resources.

Such attacks can take the form of sales promotion schemes (for example, couponing, sampling); short-term price reductions; segment-specific advertising campaigns.

Marketing strategies in the growth stage: the case of mobile telephony market in Greece

The first profitable year for Panafon and Telestet was 1996. During the growth stage, both companies based their marketing strategy on high advertising expenditures, subsidizing mobile telephone purchases and provision of complementary offerings (for example, televisions, electrical appliances, etc.). The cost of acquiring a new customer was considerably high for Telestet and Panafon. Both companies, but especially Panafon, created strong distribution channels, which followed an offensive commercial policy. At this stage, Cosmote entered the market.

Panafon's marketing strategy

Panafon is the market leader with a market share of 60% with the aim of maintaining its leading position in a growing market, it uses a combination of strategies, which aim at keeping existing customers and at the same time acquiring a larger share of the new customers market. More specifically:

Implementing a fortress or position defence strategy, Panafon continues the expansion of its telecommunications network, and the improvement of its service quality. Moreover, it invests further in quality emphasis on customer service, marketing information systems and quality accreditation for its services. In addition, it broadens its product portfolio by adding new value-added services with the objective of increasing customer satisfaction and loyalty. The distribution strategy is quite successful. It continues further building up the distribution channel with new dealership agreements, aiming at the extensive presence in the mass market. What is more, in an attempt to take control of distribution, Panafon proceeds in the acquisition of various companies.

Additionally, Panafon combines a fortress or position defence strategy with a market expansion or mobile strategy, following a sales strategy that is targeted to large corporate clients using its own sales force as well as the sales force of its Partners Panavox and Q-phone. This strategy allows the company to maintain and further extend its upper market.

As far as promotion is concerned, Panafon keeps its advertising expenditures high, emphasizing its high quality of service, and leading position. In some cases, it uses comparative advertising for confronting Telestet, while it differentiates its strategy towards various market segments accordingly. Further, following a flanker strategy, first it develops economy programmes especially for large corporate clients, and secondly, it gradually

(Continued)

(Continued)

begins to subsidize the purchase of mobile phones in order to encourage new purchases in segments which are more price sensitive. In this context, Panafon is occasionally engaged in promotional activities with the aim of gaining a larger share of the new subscribers' market, and confronting respective competitive activities (*confrontation strategy*).

In order to cope with Telestet's competitive offerings that have been available earlier in the market, and to attract new price sensitive subscribers, Panafon combines flanker with confrontation strategy. As a result, it launches a second brand, Panafon à la carte (mobile telephony with a prepaid card), targeting the market with two more economical pro- grammes. This strategy proved to be quite effective and soon, Panafon takes the lead in the market.

Next, it enriches its prepaid card offering by launching two more packages, 'à la carte junior' (a package targeted to young customers) and 'thrilos à la carte' (a package targeted to Olympiakos FC fans) for attracting new subscribers (*flanker strategy*).

Initially, Panafon underestimates Cosmote, which entered the market in April 1998 and delays enormously in reacting to its offensive strategy. Further, Panafon reduces its price list twice in a period of eight months in order to confront the offensive pricing strategy of Cosmote (*confrontation strategy*).

In an attempt to cope with Cosmote, Panafon follows the same strategy and creates customer loyalty award schemes to discourage disconnections (*confrontation strategy*). Finally, using a market expansion strategy, Panafon expands its presence in the leased lines market with Panafon Link, which is targeted at large corporate clients.

Telestet's marketing strategy

Telestet has a lower market share than Panafon, which makes it a market challenger. Its main objective is to increase its market share by gaining customers from competition and attracting new subscribers. For meeting this objective it combines various strategies. More specifically:

Using *encirclement strategy*, Telestet is the first to design and offer pricing programmes aiming at attracting new subscribers, covering different customer needs, which are not satisfied up to that moment in time. This strategy is not considered successful as there are several pricing programmes in the market that cause confusion to the customers, instead of making buying decisions easier.

For attracting new customers, Telestet makes a *flanking attack* to Panafon by gradually subsidizing the purchase of mobile phones, targeting market segments that are more price sensitive. In the context, it is occasionally engaged in sales promotional activities with the objective of acquiring a larger share of new subscribers.

Advertising expenditures are high, but the result is not considered particularly successful. It uses comparative advertising in an attempt to gain a more favourable position than Panafon, emphasizing in various ways the superiority of its offer over competition (*frontal attack*).

Moreover, Telestet follows a *bypass strategy*, as it launches first a number of value added services in order to attract new customers who seek augmented benefits, but also to motivate the users of mobile phones to replace their service packages with new superior offerings offered by the company. These services comprise voice dialling, voice mail, family and friends, roaming to prepaid card holders, which cover the needs of various market segments aiming at a differentiated positioning in relation to Panafon.

Furthermore, in order to confront the preference of early adopters of mobile telephony for Panafon's services, Telestet is launching a *flanking attack*, by introducing in May 1997 'B-free by Telestet' for the mass market, which is the first prepaid card service. This service is more attractive to those wishing to use their mobile phone less, and they are more price sensitive. However, Telestet manages to keep its lead in this market for a short time, as Panafon à la carte proves to be much more competitive.

In addition, it seems to realize with some delay that exclusive distribution is a wrong strategy, breaking its exclusivity contract with Mobitel and signing new distribution contracts. After terminating its cooperation with Mobitel, it creates a chain of company-owned stores. At the same time, Telestet expands the distribution for mobile telephony with a card, aiming at an extensive presence, including points of sale like kiosks (the so-called 'periptero' in Greek), Kodak stores and ATMs of the National Bank of Greece (*flanking strategy*).

What is more, just like Panafon, it underrates Cosmote and although it delays in reacting to its offensive pricing strategy, it reduces twice its price list in a period of seven months (*frontal attack*). Finally, Telestet copies, like Panafon, Cosmote's customer loyalty programmes.

Cosmote's Marketing strategy

Cosmote started its business operation with considerably unfavorable terms. Its telecommunication network had a limited geographical coverage and its distribution channel comprised OTE's stores, which did not have suitable opening hours (they are open only in the morning), while their employees were not highly motivated.

Having as an objective to build up its market share, Cosmote mades the following strategic moves:

First of all, the use of DCS1800 technology for its telecommunication network proves the implementation of leapfrog strategy, since this technology has a unique competitive advantage over GSM900 (used by competition), regarding quality of transmission and other technical characteristics of the network.

Furthermore, Cosmote gives priority to the expansion of its telecommunications infrastructure for achieving nationwide coverage. Relatively soon and despite the initial delays, it creates a telecommunications network with satisfactory coverage in terms of population and geography.

The above actions are coupled with a frontal attack, as Cosmote offers its services in much lower prices than competition. Its pricing programmes are simple and easily understood. Its pricing strategy is quite successful. During the first year of its operation, Cosmote attracts new customers, basically among late adopters, that are price sensitive. After a while, it gains customers from competition, which is forced to respond accordingly.

Cosmote spends less in advertising and mobile phone subsidy than competition, as an offset to the loss revenues due to reduced prices, and as a way to put down costs. However, the limited advertising budget does not allow the company to communicate effectively its geographical coverage losing significant customers.

On the contrary, Cosmote devotes considerable resources for expanding its distribution channel. New trade partners are added, and a direct sales force is recruited for large corporate clients. It gradually introduces value-added services in the market and at the end of 1997 it launches Cosmocarta (a prepaid mobile phone card). These actions describe the flanking attack, which is made by the company.

Additionally, it launches a frontal attack and by positioning against competitive offerings, it further reduces prices (1999) with the implementation of a pioneering

(Continued)

(Continued)

pricing method, what is known as volume pricing (the more you talk, the less you pay). With the objective of maintaining its customers and reducing disconnections, Cosmote is the first to develop a customer loyalty plan offering a reduction in the fixed cost for the subscribers who stay with the company for more than a year. This action is soon copied by competition.

At the end of this period, Cosmote's strategy is proved to be quite effective. Telestet and to a lesser extent Panafon have witnessed considerable losses in their market shares to the advantage of Cosmote. Panafon maintains its leading position with a market share of 43 per cent, while Telestet is second with a share of 30 per cent and Cosmote is third with 27 per cent.

Source: Avlonitis and Nikiforaki (2000)

Marketing strategies at the maturity stage

When a company is the leader in a mature market, it must aim at maintaining and protecting its market share. In this case, the marketing strategies that can be followed coincide with those in the growing markets.

However, there are markets, which are characterized as mature due to the inability of the competing companies to offer products that satisfy customer needs. In such markets, a company can implement one or more of the following strategies in order to increase the total sales volume:

- extensive penetration strategy;
- use expansion strategy;
- new market strategy.

Extensive penetration strategy

This strategy aims at converting current non-users to users in the target market. The conditions favouring the implementation of this strategy are the following:

- there is a large number of non-users;
- competitors hold relatively small market shares, and have limited resources;
- the market leader has R&D and marketing skills for producing modified products of line extensions and also has the necessary promotion resources for stimulating primary demand among current non-users (Walker et al., 1999).

The marketing tools that can be used as part of the extensive penetration strategy include, among others: increasing the value of the product by adding new features or services; enhancing distribution coverage through innovative networks; sales promotions in the form of couponing, tie-in sales and sampling.

Use expansion strategy

The main objective of this strategy is to expand the use of the product by current users. This can be achieved through the following three methods:

- increases in the frequency of use;
- increases in the quantity used;
- development of new product uses.

Aaker (1998) proposes certain strategies that can be sought in each of these three methods. More specifically, the *increases in the frequency of use* can be obtained by first, providing reminder communications, secondly, positioning for frequent or regular use, thirdly, making the use easier or more convenient, fourthly, providing incentives, and fifthly, reducing undesirable consequences of frequent use. Moreover, the *increases in the quantity used* can be attained by first, providing reminder communications, secondly, using incentives, thirdly, affecting the usage level norms, fourthly, reducing undesirable consequences of increased use level, and fifthly, developing positive associations with use occasions. Also, the *development of new product uses* can be accomplished through using the product first, on different occasions, secondly, at different locations, and thirdly, for different purposes.

New market strategy

This strategy aims at serving yet unreached segments. This strategy can take the form of geographic expansion, by targeting another region within a country or even expanding operations to other countries. Apart from geography, other criteria can also be used for define a new market like for example age (for example, Kinder chocolate is now targeted to parents as well as children) and distribution channel (for example, HSBC targets interactive digital television, 'idTV' users, apart from traditional bank branch customers).

There are certain conditions under which the new market strategy is highly applicable, namely:

- certain regions are underserved;
- the market can be segments using a variety of segmentation criteria;
- the market leader has sufficient resources to cultivate underdeveloped new market segments;
- competitors have insufficient resources to preempt underdeveloped segments.

Some marketing tactics, which can be used as part of the new market strategy, include among others: line extensions especially developed with new features for regional or applications segments; advertising and sales promotions emphasizing product features and applications; distribution networks that allow access to the underserved segments.

Marketing strategies in the maturity stage: the case of the mobile telephony market in Greece

By the year 2000, more than half of the potential customers are using mobile phones. The passing of the mobile telephony market from growth to maturity is marked by a significant reduction in the average monthly fixed cost of mobile telephony, and a significant decrease in service differentiation, increased competition, further price reduction, and the development of new value-added services with the objective of differentiating its offering, extending use and consequently revenues.

(Continued)

(Continued)

It is noted that, according to estimations WAP and GPRS Internet-related technologies will extend the life cycle of the mobile telephony market.

During the first semester of 2000, Cosmote surpasses Telestet and reaches the second place, while Panafon remains first, though having considerable losses especially in the new subscribers market.

All three companies aim at expanding the market further. The strategies followed are as follows:

- They follow extended use strategies of mobile phones by launching new value-added services, which are based on WAP technology.
- Panafon adopts an increased penetration strategy by introducing the CU prepaid card service that is targeted to youngsters, aged 15–25.
- Having as an objective to increase the amount of service used by the average customer, they continue their effort of further expanding the distribution network, especially for card-related services by signing contracts with large supermarket chains.
- Telestet introduces a new pricing scheme. According to this scheme as the duration of a call increases, its price falls accordingly. It must be noted, though, that such a tactic is aimed more at making an impression, since the average duration of a call does not exceed 60 seconds.
- Panafon is late to realize that offering several different pricing programmes causes customer confusion, and therefore it eliminates its programmes, replacing them with new ones copied from competition.
- Panafon aims at exploiting better its telecommunications network. For achieving this objective, it enters the data transmission market, offering Internet provider services, frame relay services, and leased line services through its Panafonet Company.
- Telestet launches the B-best service, offering complete telecommunication solution for corporate clients, like leased lines and virtual private networks (VPN), and so on.
- Cosmote makes similar moves, offering advanced B2B value-added services, like VPN, and so on.
- Finally, Cosmote follows a market expansion strategy by acquiring the Albanian mobile telephony company AMC, where mobile telephony is at the introduction stage of its life cycle.

Source: Avlonitis and Nikiforaki (2000)

Marketing strategies in the decline stage

The final stage of a product's life cycle refers to its decline. Although a declining market is not particularly attractive, under certain circumstances, a market in decline can be relatively attractive.

Harrigan and Porter (1983) have identified three groups of factors that can be used to determine the attractiveness of a market, namely:

1 demand conditions;
2 ease of market exit;
3 competitive rivalry.

A declining market can be characterized, for example, as highly attractive when the following conditions occur. In terms of demand conditions are concerned: speed of decline is slow; predictability of decline is certain; there are several market niches; there is extensive product differentiation; premium pricing is followed; prices are stable. As far as ease of market exit is concerned: assets are fully depreciated; there is little excess capacity; there is limited vertical integration; and no re-investing. Regarding competitive rivalry; there are high switching cost and limited customer bargaining power.

All in all, a company in a declining market can use the following five strategies (Harrigan, 1980; Aaker, 1998):

- profitable survivor strategy;
- milking or harvesting strategy;
- hold strategy;
- niche strategy;
- divesting or exit strategy.

Profitable survivor strategy

This strategy is considered as most appropriate for market leaders in declining markets that may invest in such markets in order to strengthen further their competitive position. This can be achieved by encouraging competitors to exit the market.

The market conditions favouring the implementation of a profitable survivor strategy are as follows:

- Market decline is inevitable, but it will occur at a rather slow and steady rate.
- Pockets of enduring demand continue to exist.
- Barriers to exit are low and can be further reduced by the firm's intervention.
- The company has the resources to afford a deliberate rise in the costs of competing for encouraging competitors to exit the market.

The following marketing actions can be considered part of a profitable survivor strategy: launch product line extensions, price reduction, increased distribution coverage, increased promotion.

Milking or harvesting strategy

This strategy aims at maximizing returns, even at the expense of market share. The conditions supporting the implementation of this strategy are as follows (Aaker 1998; Walker et al., 1999):

- The decline rate is pronounced and unlikely to change, but not excessively steep.
- Pockets of enduring demand ensure that the decline rate will not suddenly become precipitous.
- Competitive rivalry is not expected to be intense.
- The price structure is stable at a level that is profitable for efficient firms.
- The company's market position is weak, but there is enough customer loyalty, perhaps in a limited part of the market, to generate sales and profits in a milking mode.
- The market is not central to the current strategic direction of the firm.

The harvesting strategy presupposes avoiding additional investments and reducing operational costs. More specifically, this strategy requires:

- considerable reduction in advertising, sales promotion, as well as trade promotion costs;
- sales force efforts directed to maintaining repurchases from current customers;
- reduction in production costs;
- maintaining or even increasing prices to increase margins.

Marketing strategies in the decline stage: the case of a medium-sized cosmetics firm

Over the years, various companies have followed the harvesting or even the profitable survivor strategies and they had managed to improve their profitability.

One such example refers to a Greek medium-sized enterprise operating in the cosmetics market. Among other products this firm had unpacked eau de cologne. This product is targeted at older people, with medium to low incomes. The product showed continuous decline for seven successive years (in 1994: sales totalled 95 million drachmas or £175,000; in 2000: sales totalled 57 million drachmas or £104,000). Competition is not particularly intense despite the fact that recently there are many imitations in the market. Basically, these products come from small firms, which produce hair salon products. The company of our example remains leader in a declining market and two alternative strategies can be used: harvesting and profitable survivor.

The strategy selected is the profitable survivor strategy, which was implanted through:

- concentrating part of the selling effort to acquiring customers from competition;
- launching product line extensions with new types of unpacked eau de cologne for attracting the remaining market segments;
- continuing R&D activities at a product level, improving the functional characteristics of the jars containing the eau de cologne;
- maintaining prices at the same level.

Hold strategy

This strategy aims at maintaining market share, even if that causes a reduction in profit. Conditions favouring the implementation of the maintenance strategy include:

- The market lacks growth potential.
- Market conditions are not expected to change dramatically.
- Pockets of enduring demand still exist.
- Competitive rivalry can not be accurately predicted.
- There are no significant price pressures.
- The company holds a relatively strong position in the market.

A company that has decided on the maintenance strategy must do the following:

- maintain R&D expenses;
- focus promotion efforts on maintaining repeat purchases;
- reduce prices if necessary.

Niche strategy

The objective of this strategy is to strengthen market position in one or few promising segments. The conditions favouring the implementation of a niche strategy are as follows (Walker et al., 1999):

- The market declines quickly, but one or more segments will remain as demand pockets or decay slowly.
- There are one or more strong competitors in the mass market, but not in the target segment.
- The company has a sustainable competitive advantage in the target segment, but all in all its resources are limited.

In order to implement a niche strategy, the following marketing actions may be considered: improving product to make it appealing to the target segment; focus promotion (namely, advertising, personal selling, sales promotion, public relations) on the customers of the target segment; keep appropriate distribution coverage.

Divesting or exit strategy

When market attractiveness is particularly low, a company may seriously consider exiting the market. The conditions favouring a divesting or exit strategy are the following (Aaker, 1998):

- The decline rate is rapid and accelerating.
- No pockets of enduring demand are can be accessible anymore.
- The price pressures are expected to be extreme, caused by determined competitors with high exit barriers and by a lack of brand loyalty and product differentiation.
- Few dominant competitors have achieved sustainable advantage.
- The firm's strategic direction has changed, and the role of this market is peripheral or even unwanted.
- Exit barriers can be overcome.

Summary

- Despite the criticism the product life cycle (PLC) model has received, it remains a useful tool of strategic planning.
- Depending on the stage of the product's life cycle, different marketing strategies must be pursued.
- The most appropriate marketing strategies also depend on whether the company is a market leader or follower.
- The market characteristics, marketing objectives, marketing strategies as well as marketing tactics of each stage in the PLC are summarized in Table 3.1.

Questions

1 Select three products or services you have bought lately and list the product-related decisions that should have been taken depending on their product life cycle stage.
2 Give two examples of products that do not follow the S-curve life cycle model.

Table 3.1 Summary of stage characteristics, marketing objectives, strategies and tactics over the product life cycle

Theoretical model	Introduction	Growth	Maturity	Decline
Stage characteristics				
• Market growth rate	Moderate	High	Stable	Negative
• Financial outcomes	Loss	Increasing profitability	Decreasing profitability	Decreasing profitability
• Customers	Innovators	Early adopters and early majority	Late majority	Laggards
• Competition	Limited	Increasing	Decreasing	Steadily diminishing
Marketing objectives	Encouraging demand	Building market share	Maintaining market share	Limiting expenses
		Market leader's strategies: • Fortress or defence position • Flanker • Confrontation • Market expansion or mobile • Contraction or strategic withdrawal Market follower's strategies: • Frontal attack • Bypass or leapfrog • Flanking • Encirclement • Guerrilla attack	Strategies for maintaining market share: • Fortress or defence position • Flanker • Confrontation • Market expansion • Contraction or strategic withdrawal Strategies for further growth: • Extensive penetration • Use expansion • New market	• Profitable survivor • Hold • Milking or harvesting • Niche • Divesting or exit
Marketing strategies	• Rapid skimming • Slow skimming • Rapid penetration • Slow penetration			
Marketing tactics				
• Product	Core product, emphasis on quality	Improvements in quality, line extensions, warranties, customer service	Differentiation Maintaining brands and models	Offer minimization Withdrawal
• Price	High/Low	Aiming at penetration	Maintenance or selective reduction	Price reduction
• Place	Selective	Building distribution channels-intensive	Intensive	Selective
• Advertising	High expenses Building awareness early adopters and channel members	High expenses Building awareness in the mass market	Decreasing expenses Emphasis on differential benefits	Reduction to necessary level for maintaining loyal customers
• Promotion	Limited	Decrease with the aim of exploiting increasing demand	Increase with the aim of encouraging brand switching	Minimization

3   Why should the marketing strategies of the leaders be different from the marketing strategies of the followers over the product life cycle?
4   A pension scheme is in a high growth rate market, with increasing profitability, increasing competition, and targeted to early adopters. Discuss the alternative marketing strategies and tactics for this service.

References

Aaker, D. (1998) *Strategic Market Management*, 5th edition. Chichester: John Wiley & Sons.

Avlonitis, G. and Nikiforaki, L. (2000) 'Marketing strategies over the product life cycle: The case of mobile telephony in Greece', Working Paper, Athens University of Economics and Business.

Buzzell, R. and Gale, B. (1987) *The PIMS Principles: Linking Strategy to Performance*. New York: The Free Press.

Cox, W. (1967) 'Product life cycle as marketing models', *The Journal of Business*: 375–84.

Dhalla, N.K. and Yuspeh, S. (1976) 'Forget the product life cycle concept', *Harvard Business Review*: 102–110.

Doyle, P. (1976) 'The realities of product life cycle', *Quarterly Review of Marketing*): 1–6.

Flides, R. and Lofthouse, S. (1975) 'Market share strategy and the product life-cycle: a comment', *Journal of Marketing*: 57–60.

Harrigan, K. (1980) 'Strategies for declining industries', *Journal of Business Strategy*: 27.

Harrigan, K. and Porter, M. (1983) 'End-game strategies for declining industries', *Harvard Business Review*: 117.

Hooley, G., Saunders, J. and Piercy, N. (2004) *Marketing Strategy and Competitive Positioning*. Harlow: Pearson Education Limited.

Kotler, P. (2003) *Marketing Management: Analysis, Planning, Implementation and Control*, 11th edition. Englewood Cliffs, NJ: Prentice Hall.

Kotler, P. and Singh, R. (1981) 'Marketing warfare in the 1980s', *Journal of Business Strategy*: 30–41.

Rink, D. and Swan, J. (1979) 'Product life cycle research: A literature review', *Journal of Business Research*, 219–242.

Swan, J. and Rink, D. (1982) 'Effective use of industrial product life cycle trends', in *Marketing in the '80s*, Proceedings of the American Marketing Academy Conference, pp. 198–9.

Walker, O., Boyd, H. and Larreche, J. (1999) *Marketing Strategy: Planning and Implementation*. Irwin: Mc-Graw Hill.

Further reading

Aaker, A. and Day, S. (1986) 'The perils of high-growth markets', *Strategic Management Journal*, 7: 409–21.

Anderson, C. and Zeithaml, C. (1984) 'Stages in the product life cycle, business strategy, and business performance', *Academy of Management Journal*, March: 5–25.

Doyle, P. (1995) Product life cycle management, in M.J. Baker (ed.), *The Companion Encyclopedia of Marketing*. London: Routledge.

Treacy, M. and Wiersema, F. (1995) *The Discipline of Market Leaders*. Reading, MA: Addison-Wesley.

4 Evaluation of Product/Service Portfolio

Introduction

One of the main marketing activities of a company is the evaluation of its existing products/services so as to achieve an allocation of resources (financial, production, marketing, and so on) that leads to maximizing future returns for a given risk level.

In this sense, evaluating a company's existing products/services is a vital activity since it provides critical information for decision-making, which ensures survival and further development of the company. These decisions may refer to new product/service development, modification and/or elimination of existing products/services and allocation of the company's resources among different products/services and markets.

For evaluating product/service portfolio, one or more approaches can be used. In this chapter, the following questions that are related to these approaches are addressed:

- What is the multidimensional 'screening' approach?
- What is the index approach?
- What is the product portfolio classification/matrix approach?

In this chapter, these approaches are presented in detail. Special emphasis is given to the product portfolio/matrix approach and particularly to the financial and non-financial models that have been developed as part of this approach.

Multidimensional 'screening' approach

This approach, which was developed about five decades ago, advocates a systematic review of the product line in which every product is subject to performance evaluation on a number of key performance dimensions/criteria (for example, sales volume, profitability, market share). In Table 4.1, we provide the 'screening' dimensions/criteria and the procedures proposed.

'Index' approach

According to the 'index' approach, there is a routine evaluation of product performance on a number of key dimensions/criteria, which is summarized in a single overall performance index. Table 4.2 presents the main indices that are available in the literature.

Table 4.1   The multidimensional 'screening' approach

Author	Proposed 'screening' criteria	Procedural approach
Houfek (1952)	Sales value, composite costs (direct materials and labour; variable overhead; marketing costs).	Suggests that weak products should be identified on the basis of their incremental profit, which is the difference between their sales value and composite costs.
Sonnecken and Hurst (1960)	Profitability, product-line scope, marketing efficiency, production efficiency, cost/price, value/quality, service, competition.	Propose that weak products should be identified on the bases of these criteria which management should carefully consider in conducting a periodic product-line audit.
Alexander (1964)	Price trend, profit trend, substitute products, product effectiveness, executive time.	Advocates a systematic and periodic search for elimination candidates on the basis of these criteria and provides an additional, in-depth analysis of situations and opportunities regarding candidates for elimination.
Kotler (1965)	Share of company sales, sales decline, market decline, gross margin, product's coverage of overhead.	Proposes a computer-aided product review system, which consists of a creation stage and six operational steps. The identification of 'dubious' products is the objective of the first two operational steps in which product data sheets containing information pertinent to the proposed criteria are screened by means of a computer program.
Eckles (1971)	Inventory requirements, past sales volume, future sales volume, profit margin, competitive activity, total generic demand trend.	Suggests a four-state approach to product elimination. The first state is a monthly review of each product along the proposed criteria. The products identified as candidates for elimination at state 1 are subject to further analysis in states 2, 3 and 4 to determine their elimination/retention status and the timing of their elimination.
Worthing (1971)	ROI (product's profit as a percentage of its production and marketing costs), profitability (product's profit as a percentage of its sales value), sales volume (product's sales as a percentage of company sales).	Proposes a computer-aided two-phased product evaluation procedure. The first phase (Program SCREEN) identifies those products whose performance along the proposed criteria is worse than that of the previous year. These products are subject to further evaluation in the second phase (Program MODROP) to determine their elimination/retention status.
Kratchman et al. (1975)	Development costs, variable expenses, past unit sales, sales revenues, sales revenues of competitive products, unit sales of competitive products, current and past pricing structure, inventory turnover, competitive pricing policies, executive man hours, future sales volume.	Suggest the transformation of these accounting-based 'screening' criteria into 'warning signals'; that is, indication as to whether a product should be considered for elimination. They also propose the establishment of minimum standards of performance for these 'warning signals' which should be computerized so that any product failing to meet any standard can be 'red-flagged' as soon as possible.

(Continued)

Table 4.1 (Continued)

Author	Proposed 'screening' criteria	Procedural approach
Browne and Kemp (1976)	Sales volume, profitability, ROI, cost and availability of raw materials, average order size, rate of market penetration, number of sales calls required per sale.	Advocate a three-stage product review system. The first stage is basically a product-line monitoring system, which uses the proposed criteria to identify weak products as candidates for elimination. The products identified at this stage are evaluated in much greater depth in the following two stages to determine their elimination/retention status.

Table 4.2 The 'Index' approach

Author	Proposed framework			Proposed action
		Weight the factors	Add the weights	Act on ΣV
Berenson (1963)	Factors affecting financial security $\longrightarrow V_1$			
	Factors affecting financial opportunity $\longrightarrow V_2$			i If ΣV is approximately X_1 take action A_1
	Factors affecting marketing strategy $\longrightarrow V_3$		ΣV	ii If ΣV is approximately X_2 take action A_2
	Factors affecting social responsibility $\longrightarrow V_4$			iii If ΣV is approximately X_3 take action A_3
	Factors affecting organized intervention $\longrightarrow V_5$			iv If ΣV is approximately X_4 take action A_4

Clayton (1966)		
SURVIVAL SCORE INDEX (SSI) $= \dfrac{A \times B \times C \times (D - E) \times F}{G + H + I}$		If SSI > 1 the product should be retained in the line
where: A = % chance of product meeting is ROI goal B = % chance of continued sales success C = Projected sales volume – units/year D = Sales price/unit E = Manufacturing costs/unit F = Remaining market life (1–5 years) G = R&D costs to continue product line H = Process and product engineering costs to continue product I = Marketing costs to continue product line		If SSI > 1 the product should be dropped from the line

Table 4.2   **(Continued)**

Author	Proposed framework		Proposed action
Hamelman and Mazze (1972)	PRESS 1 – Primary model		

Inputs (per product)	Outputs	The products with the lowest SIN numbers are the most promising candidates for elimination. These products are subject to further evaluation through the supplemental models PRESS II, III and IV to examine the effects due to price changes, sales growth trends and product complementarity/substitutability factors, respectively. The revised SIN listing of products produced is used by the PRESS IV model which, starting with the products with the lowest SIN numbers, eliminates products one at a time till a reduction in a cost element, previously specified, is reached.
Materials cost Labour cost Variable overhead Sales price Quantity sold/period Sales and admin charges Manufacturing runs/period	a Performance ratios: % expressions of how much labour and variable overhead become available should product be dropped. b Selection Index Numbers – SIN	

$$SIN_i = \frac{(CM_i/\Sigma CM^2)}{(FC_i/\Sigma FC)}$$

where:

CM_i = contribution margin for product i

ΣCM = summation of contribution margin for all products

FC = facilities cost for product i

ΣFC = summation of facilities costs of all products

Product portfolio classification/matrix approach

The third approach of evaluating a company's existing products/services advocates the joint consideration of a number of key product performance dimensions which leads to the development of a product portfolio classification/matrix scheme.

When using this approach, the company examines combinations of products/markets taking into consideration its strengths and the opportunities for high financial returns, which arise in the changing external environment.

A basic characteristic of the product portfolio classification/matrix approach is that it supposes that the company manages a portfolio of products/services that:

1 are in different stages of their life cycle;
2 have their own special contribution to the prosperity and financial performance of the company and therefore,
3 require different marketing strategies.

The pioneering portfolio theory of Nobel laureate H. Markowitz (1952) in the field of financial management formed the basis for developing product portfolio management models. Markowitz defines 'portfolio' as the combination of investments (for example, stocks, bonds, cash, and so on), with various levels of risk and return. According to his theory, national investors select efficient portfolios, that is portfolios that maximize the expected return for a given risk level or alternatively minimize the risk for a given level of expected return.

However, the criteria of return and risk which are used in financial management are not good enough for the marketing manager who also needs to base its product/service portfolio's evaluations on market-related criteria as well. Therefore, in the late 1960s models of product/service portfolio evaluation appeared in the literature, which incorporated both market and not market-related criteria. These models, which are expressed in the form of matrices, are based on criteria such as market share, profitability, competitive position, market growth rate, and so on. What criteria will ultimately be used depends on the company's resources, markets, competitive position and objectives. However, the usefulness of a product/service portfolio matrix depends on its relative simplicity. The larger the number of criteria used, the more difficult is the collection of the necessary data.

Before proceeding with the presentation of the product portfolio classification/matrix models it must be pointed out that such an evaluation can be made on a product line, product mix or strategic business unit level, depending on the structure and size of the company.

Non-financial models of product portfolio

Product classification by Peter Drucker

The initial idea of classifying products for resource allocation reasons belongs to Peter Drucker (1963), who proposed that products tend to be classified in six categories:

- 'Tomorrow's breadwinners': new products or 'today's breadwinners' modified and improved, already profitable with large market and wide acceptance, much more growth ahead without substantial modification, most companies ought to have at least one of these around.
- 'Today's breadwinners': the innovations of yesterday, substantial volume large profit earners. They still have more potential growth ahead after modification or change in design, promotion or selling methods.
- Products capable of becoming net contributors if something drastic is done, for example, converting a good many buyers of 'special' variations of limited utility into customers for a new, massive 'regular' line.
- 'Yesterday's breadwinners': typically products with high volume, but badly fragmented into 'specials', small orders, and the like and requiring such massive support as to eat up all they earn plus plenty more. Yet this is – next to the category following – the product class to which the largest and best resources are usually allocated.
- 'Also rans': typically the high hopes of yesterday that, while they did not work out well, nevertheless did not become outright failures. These are always minus contributors, and practically never become successes no matter how much managerial and technical ego involved in them to drop them.
- 'Failures': these rarely are a real problem, as they tend to liquidate themselves.

Having categorized products into groups, Drucker proceeds to propose that the ranking of these six groups suggests the line that decisions ought to follow. To begin with, the first category should be supplied the necessary resources and usually a little more than seems necessary. Next, 'today's breadwinners' ought to receive support. Of the products capable of becoming major contributors, only those should be supported which have either the greatest probability of being reformed successfully or would make an extraordinary contribution if the reform were accomplished.

The lower half of the third group and also groups four, five and six either have to produce without any resources and efforts or should be allowed to die. 'Yesterday's breadwinners' for instance, often make a respectable 'milk cow' with high yields for a few more years. To expect more and to plough euros into artificial respiration when the product finally begins to fade is just plain foolish.

Although Drucker's model is a valuable tool for evaluating product portfolios, it is far from a complete synthesis of the underlying analyses and judgements as to the product's position within the company's activities and in the market where it competes.

Product classification by Fluitman

A somewhat similar classification to that of Drucker has been suggested by Fluitman (1973). He argued that a company could use four dimensions for evaluating its product portfolio, namely: sales volume, average annual growth rate, utilization of key resources, and return on investment (ROI). On the basis of these dimensions, products within a company's portfolio can be classified into the following eight categories:

- failures;
- products of tomorrow;
- products of today;
- investments in managerial ego;
- sleepers;
- fade out products;
- specialties;
- yesterday's products.

Management should classify all its products along the recommended dimensions. 'Failures', 'investments in managerial ego', 'fade-out products' and 'yesterday's products' which account for a low percentage of the company's sales turnover, experience zero growth, absorb a high percentage of the company's resources and exhibit negative profitability, should be considered as candidates for elimination. Resources should be taken to cut down such products in order to allow the company to achieve its profit objectives and to pay more attention to the 'bread and butter' products of today and tomorrow, which guarantee the continuity of the company. Our comments regarding Drucker's classification apply equally to Fluitman's classification.

Market growth – market share matrix by Boston Consulting Group

The multinational consulting firm Boston Consulting Group (BCG) has developed a strategic model for companies with many products in different markets (Boston Consulting Group, 1976). This model is known as the 'market growth-market share matrix' (Figure 4.1).

According to this BCG model, company products/services can be classified in four categories depending on the rate of market growth and the relative market share of the product/service.

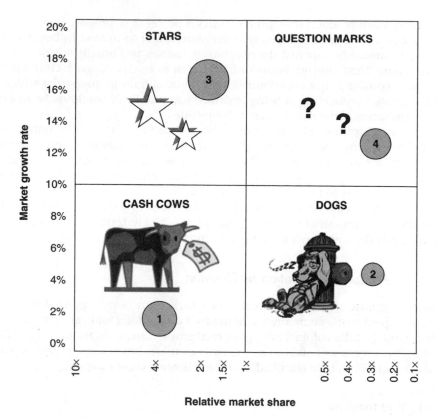

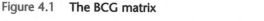

Figure 4.1 **The BCG matrix**

Source: Boston Consulting Group (1976); Hedley (1977)

More specifically, the market growth rate in the vertical axis represents how the market grows annually from 0 per cent to 20 per cent. A market growth rate above 10 per cent is considered high. The relative market share in the horizontal axis represents the market share that the company's product possesses compared to its main competitor. A relative market share of 0.2× means that the product's sales are only 20 per cent of sales of the main competing product, while 4× means that the company's product is the market leader having four times the market share of the next stronger competing product.

In the BCG model, the market growth rate represents an approximate estimation of the product's life cycle (and therefore, its attractiveness), while the relative market share reflects the product's market performance (and, therefore, its position in the market).

It must be noted that, a third criterion is also used which refers to the product's contribution to the overall sales of a company. In Figure 4.1, the circles represent the four products of a hypothesized company. The size of the circle is analogous to the sales achieved by the respective product in relation to the overall company sales.

The basic characteristic of the BCG matrix is its simplicity. The matrix attempts to accommodate the complexities of a company's product portfolio in a graphical representation by using only three criteria/variables.

The products of each of the four categories have different names like stars, cash cows, problem children or question marks and dogs. These categories present different cash flows and are related to different marketing strategies. More specifically:

- *'Stars'* (high market growth/high relative market share): products categorized as stars are leaders in fast growing markets. Despite the fact that these products are profitable, their cash flows are negative. This is because they require considerable resources for financing their rapid growth and facing competition usually through price reductions.

  High growth markets attract many companies and the battle is usually focused on acquiring new customers and developing new application for the stars. Strategies for stars can be summarized as follows: first, protecting the existing market share, secondly, re-investing cash flows (profits) for price reductions, product improvements, better market coverage and enhancing product efficiency, thirdly, acquiring a larger share of new customers.

- *'Cash cows'* (low market growth/high relative market share): As indicated by their name, these products, which are at the maturity stage of their life cycle, are the company's cash generators. Their strong competitive position allows them to enjoy economies of scale and high profit margins in low growth markets that do not require considerable financial resources. Hence, 'cash cows' provide cash flows that are much more than those needed for re-investment in R&D, market research and promotion. These positive cash flows can be used to support the other product categories of the portfolio especially 'question marks'. Strategies that can be followed for 'cash cows' are summarized as follows: first, maintaining their leading position in the market, secondly, investing for enhancing their production process and creating technological leadership and thirdly, maintaining price leadership.

- *'Problem children'* or *'question marks'* (high market growth/low market share): these products have low market share in high growth markets. They require significant financial resources in order to remain competitive, while their profit margins are limited. Most products start as 'question marks' as the company tries to enter an attractive high growth market where there exists a market leader.

  The term 'question mark' for these products is quite successful, as the company has to decide whether it will commit significant financial resources for achieving a leading position in the market or exit the market despite its attractiveness.

  The strategies, which can be used for 'problem children' or 'question marks', are as follows: first, investing considerable financial resources for building market share, secondly, building market share through acquisition of competitive companies, thirdly, de-investing through selling the product to another company, fourthly 'harvesting' which results in the maximization of cash flows through decreases in investments and promotion expenses, fifthly, segmentation and niching strategy in a market where the company can establish a strong position, lastly, product elimination.

- *'Dogs'* (low market growth/low market share): these products are weak and unattractive, as they possess a low market share in low growth markets. They are usually at the maturity or decline stage of their life cycle. They are often called 'cash traps' because they normally require more financial resources than those they generate in order to maintain their competitive position in the market. The strategies of divestment, 'harvesting', segmentation and eliminating which can be applied in 'question marks' can also be used in the case of 'dogs'.

According to the BCG matrix, the main objective of the company should be the creation of a balanced product portfolio, which will include as few 'dogs' as possible, a moderate number of 'question marks' and 'cash-cows', and as many 'stars' as possible.

Criticism of the BCG matrix

Despite the importance of the BCG matrix for evaluating product portfolios, it is not free of weaknesses, which should not be ignored. More analytically:

- The rate of market growth is not the only criterion for measuring market attractiveness. Further, negative growth rates, although possible, are not considered.
- The relative market share is not the only criterion for defining a product's competitive strength of market position.
- The BCG model presupposes that there is a positive relationship between relative market share and product profitability. This assumption has been heavily criticized (Wensley, 1981; Jacobson and Aaker, 1985; Morrison and Wensley, 1991). For example, in the case of 'cash cows' the model hypothesizes that because of their high relative market share they are 'cash generators' that can finance 'question marks' and 'stars'. However, this is not always true as there are companies that are unable to control their costs and despite increased sales, the product's profitability remains low.
- This model simply suggests the reallocation of resources among products, without presenting information about market sizes, and the resources required. For example, a 'cash-cow' may compete in a small size market and consequently, the high sales or large market share achieved, may not be enough for financing the necessary marketing activities of a 'question mark' which competes in a market five times the size of the 'cash-cow'.

All in all, the Boston Consulting Group Matrix is a tool of a preliminary evaluation of product portfolios that allows the company to combine graphically three types of information, namely market growth rate, relative market share, and percentage of product sales on total company sales. This information is certainly necessary for decision-making. Nevertheless, it should not be considered as sufficient for achieving a rational allocation of business resources to the various company products.

Product profitability grid by Philip Kotler

Kotler (1974) developed what he termed the 'product profitability grid' where each product is plotted in terms of its rates of return on investment (ROI) and sales growth, which are two useful dimensions for judging the long-term profitability of a company's product (Figure 4.2).

The grid is further divided into three parts, reflecting management's view of strong, satisfactory and weak products. The best products are those strong in both sales growth and current return on investment. But management also considers products strong if they have an exceptional sales growth rate or return on investment. The dividing line between strong products and satisfactory products, and between satisfactory products and weak products reflects the trade-off between these two dimensions in management's mind. Any products that show up as weak can be checked for their behaviour over time. The typical product shows a life cycle trajectory similar to that shown in Figure 4.2.

Although Kotler's 'product profitability grid' is theoretically sound, it overlooks important marketing variables, including that of market share, which is necessary for the identification of the product as a candidate for elimination. In fact, a product's market share assists management to determine whether a downward trend in sales growth and return on investment reflects a fundamental change in the environment or is merely due to temporary fluctuations. Furthermore, the consideration of a product's return on investment and sales growth in terms of the standard concept of the product life cycle introduces some additional practical problems. In fact, there is clear evidence that while most products do follow a broad life cycle pattern, the product life cycle itself is insufficiently uniform to provide a rational basis for prediction and therefore, for product planning.

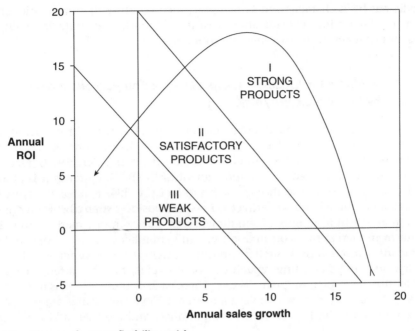

Figure 4.2 **The product profitability grid**

Source: Kotler (1974)

Product evaluation matrix by Wind and Claycamp

Another model for evaluating products is the 'product evaluation matrix' proposed by Wind and Claycamp (1976). According to this model, the product is evaluated on the basis of profitability, product sales, industry sales and market share.

These researchers propose an approach for making strategic product/market decisions with two definitional phases and five analytical stages. At the first two stages of analysis, the past and present strategic position of each product is determined through the integration of the four dimensions into a product evaluation matrix. At succeeding stages, the performance of each product is presented for alternative marketing strategies based on key assumptions about competition and other external influences.

The product performance matrix allows the marketer to systematically address two basic questions: 'Where are we now?' and 'Where should we go from here?'. Overall analysis reveals strong performers as well as candidates for remedial action of some kind or elimination.

Wind and Claycamp (1976) identify five strategies that might be appropriate for a particular product, or for an entire line of products, depending on market conditions, for example, market size, competition, customer needs and so on. These strategies are as follows:

1 maintain the product and its marketing strategy in the present form;
2 maintain the present form of the product, but change its marketing strategy;
3 change the product and alter the marketing strategy;
4 drop the product or the entire product line;
5 add one or more products into the line or add new product lines.

This model has been characterized as dynamic, incorporating the future orientation of the company, taking into consideration a variety of marketing strategies, competitive activities and changes in the external environment.

Market attractiveness – competitive position portfolio model by General Electric/McKinsey

Another model developed and popularized by General Electric in cooperation with the leading consulting firm McKinsey is the Business Assessment model or Market Attractiveness – Competitive Position Portfolio classification (Allen, 1979) (Figure 4.3).

This model can be viewed as an improvement of the BCG matrix as it is based on a multifactor analysis. More specifically, each product (or SBU) is rated in terms of two main dimensions, namely market attractiveness and business strengths. Each dimension is further analysed in a number of sub-dimensions. For example, market attractiveness may result from market size, contribution margins, number of competitors, and rate of market growth, among others. Similarly, business strengths involve market share, product quality, unit cost, marketing capabilities, brand value, to name a few. Management should identify the most appropriate factors. Then, each of these factors is rated on a five-point scale (1: very unattractive, 5: very attractive). Next, the ratings are multiplied by weights representing the factors' relative importance, and are then added up for each dimension.

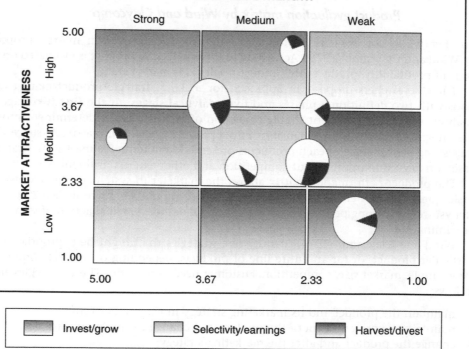

Figure 4.3   **The GE/McKinsey matrix**
Source: Day (1986). Reprinted with permission.

Each of the two dimensions of the McKinsey/GE matrix is divided into three categories, namely low, medium and high. This results in a nine-cell matrix. The position of each product in the matrix is represented in circles. The size of the circle reflects the size of the product's market. A shaded part of the circle can be drawn representing the product's market share.

The McKinsey/GE matrix is divided in three distinctive zones: the three upper-left cells indicate opportunities in which the company should invest/grow. The three diagonal cells (lower left to upper right) reflect moderate attractiveness. Thus, the company should be selective in the investments made. Finally, the three cells at the lower-right end of the matrix reflect unattractive markets in which the competitive position of the company is rather weak. In this case, the company should seriously consider following a divesting or harvesting strategy.

The McKinsey/GE matrix suggests certain strategies that the company should pursue depending on market attractiveness and its business strengths. These strategies are as follows:

- protect position (high market attractiveness-high business strengths);
- invest to build (high market attractiveness-medium business strengths);
- build selectively (medium market attractiveness-low business strengths);
- build selectively (medium market attractiveness-high business strengths);
- selectivity/manage for earnings (medium market attractiveness-medium business strengths);
- limited expansion or harvest (medium market attractiveness-low business strengths);
- protect and refocus (low market attractiveness-high business strengths);
- manage for earnings (low market attractiveness-medium business strengths);
- direct (low market attractiveness-low business strengths).

Shell International directional policy matrix

Another model for evaluating product portfolios has been developed by the Dutch oil company Shell under the name Shell International directional policy matrix (Seidl, 1979) (Table 4.3).

This matrix has two dimensions: prospects for sector profitability (horizontal axis) and company's competitive capabilities (vertical axis). Each dimension is divided into three zones. Prospects for sector profitability may vary from unattractive, through average to attractive, while the company's competitive capabilities may be weak, average or strong. Thus, the Shell matrix has nine cells with different combinations of prospects for sector profitability and company's competitive capabilities. Each cell reflects a different strategic option. For example, when the prospects for sector profitability are unattractive, and the company's competitive capabilities are weak, then the most appropriate strategy is divestment.

Ben Enis's product/market matching matrix

In 1980, Ben Enis has developed the product/market matching matrix. This matrix has two dimensions: product life cycle (PLC) stage and market phase (Figure 4.4). The first dimension is divided into introduction, growth, maturity and decline, whereas the latter dimension is divided in new, expanding, stable and contracting.

On the basis of this matrix, the company has to select between three alternative strategies: market extension, market development and market exploitation. Enis (1980) notes that many authors hypothesize that the stages of product life cycle and the market stage coincide. In such a case we refer to market development. However, this is not always true. It is possible that due to aggressive marketing the PLC may be pushed ahead

Table 4.3 Shell International directional policy matrix

		Prospects for sector profitability		
		Unattractive	Average	Attractive
Company's competitive capabilities	Weak	Disinvest	Phased withdrawal Custodial	Double or quit
	Average	Phased withdrawal	Custodial growth	Try harder
	Strong	Cash generation	Growth leader	Leader

Source: Seidl (1979)

Table 4.4 A.D. Little business portfolio matrix

		Stage of industry maturity			
		Embryonic	Growth	Maturity	Ageing
Competitive position	Dominant				
	Strong				
	Favourable				
	Tentative				
	Weak				

Source: Wind (1982)

of market stage. For example, a mature product is introduced in an expanding or stable market. This is called 'market extension'. Similarly Enis also recognizes that the PLC may lag behind the market stage, when, for example, a new product-introduction stage of PLC – is launched in a market that competitors have already entered. In such case, 'market exploitation' occurs.

Business profile matrix by A.D. Little

The leading consulting firm A.D. Little has developed the 'business profile matrix' (Wind, 1982). This model which is similar to the BCG Matrix is based on two dimensions (Table 4.4), the company's/product's competitive position and the stage of industrial maturity.

The competitive position is further broken down into five stages ranging from weak to dominant. The stage of industrial maturity has four steps, namely 'embryonic', 'growth', 'maturity', and 'aging'.

The A.D. Little business profile matrix implies that risk increases as products are aging and competitive position becomes weak. According to this model, there are certain strategies that could be followed depending on the competitive position and the stage of industrial maturity. For example, market penetration is most suitable when industry is in the embryonic or growth stage.

Barksdale and Harris model

In the classic paper of Barksdale and Harris (1982) in long range planning, a complete model of product portfolio evaluation was presented, which combines the BCG Matrix and the Product Life Cycle Concept (Figures 4.5 and 4.6). This model recognizes the

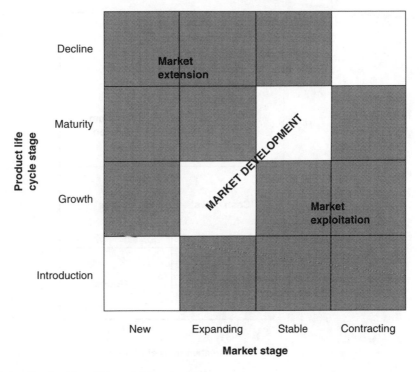

Figure 4.4   **Product/market matching matrix**

Source: Enis (1980)

importance of both the initial as well as final stages of the PLC when evaluating product portfolios. Thus, they propose three new categories of products, namely: pioneering products that are called 'infants', products with large market shares in declining markets, which are called 'war horses' and products with small market shares in declining markets, that are called 'dodos'.

'Infants' are pioneering products that require niche marketing. Usually, they do not generate profits for a period of time, while they require considerable financial resources. In a declining market, 'cash generators' (of the BCG model) become 'war horses'.

These successful 'veterans' have a strong competitive position in the market and with good management may remain significant sources of cash flow for the company.

According to the authors, Maxwell House coffee of General Foods is an excellent example of a 'war horse'. For many years it maintains a leading position in the instant coffee market and although this market is in decline, Maxwell House remains a successful brand.

'Dodos' are products with a small market share in declining markets and offer limited opportunities of generating cash flows. Usually, these products are deleted from the company's product portfolio. Although competition usually exits the market, it may be profitable for the company to maintain a 'dodo' in a declining market.

How effective are the models/matrices of product portfolios?

A number of researchers have attempted to empirically evaluate the effectiveness of the product portfolio models that we described earlier. In 1983, Wind, Mahajan and Swire used

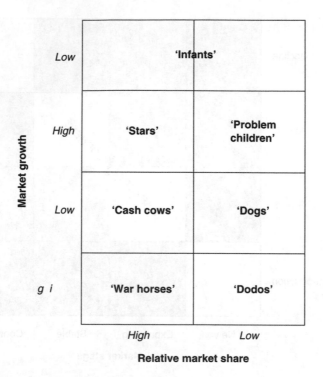

Figure 4.5   **Product life cycle portfolio matrix**
Source: Barksdale and Harris (1982)

data from the PIMS (Profit Impact of Marketing Strategy) database for fifteen SBUs of companies that belong the Fortune 500 list. Their main findings are summarized as follows:

The classification of any SBU or product in a specific product portfolio position such as low market share and low market growth rate ('dog') or high market share and high market growth rate ('star') depends on the following four specific factors:

1   the operational definition of the dimensions used;
2   the rule used to divide a dimension into categories, like high-low;
3   the weighting of the variables constituting the composite dimensions (if used);
4   the specific product portfolio model used.

Any minor change in the aforementioned factors may lead to different classification of the SBU or product involved, and, thus, in different strategies. Actually, only one of the fifteen SBUs that were examined remained in the same category regardless of the changes made in these factors.

Consequently, and given the sensitivity of SBU or product classification, it is quite risky to use a single portfolio model as a basis for product analysis and strategy. Wind and his colleagues suggest that companies should examine the sensitivity of the portfolio classification of SBUs or products to various portfolio objectives, definition of variables and weights, as well as the use of hybrid models. Following their recommendations would increase the value of portfolio analysis as an appropriate basis for marketing strategy and may avoid situations like the one revealed in their study, that the same SBU could be classified as a problem child, star, dog or cash cow depending on the model used.

In 1994, Armstrong and Brodie conducted a series of laboratory experiments in six countries over a five-year period to investigate whether decision makers might be

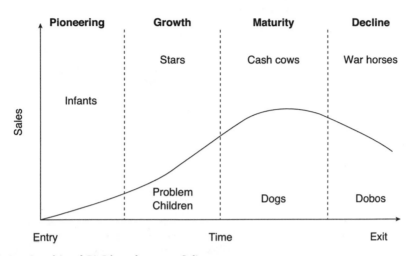

Figure 4.6　**Combined PLC/product portfolio concepts**

Source: Barksdale and Harris (1982)

misled by portfolio methods when making an investment decision. The two researchers chose an experimental design in which subjects were provided with a particular presentation (Boston Consulting Group – BCG Matrix or Net Present Value – NPV) and were then faced with a choice between two different investment opportunities. To determine whether the BCG Matrix would mislead people, the profitable investment was labelled 'dog' (its commercial name was digits), while the bad investment was labelled 'star' (its commercial name was sunbars). This study revealed that information about the BCG matrix increased the subjects' likelihood of selecting the investment that was clearly less profitable. Of subjects who were exposed to the BCG matrix, 63.5 per cent selected the unprofitable investment, while 37.1 per cent of subjects exposed to NPV made the wrong decision. Of subjects who used the BCG matrix in their analysis, 86.8 per cent selected the less profitable investment. In contrast, only 15.3 per cent of those using the NPV selected the bad investment. On the basis of their findings, Armstrong and Brodie (1994) suggested that the BCG model should not be used for product portfolio analysis.

This extreme position has been questioned by Wensley (1994) by criticizing both the nature of their experiments and the data analysis method used. More specifically, he argued that Armstrong and Brodie (1994) chose a relatively simple experimental design, and their finding that the BCG treatment generally results in a substantial preference for sunbars is not surprising, since sunbars are somewhat modelled on the BCG 'star' category and the digits on the 'dog' category. However, Wensley (1994) agreed that additional research is required before one can conclude that matrix techniques indeed improve the nature of decision-making.

Financial models of product portfolio analysis

As we mentioned at the beginning of the chapter, the financial portfolio theory, as reported by Markowitz (1952) forms the basis for developing models of product portfolio analysis.

Using techniques of non-linear programming, Markowitz has shown that, from an available population of alternative investments, an efficient portfolio can be developed.

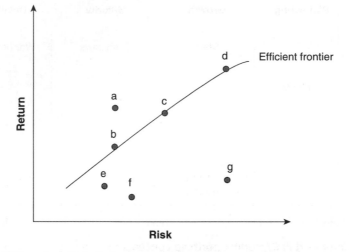

Figure 4.7   'Efficient frontier' of alternative investments

This portfolio is composed by all the investments that lie in a curve known as the 'efficient frontier' of alternative investments (Figure 4.7).

In order to identify the 'efficient frontier' one should calculate the following:

*   the expected return of the portfolio measured as the average return of all investments in the portfolio;
*   the risk of the portfolio measured as the standard deviation or the variance of the portfolio's return;
*   an additional risk of the portfolio, measured as the covariance or correlation coefficient between the expected returned of the portfolio's investments with the expected return of every alternative investment that is available.

The first empirical study that explored the feasibility of using concepts from financial portfolio theory to design and manage product and service portfolio has been undertaken by Cardozo and Smith (1983). These researchers found that return and risk measurements of product-market investments demonstrate high positive covariance, and therefore are candidates for use in a consistent constrained optimization approach similar to that developed in modern portfolio theory. More specifically, they concluded that, it is possible to create the product portfolio equivalent of an efficient frontier using non-linear optimization techniques. However, the decision rules from financial portfolio theory need to be modified so as:

*   to avoid premature divestment of new and growing product lines;
*   to take into account the discontinuities in abilities of product lines to surrender or absorb resources without jeopardizing productivity of individual product-market investments, and
*   to provide for addition of new product line.

According to Cardozo and Wind (1985), knowledge of the 'efficient frontier' can help companies to increase the productivity of their resources. The 'efficient frontier' consists of the most productive investment opportunities that are available to the company at a particular point in time. Hence, it constitutes a benchmark against which investments in product lines may be evaluated. Any investment that lies to the left of the 'efficient frontier' yields higher returns for similar risk levels, or alternatively lower risk for similar returns. Investments to the right of the efficient frontier offer lower return than other investments of comparable risk or higher risk for investments of similar return.

Cardozo and Wind (1985) also introduce the concept of 'hurdle rate', which represents the minimum accepted rate of return.[1] In some instances, the use of the 'efficient frontier' will lead to different decisions from the 'hurdle rate' criterion. For example, an investment opportunity may lie below the 'hurdle rate', which means that if this criterion is used, this investment should be rejected. However, the same investment may also lie to the left of the 'efficient frontier', which means that, on the basis of this criterion, it should be accepted.

Ideally, the two concepts should be combined to form a composite criterion in which the hurdle rate is used for low-risk investments, while the efficient frontier is used for high-risk investments. This criterion is more exact than multiple hurdle rates which some companies use (namely, lower for low-risk investments, higher for high-risk investments).

In order to improve portfolio productivity, the following process could be used:

- *Definition of investments* that are product-market combinations whose returns are independent of one another. Products may include technologies, product classes, product lines, brands and specific items, while markets may refer to product application segments, geographical areas and individual customers.
- *Estimation of returns and risks* on the basis of managerial judgement, historical performance and forecasts of future performance under different environmental conditions (for example, competitive activities, customer reactions).

More specifically, managers should first, forecast return for each investment; and secondly, identify the main factors that affect these returns, construct scenarios around these factors (based on the probability of their occurrence) and quantify these estimations and arrange them in a tabular and graphical form. Further, managers should compute risk, which is the variation in level of return either among sets of environmental conditions, or time periods. For each investment, risk is the standard deviation of the return estimate for that investment, weighted by the probability of occurrence of each return. Once the risk and return have been computed for each investment, those values may be calculated for each set of individual product-market investments (or business units) that managers consider appropriate. Then, the 'efficient frontier' can be plotted through those investments that maximize return for any level of risk and minimize risk for any level of return.

- *Measurement of portfolio productivity* is calculated by adding the average returns of each investment weighted by the resources committed to each of them as a percentage of total resources committed.
- *Selection of desired sets of investments*: if the company wishes to avoid the possibility of large losses, it should select investments on the lower left part of the 'efficient frontier'. If, on the other hand, the company is willing to bear larger variations in returns, it should select investments along the upper right part of the 'efficient frontier'. Finally, companies that desire a balanced product portfolio should select a combination of investments from each end of the 'efficient frontier' or from its centre.

Summary

- These are the main approaches of product portfolio analysis, namely the multidimensional 'screening' approach, the index approach and the product portfolio classification/matrix approach.
- Product portfolio models can be either financial or non-financial.

- The non-financial models base the product portfolio evaluation on a number of key dimensions or criteria, such as market attractiveness, profitability, and relative market share.
- The most popular non-financial product portfolio models are the Boston Consulting Group (BCG) matrix, the General Electric (GE) matrix, the A.D. Little matrix, and the Shell International directional policy matrix.
- Empirical evidence suggests that non-financial product portfolio models must be used in combination to be more effective.
- Financial product portfolio models are based on the financial portfolio theory.
- Two basic financial criteria can be used to evaluate product portfolios, namely the 'hurdle rate' and the 'efficient frontier'.
- The 'hurdle rate' represents the minimum accepted rate of return.
- The 'efficient frontier' consists of the most productive investment opportunities that are available to the company at a particular point in time. Hence, it constitutes a benchmark against which investments in product lines may be evaluated.
- Ideally, the two concepts should be combined to form a composite criterion in which the hurdle rate is used for low-risk investments, while the efficient frontier rate is used for high-risk investments.

Questions

1   Write down three reasons why a company should analyse its product portfolio.
2   What are the similarities and differences between the BCG matrix and the GE matrix?
3   Select a product portfolio model and write down all the necessary information you need in order to use it effectively.
4   Describe the process of analysing the portfolio of an automotive company using the risk-return approach.

Note

1 For a detailed example of how one company can use the risk-return analysis, see Cardozo and Wind (1985).

References

Alexander, R. (1964) 'The death and burial of sick products', *Journal of Marketing*, 28: 1–7.

Allen, M. (1979) 'Diagnosing GE's planning for what's watt', in R.J. Allio and M.W. Pennington (eds), *Corporate Planning Techniques and Applications*, AMACOM: New York, pp. 211–20.

Armstrong, S. and Brodie, R. (1994) 'Effects of portfolio planning methods on decision-making: experimental results', *International Journal of Research in Marketing* 11: 73–84.

Barksdale, H. and Harris, C. (1982) 'Portfolio analysis and the product life cycle', *Long Range Planning*, 15(6).

Berenson, C. (1963) 'Pruning the product line', *Business Horizons*, 6: 63–70.

Boston Consulting Group (1976) *Perspectives on Experience*. Boston: Boston Consulting Group.

Browne, W.G. and Kemp, P.S. (1976) 'A three-stage product review process', *Industrial Marketing Management*, 5: 333–42.

Cardozo, R. and Smith, D. (1983) 'Applying financial portfolio theory to product portfolio: an empirical study', *Journal of Marketing*: 110–19.

Cardozo, R. and Wind, J. (1985) 'Risk return approach to product portfolio strategy', *Long Range Planning*, 18(2): 77–85.

Clayton, H.L. (1996) 'The pruning of sick products', *Management Accounting*, June: 17–18.

Day, G. (1986) *Analysis of Strategic Marketing Decisions.* St. Paul, Minn: West Publishing Company.

Drucker, P. (1963) 'Managing for Business Effectiveness', *Harvard Business Review*, 41: 59–60.

Eckles, R.W. (1971) 'Product line deletion and simplification', *Business Horizons,* 14: 71–7.

Enis, B. (1980) 'GE, PIMS, BCG, and the PLC', *Business*, 30(3).

Fluitman, L. (1973) 'The necessity of an industrial product-mix analysis', *Industrial Marketing Management,* 2: 345–52.

Hamelman, P. and Mazze, E. (1972) 'Improving product abandonment decisions', *Journal of Marketing,* 36: 20–6.

Hedley, B. (1977) 'Strategy and the business portfolio', *Long Range Planning*, 10(1): 9–15.

Houfek, L. (1952) 'How to decide which products to junk', *Printers Ink* , August: 21–23.

Jacobson, R. and Aaker, D. (1985) 'Is market share all that it's cracked up to be?', *Journal of Marketing,* 49: 11–21.

Kotler, P. (1965), 'Phasing out weak products', *Harvard Business Review*, 43: 108–18.

Kotler, P. (1974) 'Marketing during periods of shortages', *Journal of Marketing*, 38: 29–39.

Kratchman, S., Hise, T. and Ulrich, T. (1975) 'Management's decision to discontinue a product', *Journal of Accountancy*, June: 50–57.

Markowitz, H. (1952) 'Portfolio selection', *Journal of Finance*, 7 (March).

Morrison, A. and Wensley, R. (1991) 'Boxing up or boxed in? A short history of the Boston Consulting Group share/growth matrix', *Journal of Marketing Management* 7: 105–29.

Seidl, R.L. (1979) 'How useful is corporate planning today?', Corporate Finance Conference, (October), Shell Group Planning Division, Shell International Petroleum Co.

Sonnecken, G. and Hurst, D. (1960) 'How to audit your existing products for profit', *Management Methods*: 45–46.

Wensley, R. (1981) 'Strategic marketing: betas, boxes or basics', *Journal of Marketing*, 45: 173–82.

Wensley, R. (1994) 'Making better decisions: the challenge of marketing strategy techniques', *International Journal of Research in Marketing*, 11: 85–90.

Wind, Y. (1982) *Product Policy: Concepts, Methods and Strategies.* Reading, MA: Addison-Wesley.

Wind Y. and Claycamp H. (1976) 'Planning product line strategy: a matrix approach', *Journal of Marketing*, 4: 2–9.

Wind, Y., Mahajan, V. and Swire D. (1983) 'An empirical comparison of standardized portfolio models', *Journal of Marketing,* 47: 89–99.

Worthing, P. (1971) 'The assessment of product deletion decision indicators', in T.J. Schreiber and L.A. Madeo (eds), *Fortran Applications in Business Administration.* Graduate School of Business Administration, University of Michigan.

Further reading

Aaker, D. (1992) *Strategic Market Management.* John Wiley & Sons.

Walker, O., Boyd, H. and Larreche, J. (1999) *Marketing Strategy: Planning and Implementation.* Irwin Mc-Graw Hill.

5 New Product/Service Development and Portfolio Models

Introduction

The development of new products and services is one of the most critical decisions that a company may make as a result of evaluating its product portfolio. New products and services can actually be viewed as the main drivers of surviving and succeeding in the market.

Because of the critical nature of new product/service development, the scientific community around the world has turned its attention to the process of developing new products and services. As a result, a considerable number of models are available in the literature about the steps followed and the subsequent decisions made during the process of developing new products and services.

In this chapter, we will answer the following questions:

- What are the processes or models for developing new products and services?
- Which are the alternative types of new product/service development processes in terms of parallel or sequential execution of activities?
- What models could a company use for managing its new products/services portfolio? How often are they actually used and how effective are they?

New product development models

The development of new products has been the subject of research in various scientific domains such as management, industrial design and engineering, and marketing. Depending on the domain, new product development (npd) models give emphasis to different stages or activities. For example, the npd models that are drawn from the management domain underline the managerial procedures or activities, while the npd models from the industrial design domain place emphasis on the technicalities of the development process.

Basic model

The most popular new product development model, by far, has been proposed by the consulting firm Booz, Allen and Hamilton Inc. (BAH). Thirty years ago, they surveyed a sample of US manufacturing firms regarding their new product development practices (Booz et al., 1968). They were the first to suggest that a systematic process exists or should exist in the development of new products. Undoubtedly, the work of BAH is one of the most significant contributions to the management of new products.

Their initial model consisted of six steps:

1 *Exploration* – the search for new product ideas to meet company objectives.
2 *Screening* – a quick analysis to determine which ideas are pertinent and merit a more detailed study.
3 *Business analysis* – the expansion of the idea into a concrete business recommendation including product features and a programme for the product.
4 *Development* – turning the product idea into a ready-made product, demonstrable and producable.
5 *Testing* – the commercial experiments necessary to verify earlier business judgements about the product.
6 *Commercialization* – full-scale production and launching of the product into the market place.

In a later study, Booz et al. (1982) added one more step at the beginning of the process, that of New Product Strategy Development, providing a seven-step model. During this stage, the company identifies the strategic business requirements that the new product should satisfy.

New product development models from the management domain

In the management domain, Tushman (1977), based on previous work of Marquis (1982), makes a distinction between the different phases that occur within the innovation process:

- idea generation;
- problem solving and
- implementation.

During the first phase the new product idea is generated. Problem solving involves the technical activities that transform the product idea into a fully developed product, whereas implementation includes pilot production, testing and market introduction of the new product.

A few years later, Burgelmann (1983) characterized innovation process as 'the internal corporate venturing (ICV) process'. This ICV process includes the following four stages:

- conceptual (idea generation);
- pre-venture;
- entrepreneurial (product development) and
- organisational (implementation).

According to this model, in every stage different actors participate and activities take place at different levels in the organization, simultaneously as well as sequentially.

On the same grounds, Van de Ven et al. (1989) describes the innovation process as a sequence of three distinct stages:

- the idea stage;
- the design (or development) stage and
- the implementation stage.

New product development models from the industrial design domain

In the design and engineering domain, Pugh (1983) has developed the 'Design Activity Model', which begins and ends in the market. It recognizes that design is an iterative process and that the interfaces between the different activities are critical to the outcome of the design activity. The major steps of this model are:

- market;
- specification;
- concept design;
- detail design;
- manufacture and
- sell.

Similarly, Pahl and Beitz (1984) argue that an iterative process exists by placing loops between the activities. These activities are:

- task clarification;
- conceptual design;
- embodiment design, and
- detail design.

New product development models from the marketing domain

In the marketing domain, Kotler (1980) suggests a development process of eight major stages:

1 idea generation;
2 idea screening;
3 concept development and testing;
4 marketing strategy;
5 business analysis;
6 product development;
7 market testing;
8 commercialization.

It is obvious that Kotler bases its model in the work of Booz et al. with the difference that he is the only researcher who explicitly refers to the creation of a marketing strategy for the new product in a separate stage of the innovation process.

In addition, Cooper and Kleinschmidt (1986) investigated the new product development activities of 203 projects. Drawing upon a variety of new product development models, they developed a process model that comprises the following thirteen activities:

1 initial screening;
2 preliminary market assessment;
3 preliminary technical assessment;
4 detailed market study/market research;
5 business/financial analysis;
6 product development;
7 in-house product testing;
8 customer tests of product;

9   test market/trial sell;
10   trial production;
11   pre-commercialization business analysis;
12   production start-up;
13   market launch.

A more limited view of the development process is taken by Urban and Hauser (1993), who distinguish five key stages:

*   idea development and screening;
*   business and market opportunity identification;
*   technical development;
*   product testing, and
*   product commercialization.

This model also has a strong resemblance to the other models available in the literature. The only difference is that, it combines idea generation and screening in one stage and it makes no explicit reference to the new product strategy development and marketing strategy.

New service development models

A number of new service development models have been proposed in the literature (Donnelly et al., 1985; Bowers, 1986, 1989; Johnson et al., 1986; Scheuing and Johnson, 1989a, b). The differences in the development of new products and services stem from the special characteristics of services, i.e. intangibility, inseparability, heterogeneity and perishability. These characteristics can impact new service development, thus special attention is given to the execution of particular activities (Easingwood, 1986). de Brentani (1991, 2000) provides a discussion of how differences between manufactured goods and services might affect new service development. The main points of this discussion are as follows:

*   Because of intangibility, new service ideas remain conceptual throughout the new-product development process, which means that uncertainty about the exact nature of the service and, therefore, its risk of failure remain high. In order to tackle this problem, service providers should undertake detailed service blueprinting. Further, as services are mainly intangible, they are not patentable. As a result, they can be more easily imitated by competitors. In an attempt to avoid immediate service imitation, service providers often bypass the testing stage, which can increase the risk of failure. Finally, customers have greater difficulty visualizing intangible offerings. Therefore, when launching a new service, the firm must provide certain physical clues that describe the new service, so as it can be made less abstract and less difficult to perceive and evaluate.
*   In services, production and consumption occur more or less simultaneously. Hence, the interaction between the customer and the service provider during service delivery is critical. Front-line personnel not only need to know the characteristics and features of the new service, but they also have to be motivated to promote it to customers. However, front-line personnel usually view another service offering as simply added workload (Easingwood, 1986). Thus, a new service launch programme requires both external and internal marketing planning.
*   Service heterogeneity which results in variations between the actual service outcome and the customer's experience at each purchase occasion, also influences new service

development. For instance, during the development (or design) stage, much of the effort is directed to planning and controlling for the level of variation in the service outcome(s) at various points in the service delivery process (Shostack, 1984). This allows for a much greater level of fine-tuning the new service both to customer needs and to provider resources.

- Because services are perishable, that is, they cannot be produced in advance and then be kept in stock, this may create overcapacity problems during purchase lulls, while potentially strapping the organization to capacity when demand is high. Firms often respond to this problem by service-line additions that will make use of existing operating and delivery systems during periods of low demand and/or offer alternate, peak load versions of a service when the company is strapped to capacity (Berry, 1980). Some large hotels in the Mediterranean, for example, have added spa and body care services in order to make use of some of their underused capacity during the winter period, while during the summertime (period of high usage), they mainly promote the 'sea and sun' concept.

The most analytic model of new service development has been suggested by Scheuing and Johnson (1989a, b). This model is based on the extensive body of literature dealing with new product management and a number of in-depth interviews with senior executives in service firms. More specifically, it is characterized by a fifteen-step sequence of activities (Figure 5.1). The major steps of the npd models have been retained, but the sequence of activities in this proposed model goes beyond existing models as it looks separately at the design of the service and the design of the delivery process.

The fifteen activities of the Scheuing and Johnson's model can be grouped into four distinct stages:

- *Direction*: this stage includes three activities: the formulation of new service objectives and strategy, idea generation and idea screening. Direction is the outgrowth of the firm's marketing objectives and a detailed environmental analysis. Internal and external sources of new service ideas provide the input to idea generation and screening.
- *Design*: this stage comprises eight activities (from concept development to personnel training). More specifically, it involves concept development, in which the selected ideas are translated into full product concepts with the help of input from prospects and the company's customer contact personnel. Next, during concept testing customer's reactions to service concepts are examined. This activity helps eliminate ideas that are not considered attractive by potential customers. Business analysis follows which represents a feasibility study of each concept. It comprises a complete market assessment and budget development for each proposed new service concept. The next activity refers to project authorization, when top management commits resources to the development of a full service. What follows is service design and testing, an activity that requires input from both operations personnel and potential customers/users of the new service under development. Closely linked to this activity is process and system design and testing. The delivery process is designed and tested in detail in order to ensure proper provision of the new service to the customer. Next, a marketing programme must be designed and tested for potential customers. At the end of the design stage, all personnel must follow training seminars on the nature and operational details of the new service.
- *Testing*: this stage includes three activities. First, a service testing is undertaken to determine potential customers' acceptance of the new service. Secondly, process and system design and testing in the form of pilot runs ensure the service's smooth functioning. Thirdly, test marketing examines the marketability of the new service and field tests its

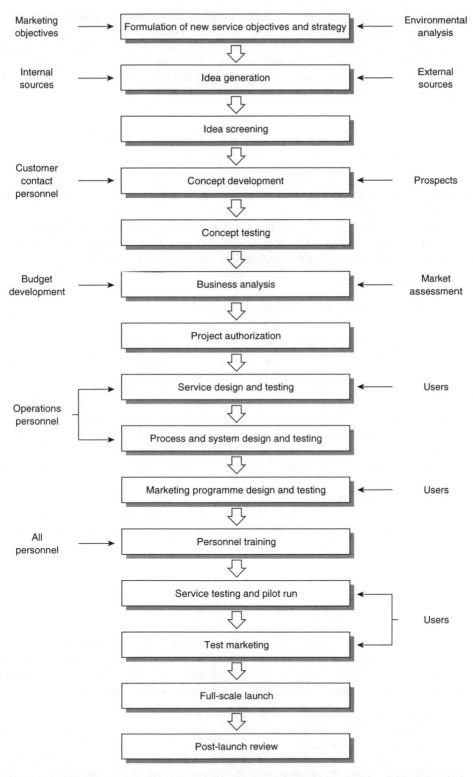

Figure 5.1   **Scheuing and Johnson's normative model of new service development**

marketing programme with a limited number of customers. Completion of test marketing is followed by a review and corrective actions in the marketing effort.

- *Introduction*: in this final stage of the new service development process, a full-scale launch is initiated, introducing the new service to the market. A post-launch review follows, with the aim of investigating whether the new service objectives are being achieved or alterations are needed.

Types of new product development models

In the previous sections we described the activities/stages of developing new products and services. An equally important issue refers to the sequence with which these activities/stages are undertaken.

Cooper (1994) distinguishes between first, second and third generation new product development process models. The first two generations describe stage-gate systems that are steadily evolving into the third generation new product processes.

First generation stage-gate models

The first generation product process was NASA's Phased Project Planning, developed in the 1960s. It was also called Phased Review Process, which broke product development into discrete phases. There were review points at the end of each phase. For instance, funding for the next phase was subject to certain prerequisites that had to be met, typically that all tasks had been satisfactorily completed for the previous phase to move to the next one. This method was rather a measurement and control methodology designed to ensure that the project was proceeding as scheduled. The process was engineering-focused since it was solely dealing with physical design and development. Marketing was absent from the development efforts, which were mainly technical, rather than business-oriented.

The first generation npd model was a more disciplined way of carrying out innovation activities compared to ad hoc development processes applied in previous years. Nevertheless, the Phased Review Process was cumbersome and slow. It had a narrow scope as it dealt with the actual development phase only, and also, it was monofunctional as it was assigned to engineering team of the company.

Second generation stage-gate models

A stage-gate system of the second generation is described as a 'game plan or blueprint' for improving the effectiveness and time efficiency of the new product process (Cooper and Kleinschmidt, 1991). In Figure 5.2, a second generation stage-gate new product system is depicted. The main characteristics of such systems are as follows:

1 The innovation process is broken down into a standard series of stages, with each comprising a number of activities (namely, a cost/benefit analysis or a market study of user needs and wants).
2 The stages transcend functions and involve marketing, R&D, manufacturing and others in every stage. In other words, the development of new products becomes a cross-functional task.

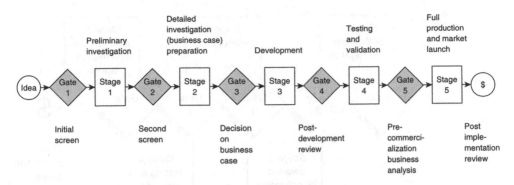

Figure 5.2   Overview of a second generation stage-gate new product system

Source: Cooper and Kleinschmidt (1991)

3   Stages are separated by go/no go decision points (or gates), which serve as review stops for the new product under development. Quality of execution checks are performed on the basis of a predetermined list of criteria. If the product meets these criteria then it moves on to the next stage, otherwise it is 'killed'.

4   In stage-gate systems of product development, the process is monitored by a cross-functional team headed by a project leader/champion.

5   Parallel processing of activities as well as speed in development also characterize these systems. Timely gate decisions keep the project moving along. Effective project evaluations focus resources on the promising projects, while quality control checks ensure that the new product project is well executed.

Although, the second generation new product process is surely more efficient than its predecessor, it has certain weaknesses too. For one thing, development activities are executed in parallel only within each stage. In that sense, projects must wait at each gate until all tasks have been completed and overlapping of stages is impossible. As a consequence, the projects must go through all stages and gates which may lead to unnecessary resources spending when a shortcut is more appropriate (namely, when developing close-to-home products). Moreover, the second generation system does not allow for project prioritization and focus as they pay little attention to resource allocation questions. Finally, it has been accused as being highly detailed and bureaucratic, causing conceptualization problems to managers.

Third generation models

The third generation models have been proposed as a way to deal with the deficiencies of the second-generation stage gate systems. Figure 5.3 represents graphically the concept of such models. A third generation model has four fundamental characteristics (Fs):

1   *Fluidity*: it is fluid and adaptable, with overlapping and fluid stages for higher speed.

2   *Fuzzy gates*: it features conditional Go decisions, rather than absolute ones, which are dependent on the situation.

3   *Focused*: it builds on prioritization methods that look at the entire portfolio of projects, rather than one project at a time, and also allocates resources on the meritorious ones.

4   *Flexible*: it is not a rigid stage-gate system, as each project is considered unique and has its own routing through the process.

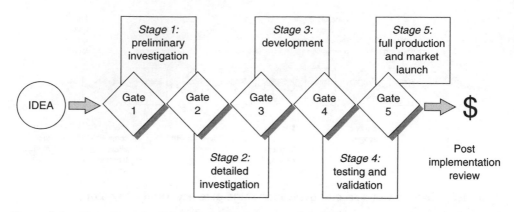

Figure 5.3   **Overview of a third generation new product system**

Source: Cooper (1994)

These four facets of the third generation process have a positive effect on the development of new products. However, Cooper (1994) recognizes that a fifth F also exist. It's *Fallibility* or failure. This advanced system introduces much more freedom and discretion to project leaders and development teams, which increases risk. This new process is also more sophisticated and therefore, it requires a more experienced, professional approach. Managers wishing to adapt such a system must bear in mind these words of caution before they expect to solve all their npd problems through the implementation of a third generation process.

Portfolio management models for new products

The technological advancements, intensity of competition and globalization of markets make new products critical for creating and sustaining a competitive advantage. However, corporate resources are scarce, and they need to be allocated effectively to achieve new product objectives. Portfolio management allows the company to allocate these resources and optimize its new product investments by defining the right new product strategy, selecting the most promising new product ideas and achieving the ideal balance of new product projects.

Cooper et al. (1998, 1999, 2000, 2001) have published extensively on this issue on the basis of an empirical study in 270 companies. Their research revealed a number of models of new products portfolio management.

These authors include this task in their stage gate process for developing new products, and they relate it to 'Gate 2' which comes before the detailed investigation stage or alternatively 'Gate 3' after which the product could move to the actual development stage.

According to the authors, portfolio management for new products goes beyond idea and project selection for further development and the go/no go decision in the various 'gates' of their npd model. More specifically, they define portfolio management as:

A dynamic decision process, whereby a business's list of active new products (and R&D) projects is constantly up-dated and revised. In this process, new projects are evaluated, selected and prioritized; existing projects may be accelerated, killed or de-prioritized; and resources are allocated and re-allocated to the active projects.

In the following sections, we present some interesting results of Cooper et al.'s study which refer to first, the goals of portfolio management for new products; secondly, the tools and techniques for achieving these goals; thirdly the frequency with which the various tools are used; fourthly the effectiveness of these tools; fifthly the behavior of best performers as far as portfolio management is concerned.

Goals of portfolio management for new products

There are three main goals of managing a portfolio of new products:

1 Maximizing the value of the portfolio: this goal aims at allocating resources so as to maximize the value of the portfolio against one or more corporate objectives (e.g. profitability).
2 Achieving a balanced portfolio: this goal seeks to obtain a desired balance of new products projects in terms of certain parameters, such as durability of competitive advantage (short-term, long-term), risk (high, low), markets, product categories, technology, and so on.
3 A strong link to strategy: this goal aims at ensuring that first, the final portfolio of new products reflects the corporate strategy, secondly, the breakdown of expenses across projects, products, markets, and so on is directly tied to corporate strategy and thirdly, all projects and products are on strategy.

Methods of portfolio management for new products

In this section, we present the methods, which are used, in relation to the aforementioned goals.

Maximizing the value of the portfolio

A number of financial and non-financial tools and methods are used to achieve this goal. The financial methods include the net present value, the expected commercial value, the productivity index, and the dynamic rank ordered list. The non-financial methods comprise scoring models, checklists and paired comparisons.

Financial methods for portfolio value maximization   Net present value is calculated when the present value of the future cashflows[1] is estimated after subtracting the initial investment made.

Expected commercial value (ECV): aims at maximizing the value of the new products portfolio subject to certain budget constraints. According to Cooper et al. (1998), this approach is one of the most well thought out financial methods, which introduces in the analysis probabilities of technical and commercial success. For calculating the expected commercial value of a new project/product the following must be taken into consideration:

- The development of a new product has a cost (D).
- In case a new product is considered an absolute technical failure, it is not considered for further development. In every other case, it proceeds to commercialization, subject to a probability of technical success (Pts).

- If the new product is technically successful, it moves into commercialization, bearing the capital and marketing costs (C).
- There is always a probability of commercial success (Pcs). In this case, the company will gain profits (sales minus costs) which can be translated into net present value (NPV).
- The new product's strategic importance (SI) for the company could also be incorporated in the evaluation of the expected commercial value of the new product. Based on the above discussion, the formula for the ECV is as follows:

$$ECV = [(NPV \times SI \times Pcs) - C] \times Pts - D$$

After calculating the expected commercial value for each new product/project, the company should decide which of these new products/projects would be included in its portfolio. This decision should be based on both the ECV and the budget constraints or scarce resources of the company (for example, R&D funds, capital investments for capital intensive projects or work months for labour intensive projects). The company should divide the ECV by the constraining resource (for example, R&D pending). Projects are then rank-ordered according to this ratio. Further, the company should calculate the sum of R&D spending for each project starting from the first rank-ordered. Those projects that cover the available R&D spending limit are included in the portfolio, while the others are placed on hold.

Productivity index is another financial method for maximizing the value of a new products portfolio, which has been popularized by the strategic decision group (Matheson and Matheson, 1994).

This index is derived from the following formula:

$$PI = [NPY \times Pts - R\&D]/R\&D$$

where PI: Productivity index
        NPV: Net Present value
        Pts: Probability of technical success
R&D: R&D costs remaining in the project (alternatively total costs remaining can be used)

New products or projects are rank-ordered according to this index in order to arrive at the preferred portfolio.

Dynamic rank ordered list: according to this value maximization method, new products or projects can be rank-ordered according to several criteria concurrently without becoming complex and time-consuming. Such criteria include net present value, return on investment, strategic importance, probability of technical or commercial success and so on.

Tables 5.1 and 5.2 presents an example of the dynamic rank ordered list prepared for a hypothesized company. The criteria used by this company to rank order new product projects are return on investment, new present value, strategic importance and probability of commercial success.

In order to rank-order projects, the probability of commercial success is multiplied by each of the return on investment (ROI) and net present value (NPV) yielding the adjusted ROI and the adjusted net present value. Then, the projects are ranked according to each of the three criteria ROI, NPV and strategic importance on a five point scale (1: not strategically importance, 5: strategically important). The overall ranking of each project is calculated by the mean of the three rankings. In our example, Zeus product was ranked first on ROI, first on NPV and second on strategic importance. Hence, the mean of these three rankings is 1.33 and this product is placed at the top of the list. Similarly, Apollon comes second, while Aphrodite is ranked third.

Table 5.1   Example of a dynamic rank-ordered list

Product/Service	Return on investment (ROI)*	Net present value (NPV) in million euros	Strategic importance	Probability of technical success
Zeus	17.3%	8.0	4	84%
Apollon	13.9%	4.0	5	65%
Aphrodite	8.7%	6.0	3	92%

*The minimum ROI is 8%.

Table 5.2   Dynamic rank-ordered list of a hypothesized company

Product/Service	ROI × probability of commercial success	NPV × probability of commercial success	Strategic importance	Final ranking
Zeus	14.5 (1)	6.7 (1)	4 (2)	1.33 (1)
Apollon	9.0 (2)	2.6 (3)	5 (1)	2.00 (2)
Aphrodite	8.0 (3)	5.5 (2)	3 (3)	2.67 (3)

Table 5.3   Scoring model for evaluating a new product

Criteria	Weighting (1)	Score (2)	Total score (1) × (2)
Market share	1.5	8	12.0
Superiority	1.2	7	8.4
Required investment	0.2	7	1.4
Market fit	1.7	8	13.6
Enhanced company image	1.3	5	6.5
Impact on customer relations	2.6	6	15.6
Use of existing technology	0.5	5	2.5
Production capabilities	0.3	6	1.8
Marketing know-how	0.7	7	4.9
Total	10		66.7

Non-financial methods for portfolio value maximization   Scoring models: the use of scoring models is based on a list of criteria, which is developed to rate new products/projects. These criteria often capture well-reported determinants of new product success (for example, product superiority, market fit). New products/projects are rated on each criterion in terms of the degree they satisfy each criterion. Typically, 1–10 scales are used (where 1 = it does satisfy the criterion, 10 = it fully satisfies the criterion). Next, these scores are multiplied by importance weights (the higher the importance, the higher the weight), and summed across all criteria to yield the total score for each new product/project. As importance weights add up to 10, the total score may range from 0–100. If the new product/project has a score of 0–50 it is rejected, if it scores between 51–70, it is re-evaluated in more detail, while if it scores from 71–100 it is usually accepted. In Table 5.3, we provide an example of the scoring model for evaluating a new product.

  Checklists: a checklist is similar to a scoring model as it evaluates a new product/project on a number of criteria. Their difference, though, is that when using a checklist the criteria are rated with a yes or no. Even one 'no' can lead to rejection of a new product. The checklist method is a useful tool to discard the highly misfit new products. A scoring model can then be used to rank and prioritize the remaining projects.

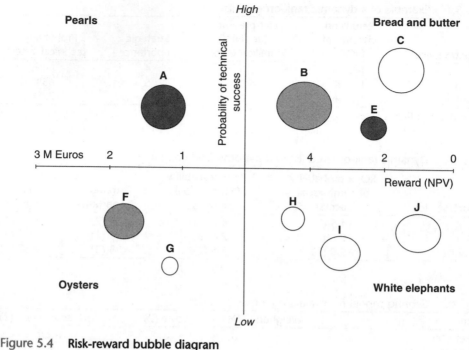

Figure 5.4 **Risk-reward bubble diagram**
Source: adapted from Cooper et al. (1998)

Paired comparisons: this method may be particularly effective in the very early stages of the new product development process (namely, idea generation) when information is still quite limited. When using the paired comparisons method, managers should compare new product ideas against each other in pairs. Their decision should be based on which of the two ideas they would select if they had a choice. This method may be criticized as time consuming. For example, if nine ideas are compared, then thirty-six paired comparisons must be made (the first idea with the remaining eight, the second idea with the remaining seven and so on).

Achieving a balanced portfolio

In order to achieve a balanced portfolio of new products, a company may use *visual charts*. These charts are preferred because of their ability to represent visually the balance of new products portfolio, something that cannot be done with the aforementioned financial and non-financial methods.

These visual charts, take the form of bubble diagrams since new products are shown as balloons or bubbles. Bubble charts must not be viewed so much as decision models but rather as information display tools. A number of parameters can be used in bubble diagrams to seek balance. These include:

- fit with corporate strategy (low, medium, high);
- strategic importance to the company (low, medium, high);
- durability of competitive advantage (short-term, medium, long-term);
- reward, expressed in qualitative (for example, modest to excellent) or quantitative terms (e.g. NPV);

- probabilities of technical or commercial success (high, medium, low);
- total cost.

In Figure 5.4 we provide a bubble diagram for a hypothetical company. Two parameters are used, namely reward and risk expressed by the probability of technical success. The size of the bubbles shows the resources to be spent annually on each new product. The four quadrants of the bubble diagram are as follows:

- *Pearls*: these are potential 'stars', products with a high likelihood of success, and expected rewards. The majority of companies wish to have more of these new products.
- *Oysters*: these are long-shot projects, with high expected payoff, but low likelihood of technical success. In this case, technical breakthroughs will prepare the way for solid payoffs.
- *Bread and butter*: these are small and simple projects with high likelihood of success, but low expected rewards. They include product line extensions, modification and updating of products.
- *White elephants*: these are low success and low reward projects.

What is quite attractive in the bubble diagrams is that it forces the company to consider its resources. Every time a new product is added to the diagram, the company must decide which other product to subtract or limit resources from, in order to ensure the necessary resources for the 'newcomer' in the portfolio.

Further, a range of additional information can be represented in a bubble diagram. For example, the shading of each circle shows the product line with which the project is associated; the colour of each circle is related to timing (for example, red circles represent late stage projects, while blue circles signify early stage projects).

Strategic direction

The goal of building a strong link to strategy can be achieved using the 'strategic buckets' model. This model is used when firms want to ensure that portfolio spending reflects their strategic priorities.

The strategic buckets model operates as follows:

- First, the company's vision and strategy are defined.
- Then, decisions are made about where the company wishes to spend its R&D and new product resources (namely types of projects, markets, etc,).
- Next, buckets with ideal spending levels, called 'envelopes of money' are defined (for example, x per cent to be spent on product platforms).
- Finally, projects are prioritized within buckets via the maximization approaches presented earlier in this chapter.[2]

Frequency use of portfolio management methods

According to the study of Cooper et al. (2001), almost all companies in their sample use multiple methods. The most popular methods are the financial methods, which aim at value maximization, followed by the strategic buckets method, which refer to the goal of strategic direction, and bubble diagrams seeking a balanced portfolio. Two non-financial methods of value maximization are also used, namely scoring models and checklists.

Financial methods: a total of 77.3 per cent of businesses use a financial approach to portfolio management and project selection while 40.4 per cent of businesses stated that they rely heavily on financial methods. From the businesses that use financial methods:

- 38.1 per cent determine each project's expected financial results or economic value, which is then used to rank order projects against each other in order to decide the preferred portfolio of projects.
- 28.4 per cent set a minimum acceptable level or hurdle rate in order to make go/kill decisions on individual projects, which, in turn, determine the final portfolio of new products.
- The remaining 10.2 per cent of businesses use both the economic value to rank projects against each other and this value is also compared to a hurdle rate to make final go/kill decisions.

Strategic buckets methods: this is the second most popular portfolio management method. A total of 64.8 per cent of businesses use it, while for 26.6 per cent of businesses this is the dominant method. On the basis of strategic priorities, a number of dimensions can be used to allocate resources into different buckets. According to frequency of mention the most popular dimensions are as follows:

1 type of market;
2 type of development (maintenance, exploratory, frontier research, systems, line extensions);
3 product line;
4 project magnitude (minor/major);
5 technology area;
6 platform types;
7 strategic thrust (against strategies in the plan);
8 competitive needs.

In order to prioritize projects within a bucket, the following approaches are used (rank-ordered):

1 financial method;
2 scoring model;
3 bubble chart;
4 senior executive's judgement;
5 checklist method.

Bubble diagrams: a total of 40.6 per cent of businesses use these diagrams for portfolio management and project selection. By far the most popular plots identified refer to risk/reward plots. Rewards are usually represented by net present value, benefits after years of launch or market value, while risk is represented by the probability of success (technical, commercial). Other plots include technical newness by market newness or technical feasibility by market attractiveness.

Non-financial methods: scoring models and checklists are the least popular methods of portfolio management as they are used by 37.9 per cent and 20.9 per cent of businesses respectively. The criteria used by firms to rank new projects were found to be as follows:

- strategic fit/leverages core competencies (90.4 per cent of business);
- financial reward pay-off (86.8 per cent);
- risk and probability of success (76.1 per cent);
- timing (65.5 per cent);

Table 5.4   Mean value of performance metrics

Performance metric	Mean value	Financial methods	'Strategic bucket'	Bubble charts	Scoring models	'Best' companies	'Worst' companies
1	3.9	3.74	4.08	4.11	3.95	4.6	2.9
2	3.6	3.37	3.77	3.70	3.82	4.4	2.6
3	3.5	3.50	3.72	3.00	3.59	4.5	2.5
4	2.9	2.79	3.22	2.90	3.13	3.8	2.1
5	2.9	2.80	3.08	3.20	3.20	4.1	1.9
6	2.7	2.50	2.93	2.50	2.70	3.6	1.6

- technological capability (62.9 per cent);
- commercialization capability (50.1 per cent);
- protectability (41.6 per cent);
- synergy between projects (35.5 per cent).

Effectiveness of new products' portfolio management methods

Another issue that has been studied by Cooper et al. (2001) is which method yields the best portfolio. Hence, they constructed the following six metrics to capture how well the company's portfolio was performing:

1 Projects are aligned with business's objectives.
2 Portfolio contains very high value projects.
3 Spending reflects the business's strategy.
4 Projects are done on time.
5 Portfolio has good balance of projects.
6 Portfolio has right number of projects.

The researchers asked respondents to rate their portfolio management method using these metrics on a 1–5 scale (1= poor, 5= excellent). Table 5.5 presents the mean values of each performance metric for all companies in the sample, for the best (top 20 per cent) and also the worst (bottom 20 per cent) companies, as well as for the dominant methods employed.

As can be seen in Table 5.4, portfolio management works well. However, it is ironic that the most popular financial methods, which are supposed to lead to projects with high returns and profitability, are related to portfolios with the worst economic value. In fact, these methods present the worst results in five of the six performance metrics.

The strategic buckets method and the scoring models lead to satisfactory results, as they are related to the best or second best results in five of the six performance metrics.

Also, the bubble charts yield moderate results in terms of most metrics, but they are better in selecting projects that are aligned with the business's objectives and creating portfolios with good balance of projects.

Further, the best companies (top 20 per cent) outperform the 'worst' companies (bottom 20 per cent) across all six performance metrics. However, the areas where the best companies really excel are: achieving the right balance of projects, and having the right number of projects for the resources available.

High-performing companies: how do they manage portfolios of new products?

As we have noted in the previous section, the best companies yield better results than the worst companies. But, what else is different between these two types of companies? Cooper et al. (2001) found that, compared to the worst companies, the best companies:

1   consider portfolio management as a much more important managerial task, particularly the technology managers compared to managers from marketing, sales and production departments;
2   have established an explicit method for portfolio management with clear rules and procedures, which is supported by top management and it is consistently applied across all new products;
3   rely less on financial methods as the dominant tool for portfolio management. In fact, 56.4 per cent of the worst companies use these methods compared to 35.9 per cent of the best companies;
4   use to a greater extent the strategic buckets method. Only 10 per cent of the worst companies use this method. By contrast, 30 per cent of the best companies use it; it is interesting to note that the strategic buckets method is the number one tool of portfolio management for the best companies;
5   use multiple methods of portfolio management; more specifically, the best companies use on average 2.43 methods, while almost half of them (47.5 per cent) use three or more methods. By contrast, the worst companies rely on fewer methods (1.83 on average) and almost half of them (46.3 per cent) focus on a single method portfolio management.

Summary

- The most popular new product development model has been proposed by the consulting firm Booz, Allen and Hamilton and it comprises seven stages, namely new product development strategy, exploration, screening, business analysis, development, testing and commercialization.
- The most analytic model of new service development has been suggested by Scheuing and Johnson. It involves fifteen stages or activities that are grouped in four distinct categories of activities, namely direction, design, testing, and introduction.
- On the basis of the sequence with which the npd activities/stages are undertaken, we recognise first, second and third generation new product development process models.
- There are three main goals of managing a portfolio of new products, namely maximizing the value of the portfolio, achieving a balanced portfolio, and a strong link to strategy.
- Value maximization can be achieved using financial and non-financial tools. The financial tools include the net present value, the expected commercial value, the productivity index, and the dynamic rank ordered list. The non-financial tools comprise scoring models, checklists and paired comparisons. For achieving a balanced portfolio bubble charts can be used, while building a strong link to strategy can be attained using the strategic buckets model.
- The most effective companies tend to use multiple methods of managing new product portfolios. The most popular methods are the financial methods followed by the strategic buckets method, and bubble diagrams seeking a balanced portfolio.

Questions

1   Select one tangible product and one intangible product (namely, service) and describe the differences in their development process.
2   What stage precedes the technical development of a new service? Discuss its necessity for the development of a life insurance plan.
3   Discuss the three main goals of portfolio management of new products and the methods associated with each of these goals.
4   Provide a list of guidelines for achieving high performance in new product portfolio management.

Notes

1 The mathematical formula for estimating the present value of future cash flows is as follows:

Future cash flows$/(1 + i)^n$
where   n: number of periods
          i: discounted interest rate for every period

2 For a detailed discussion of portfolio management methods, see Cooper et al. (1998).

References

Berry, L. (1980) 'Services marketing is different', *Business*, 30: 24–9.
Booz, Allen and Hamilton (1968) *Management of New Products*. New York: Booz, Allen and Hamilton, Inc.
Booz, Allen and Hamilton (1982) *New Products Management for the 1980s*. New York: Booz, Allen and Hamilton, Inc.
Bowers, M. (1986) 'The new product development process: a suggested model for banks', *Journal of Retail Banking*, VIII(1, 2): 19–24.
Bowers, M. (1989) 'Developing new services: improving the process makes it better', *The Journal of Services Marketing* 3(1): 15–20.
Burgelmann, R.A. (1983) 'A process model of internal corporate venturing in the diversified major firm', *Administrative Science Quarterly*, 28.
Cooper, R. (1994) 'Perspective: third-generation new product processes', *Journal of Product Innovation Management*, 11: 3–14.
Cooper, R. and Kleinschmidt, E. (1986) 'An investigation into the new product process: steps, deficiencies and impact', *Journal of Product Innovation Management*, 3: 71–85.
Cooper, R. and Kleinschmidt, E. (1991) 'New product processes at leading industrial firms', *Industrial Marketing Management*, 20: 137–47.
Cooper, R., Edgett, S. and Kleinschmidt, E. (1998) *Portfolio Management for New Products*. Cambridge, MA: Perseus Books.
Cooper, R., Edgett, S. and Kleinschmidt, E. (1999) 'New product portfolio management: practices and performance', *Journal of Product Innovation Management*, 16: 333–51.
Cooper, R., Edgett, S. and Kleinschmidt, E. (2000) 'New problems, new solutions: making portfolio management more effective', *Research Technology Management* 43(2): 18–33.
Cooper, R., Edgett, S. and Kleinschmidt, E. (2001) 'Portfolio management for new product development: results of an industry practices study', *R&D Management*, 31(4): 361–79.
de Brentani U. (1991) 'Success factors in developing new business services', *European Journal of Marketing*, 25(2): 33–59.
de Brentani, U. and Ragot, E. (1996) 'Developing new business-to-business professional services: what factors impact performance?', *Industrial Marketing Management*, 25: 517–30.

de Brentani, U. (2000) 'Designing and marketing new products and services', in K. Blois (ed.), *Oxford Textbook of Marketing*. Oxford University Press.

Donnelly, J., Berry, L. and Johnson, T. (1985) *Marketing Financial Services*. Homewood, IL: Dow Jones-Irwin.

Easingwood, C. (1986) 'New product development for service companies', *Journal of Product Innovation Management*, 4: 264–75.

Johnson, E., Scheuing, E. and Gaida, K. (1986) *Profitable Service Marketing*. Homewood, IL: Dow Jones-Irwin.

Kotler, P. (1980) *Principles of Marketing*. Englewood Cliffs, NJ: Prentice-Hall.

Marquis, D. (1982) 'The anatomy of successful innovations', in M.L. Tushman and W.L. Moore (eds), *Readings in the Management of Innovation*. Boston, MA and London: Pitman.

Matheson, D. and Matheson, J. (1994) 'Making excellent R&D decisions', *Research Technology Management*, 37: 21–4.

Pahl, G. and Beitz, W. (1984) *Engineering Design*. London: The Design Council.

Pugh, S. (1983) *Design Activity Model*. Loughborough University of Technology: Engineering Design Centre.

Scheuing, E. and Johnson, E. (1989a) 'A proposed model for new service development', *Journal of Services Marketing*, 3(2): 25–34.

Scheuing, E. and Johnson, E. (1989b) 'New product development and management in financial institutions', *International Journal of Bank Marketing*, 7(2): 17–21.

Shostack, L. (1984) 'Designing services that deliver', *Harvard Business Review*, 62: 133–9.

Tushman, M.L. (1977) 'Special boundary roles in the innovation process', *Administrative Science Quarterly*, 22: 587–605.

Urban, G. and Hauser, J. (1993) *Design and Marketing of New Products*. Englewood Cliffs, NJ: Prentice Hall.

Van de Ven, A., Angle, H. and Poole, S. (1989) *Research on the Management of Innovation*. New York: Harper Row.

Further reading

Brown, S. and Eisenhardt, K. (1995) 'Product development: past research, present findings and future directions', *Academy of Management Review*, 20(2): 343–78.

Craig, A. and Hart, S. (1992) 'Where to now in new product development research?', *European Journal of Marketing*, 26(11): 1–49.

Johne, A. and Storey, C. (1998) 'New service development: a review of the literature and annotated bibliography', *European Journal of Marketing*, 32: 184–251.

Wheelwright, S. and Clark, K. (1992) *Revolutionizing Product Development*. New York: The Free Press.

6 Pre-Development Activities of New Products and Services

Introduction

As we discussed in the previous chapter, the development of new products/services is one of the most important managerial tasks, which requires a systematic involvement and allocation of the necessary resources in the context of a pre-defined new product development strategy.

Following a combination of Kotler's and Booz et al.'s (BAH) models that have been presented in Chapter 5, we envisage the whole new product development process as follows:

- new product strategy development;
- idea generation;
- idea screening;
- concept development and testing;
- marketing strategy;
- business analysis;
- technical development;
- testing;
- commercialization – launching.

These stages can be grouped into first, the pre-development stages, namely new product strategy development, idea generation, idea screening, concept development and testing, marketing strategy, business analysis, and secondly the development and post-development stages, that is technical development, testing and commercialization – launching.

In this chapter, we will present the pre-development stages, while in the next chapter we will be dealing with the stages of development, testing and launching. The following questions will be addressed in this chapter:

- What is the usefulness of a new product development strategy, before the development and full-scale launching of a new product is decided?
- Which activities are undertaken during the stages of idea generation, idea screening, concept development and testing, marketing strategy and business analysis?

Before answering these questions, we should note that, while the new product development process has been studied extensively in the cases of tangible goods, the relevant studies for services are limited.

New product strategy development

The stage of new product strategy development sets the strategic requirements to be satisfied by the new product/service. In other words, during this stage the company makes decisions about the strategic roles of the new products/services.

The addition of this stage altered the nature of the early stages of the new product development process. As a result, the idea generation stage is now focused on ideas that are close to the strategic objectives of the company. Similarly, the criteria used for idea screening reflect these objectives. Consequently, the first three stages of the new product development process are more closely related and interlined.

As mentioned in the previous chapter, Booz et al. (1982) have added the stage of new product strategy development at the beginning of the npd process. In their study, 77 per cent of the companies surveyed had included this stage in their new product process. The strategic roles that companies may set for their new products can be classified in two broad categories, externally driven and internally driven. Booz et al. (1982) reported the percentages of companies that followed each strategic role/objective for their most successful products. These results are as follows:

Externally driven strategic roles/objectives:

- defend market share position (about 45 per cent)
- establish foothold on new market (approx. 38 per cent)
- preempt market segment (around 34 per cent).

Internally driven strategic roles/objectives:

- Maintain position as product innovator (about 47 per cent);
- Exploit technology in a new way (approx. 28 per cent);
- Capitalize on distribution strengths (almost 25 per cent);
- Provide a «cash generator» (around 13 per cent);
- Use excess or off-season capacity (about 8 per cent).

In a more recent study, Mahajan and Wind (1992) have found that increasing market penetration was the most frequently cited objective of new products (77 per cent of the companies), followed closely by capitalizing on existing markets (74 per cent). Other objectives were combat major competitive entry (58 per cent), capitalize on a new technology (53 per cent), establish a foothold in a new market (46 per cent), preempt emerging market segment (32 per cent), utilize excess capacity (17 per cent), offset seasonal cycle (13 per cent), utilize by-products of existing products (10 per cent), and produce products at lower cost (4 per cent).

Innovation objectives at BMW

BWM, the leading German automobile manufacturer has a commitment to maintain its leadership in technology and the continuity of its brand. More specifically, they have three innovation objectives. First, they want to have more than one unique selling proposition (USP) in each of the cars they launch, regardless of the model series. Secondly, they plan to complete as many breakthrough innovations as possible, as they prepare their products for the market. Thirdly, they want to develop concept cars to convey their brand image at motor shows.

Source: Seidel et al. (2003)

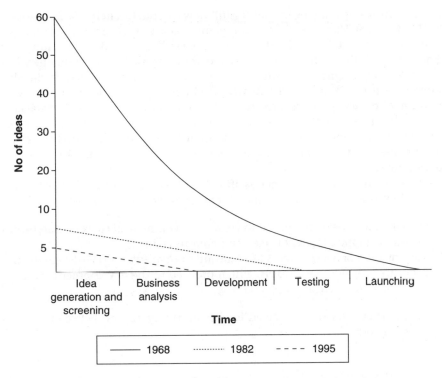

Figure 6.1 **Mortality curve of new product ideas**

Source: Booz, Allen and Hamilton (1968, 1985); Griffin (1997)

In a service context, one of the first studies regarding new service development practices has been conducted by Easingwood (1986). In a sample of thirty-one service companies, it was revealed that:

- 71 per cent had clearly defined objectives for their new product program, whereas the relevant percentage was 63 per cent and 77 per cent for small and large firms, respectively.
- Some 94 per cent considered the role of npd in the company's overall strategy as, either very important or important. The percentage rises to 88 per cent and 100 per cent for small and large firms, respectively.
- 55 per cent did have an expectation with regard to the new product contribution written into the company's strategic plan.

In addition, Easingwood (1986) revealed that new product objectives of service companies tended to be industry specific. For example, exploiting new technology was a main objective of the communications industry, while using excess off-season capacity was a main aim of hotel chains and defending market share a principal concern for building societies.

The importance of the new product strategy development stage can be substantiated by the so-called 'mortality curve' of new product ideas. This concept, which has been popularized by Booz et al. (1968, 1982), displays the rate at which new product ideas are screened out (or 'die out') at successive steps in the new product development process.

Figure 6.1 presents the 'mortality curves' drawn from studies published in 1968, 1982 and 1997. In their 1968 study, BAH found that, fifty-eight new product ideas are considered on average for every successful new product. Their 1982 study, which involved in total 850 US and European companies, took only seven ideas to generate one successful new product. The 1997 study by Abbie Griffin showed a slight improvement over Booz et al.'s 1982 results, as only 6.6 ideas were required to generate one successful product. However, a significant difference between 1982 and 1995 lies in the shape of the 'mortality curve'. While the 1982 curve declines slowly at the beginning, with the largest number of new product ideas to be discarded at the development stage, in the 1997 study the largest number of new product ideas is weeded out at the idea screening stage, that is much earlier in the npd process, mainly because clearer strategic objectives exist that guide the development process. Hence, fewer resources are wasted on unsuccessful products.

It is also worth noting that, when Griffin (1997) compared the 'best practice firms' with the rest of the sample, she concluded that for 'best practice firms':

- Statistically fewer ideas are needed to create one commercial success than for the rest of the sample (approximately three compared to eight).
- The vast majority of new product ideas 'die out' prior to entering the development stage.
- For every three new product ideas, which proceed to the development stage, two go on to become commercial successes.

However, no differences were detected in the 'mortality curves' between services and manufactured goods.

Idea generation

After the new product strategy development, idea generation follows. This stage together with the next one which involves idea screening are usually referred to as the 'fuzzy front end' of the new product development process. In the following paragraphs, we will discuss the sources of new product and service ideas, as well as the most popular techniques for idea generation.

Sources of new product and service ideas

An idea for a new product or service can derive from a variety of sources, both internal and external to the company, and can be driven by market or technology forces. Internally, new product ideas may flow from the sales force and service engineers who are close to customer needs, production and R&D specialists who are close to new technological developments, and top management who know the company's strengths and weaknesses. 3M Corp. is one of the first companies to involve its employees in the generation of new product ideas. Actually, the company allows its employees, both marketing and technical, to spend up to 15 per cent of their work time on a new product project of their own. Royal Dutch Shell's Exploration and Production division went so far as to set up an internal 'venture board' to review new ideas and business plans created by division employees. Also, Siemens's strategic business development group sponsors business-plan competitions among employees. Externally, ideas may come from customers, competitors, or channel members like industrial distributors.

How new product ideas are generated in BMW

Technis, an intranet system US, European and Japanese scouts send in regular reports of their impressions and discoveries. These reports go into Technis, the central intranet database, and they are available to all BMW Group associates. By providing general access through its Intranet, BMW capitalizes on the technical advances discovered by its scouts, thus providing new ideas and flashes of inspiration in their daily work.

Virtual Innovation Agency (VIA) Internet portal The company has also created the VIA Internet portal to make sure that it does not rely alone on the creativity and scouting abilities of its own associates. Universities or other companies can use the VIA portal to provide the company with suggestions for their own innovation projects which they believe will drive the BMW Group forward.

VIA has become a greater success than anybody expected. Although the portal has been in place for about three years, and it has never been promoted, it has received more than 1,000 suggestions through it. And some of the ideas that have come through VIA have already been transformed into concrete, operative development projects.

Source: Seidel et al. (2003)

The majority of studies reported in the literature highlight the importance of customer involvement in idea generation for both manufactured goods and services (these include Von Hippel 1978, 1986; Cooper and Kleinschmidt 1986; Sanchez and Elola 1991; Neal and Corkendale 1998; Gruner and Homburg 2000; Alam 2002).

In his classical work, Eric Von Hippel (1978, 1986) has developed the 'customer active paradigm' (CAP) according to which the role of industrial customers as a source of new product ideas is central in the scientific instrument industry and the semiconductor and electronics sub-assembly process equipment industries, computer software and medical products. In the CAP, it is the role of the would-be customer to develop the idea for a new product, select a supplier capable of making the product, and take the initiative to send a request to the selected supplier. The role of the manufacturer in this paradigm is to wait for a potential customer to submit a request, to screen ideas for new products, and to select those for development, which seem to offer the most promise from the manufacturer's point of view. Generally speaking, this customer dominated new product development process which provides an excellent example of the buyer-seller interdependence characteristic of industrial markets, is common in those industries where suppliers do not control the technology of the manufacturing process in customer industries and customers depend on material and equipment suppliers for improvements in their production methods. In the same work, Von Hippel (1986) introduces the 'lead-user' method for idea generation. When using this method, the company collects information on both needs and ideas for solutions from 'lead users'. 'Lead users' are defined as users of a given product or service that first, expect attractive innovation-related benefits from the solution of their needs and so are motivated to innovate, and secondly, experience needs for a given innovation earlier than the majority of the target market. 'Lead users' may actually come from other markets that face similar problems in a more extreme form.

Identifying 'lead users' for new braking systems

If an automotive manufacturer would like to apply the 'lead user' method to improve car braking, they might start looking among auto racing teams that are at the leading edge with respect to this need. The automaker would not stop there, though. They would look for innovative ideas and solutions in other fields that might have a similar need, such as aerospace. In fact, it was in this field that the antilock braking systems (the so-called ABS) were first developed, as it is very important for military and commercial aircraft users to design mechanisms that would prevent their expensive vehicles from runway overrun.

Source: Von Hippel et al. (1999)

Some years later, Foxall (1989) extended the work of Von Hippel using a case study approach. Foxall put forward the concept of user-initiated or reverse innovation, which is broader than that of the CAP and embraces situations of industrial npd in which a user not only invents and applies a novel device as an internal process innovation, but is entrepreneurially alert to the possibility of gaining maximally from its wider diffusion as a product innovation. Rather than passively allowing a manufacturer to benefit from marketing the innovation, the user-initiator actively seeks to gain, as fully as possible, from its marketing by concluding the most favourable leasing or licensing deals (quasi-vertically integrated user-initiated npd) or by directly manufacturing and marketing the item (fully-vertically integrated user-initiated npd). According to Foxall, reverse innovation is already a fact for many companies and its potential benefits stem from the commercial use of available technologies, which are often already applied, tried and tested.

'Lead user' method effectiveness in 3M Company

In exploring how the 'lead user' method actually performs relative to more traditionally used methods, a natural experiment with the 3M Company has recently been conducted. The results of this experiment clearly showed that the 'lead user' method generated breakthrough new products at a higher rate than the methods traditionally used at 3M. Further, annual sales for the average new product idea that was generated using the 'lead user' method were forecasted to be more than eight times higher than the projected sales for contemporaneous conducted 'traditional' new product projects. Finally, each 'lead user' generated new product project was projected to create a new major product line for 3M.

Source: Lilien et al. (2002)

In the service environment, Easingwood's study (1986) revealed that, on average, the sampled companies generated twenty-six new service ideas per year. This number fell to twenty-two for small companies and it rose to thirty-two for large firms. Further, over half of the sampled companies indicated that it is a rather easy task to generate many more ideas. The relative importance of the alternative sources does not vary much among large and small companies, with the exception of 'competitors' which is a more important source of ideas for the former than the latter firms. Marketing and market research account for 44.2 per cent of ideas for all companies. Operations, however, seem to be a source of relative fewer ideas (13.5 per cent). This means that, companies do not take advantage of its proximity to the customer. Discussions with the npd managers indicate that a good explanation can be that the new products developed as translated to increased workload by the operations people. Thus, they prefer not to make any relevant suggestions.

In a study of the development practices of new personal financial services, Davison et al. (1989) found that top management and the marketing department were identified as being the main internal idea sources, while the most popular external source of new product ideas was found to be the competitors. Further, Teixeira and Ziskin (1993) reported the results of a study conducted by the consulting firm Ernst and Young on product development approaches in banks. Approximately 80 per cent of the banks surveyed viewed their competitors as the main source of new product ideas.

Idea generation techniques

The techniques that can be used for generating new product ideas can be grouped in the following two categories:

- the creative techniques that emphasize creativity and imagination (for example, brainstorming) and
- the analytical techniques that put emphasis on the analysis of a specific situation (for example, market analysis).

In order to generate new product ideas there is a myriad of different formal techniques/methods that could be used. Hubka (1983) provides a summary of thirty-one idea generation techniques presented in Table 6.1.

Idea generation in Texaco Inc.

In the fall of 2000, the E-business unit of Texaco Inc. (now Chevron Texaco) launched an E-business contest. All of Texaco's employees were offered cash prizes for ideas on how Internet technologies could help Texaco improve the company's performance. In order to persuade company employees to take part in the contest and share their innovative ideas, the payout structure favoured ideas submitted as a team, rather than those submitted by an individual. Two hundred twenty ideas were eventually submitted. Five ideas ultimately won and the teams behind these five winning ideas each received $20,000. An Internet consulting company was also hired to act upon these innovative ideas. The submissions included multiple online customer services, a web-based reservoir for Texaco's management training programmes, and online reporting systems for machinery in refineries.

Apart from communicating to its employees a renewed corporate focus on innovation and Internet technologies, the contest also informed Texaco what could be improved upon. More specifically, Texaco realized it had to create an ongoing mechanism that would allow all ideas to be continually generated, discussed and improved, and further lead to the development of successful new products. For this purpose, the idea-X tool was developed by The Cap Gemini Ernst & Young Center for Business Innovation (CBI).

After customizing the idea-X tool for Texaco and naming it ideamarket, the CBI and Texaco embarked on a Beta phase that allowed a considerable number of employees to participate in a web-based idea generation process. This phase successfully engaged a group of Texaco employees from different business units and with diverse expertise in multiple online conversations. Employees had the ability, for example, to submit ideas comment on ideas or champion ideas and try to turn them into more concrete business solutions.

Source: Abraham and Pickett (2002)

Table 6.1 Idea generation techniques

Technique	Characteristics	Objectives	Technique	Characteristics	Objectives
• Abstraction (progressive abstraction)	Make problem or situation more abstract	Insights into new solutions	• Interaction	Starting from assumed values, obtain progressively closer approximation of all values	Solution of a system with complicated interactions
• Adaptation	Modifying or partial transformation of an existing product for different conditions	Reliable solution for new conditions	• Market research	Systematic collection and classification of market information	Establishing market conditions and opportunities
• Aggregation	Combination of product characteristics into a single product or of functions of a number of products into one product	New properties simplified structure	• Mental experiment	Observe and idealised mental model at work	Testing of an idea, determination of behaviour
• Analysis of properties (attribute listing)	Thorough analysis of every property of the product	Improvement of an existing product	• Methodical doubt (scientific scepticism)	By systematic negation of existing solution, search for new solution paths	Find new solutions, opportunities
• Application	Application of an existing product for new functions	Application of a proven product to new areas of use	• Method '6-3-5'	6 participants, each write down 3 ideas within 5 minutes, passes ideas on to the next person for 3 similar ideas, working all the way around the group	Find many solutions, ideas

(Continued)

Table 6.1 (Continued)

Technique	Characteristics	Objectives	Technique	Characteristics	Objectives
• Attribute-based discriminant analysis (PREFMAP)	Market segments developed on basis of brand preferences, geometric representation developed by discriminant analysis from brand's effective attributes, then mapped and analysed	Market structure general and searched for new product opportunities	• Morphological analysis/matrix	Split up problem into parts and look for partial solutions to each, leading to generation of solutions to original problem	New solutions by combinations of functions
• Brainstorming	Collect ideas in freewheeling discussion without criticism	Find many new ideas	• Problem inventory analysis (reverse brainstorming)	Generate list of negative attributes of existing products	Find product improvements
• Combinations with interactions	Combining of a product or of properties to obtain new and more complicated effects	Derive new solutions from existing products	• Problem-purpose expansion	Expand problem, reformulate by stating objective in standard format	Look for new solutions
• Critical path network	Graphic representation of activities and their duration	Create an overview of the sequence and timing and find the critical path to identify opportunities	• Questioning	By applying a system of questions, find gapless information or produce mental stimulation	Obtain most complete information possible
• Descartes	Four principles: criticism, division, ordering, create overview	Correctness and effectiveness of thought process stimulates ideas	• Step forwards/backwards	Attempt both solution directions from 'is' to 'should be' and reverse	Find most favorable path to a solution
• Dimensional investigation	Technical and economic properties of the product brought together into a mathematical relationship and extreme values found	Find optimal solution on product properties	• Synetics	Team analyses problem and searches for new solutions through analysis	Discover new solutions, opportunities

(Continued)

Table 6.1 (Continued)

Technique	Characteristics	Objectives	Technique	Characteristics	Objectives
• Division of totality	Tactical procedure based on division of a whole concept or problem into component parts	Create overview generate partial solutions	• Systems approach	Systematic working in every situation requiring a solution or decision	As far as possible complete investigation
• Evaluation	Find technical and economic valuation by point counting	Find best variant among a few	• Technoeconomic design	By technical and economic evaluation find and improve the strong features of the product	Improve product
• Experimentation	By measuring and testing, obtain desired values	Determination of product	• Technological environment forecasting	Develop broad scenarios about the future in general, then technology in particular	Insight into the future
• Incubation	After thorough preparation of the problem, take a break	Find ideas by intuition	• Value analysis or engineering	Analysis and criticism of the existing solution from the economic viewpoint	Improve economic properties of the product
• Systematic search of field	Research all directions starting from fixed points of the region	Obtain most complete information possible			

Source: Hubka (1983). Reprinted with permission from Elsevier.

Idea screening

The screening stage of new product development comprises the activities of selecting the new product ideas that will be forwarded to the following phases of the npd process. During this stage, new product ideas go through a screening process by considering whether they can satisfy their strategic goals with the available corporate resources and know-how.

In the literature, there are many normative approaches for new product screening, such as ranking, checklists, scoring models, profitability index models, to name just a few. The criteria used to screen new product ideas usually refer to the technical capabilities of the new product and its market potential (for example, market attractiveness, availability of necessary resources, existence of competitive advantage).

In order to identify the most important criteria for evaluating a new product idea, a market study can be very useful. Such a study can provide information about the following questions:

- What do the customers want to buy?
- What choice criteria do the customers use?
- Where do customers buy similar products?
- How much money are customers willing to pay for the product?
- How often do customers plan to buy the product?

Further, a market study includes an analysis of competitive conditions such as the number of competitors, the competitive products, the strategies followed by competitors and their results. Such information can help the company to evaluate how intensive the competition is and whether it can be a serious threat to its new product introductions.

In his seminal study, O'Meara (1961) classified seventeen screening criteria into four categories, namely marketability, durability, productive ability and growth potential. Marketability criteria include relation to present distribution channels, relation to present product lines, number of sizes and grades, merchandizability, quality/price relationship, effects on sales of present products. Durability criteria comprise, stability, breadth of market, resistance to cyclical fluctuations, resistance to seasonal fluctuations, and exclusiveness of design. Productivity ability reflects criteria such as necessary equipment, necessary production knowledge and personnel, availability of raw materials, while growth potential includes place in the market, expected competitive situation-value added, and expected availability of end users.

According to O'Meara's model, the evaluation of each criterion may range from 'very good' to 'very poor'. For example, a very good idea in terms of its relation to present product lines means that this new product complements a present line which needs more products to fill it. By contrast, a poor idea means that it will have to be distributed entirely through new channels in order to reach major markets. Similarly, an idea as far as resistance to seasonal fluctuations is concerned can be characterized as good if it may yield steady sales throughout the year, and poor if it involves severe seasonal fluctuations that will necessitate layoffs and heavy inventories.

All in all, Cooper and de Brentani (1984) proposed the following general screening criteria for new product ideas:

1 *economic performance/financial potential*: assessment of the project's market potential; expected sales growth, market growth and market share; ROI; and probability of success);
2 *corporate/internal synergy*: utilization of the company's experiences, capabilities, and already established marketing facilities;

3   *technological synergy/production-design synergy*: utilization of current production facilities and methods and engineering/design resources);
4   *product differential advantage*: product uniqueness and superiority achieving a competitive and/or technological edge.

Regarding the screening stage of new service ideas, Easingwood (1986) found the following interesting results:

- 26 per cent of the sampled companies had formal reviewing procedures;
- 52 per cent had a partly formal process;
- 23 per cent regarded their reviewing system as entirely informal;
- 77 per cent collected some customer response to the proposed new product idea;
- only 53 per cent would base their financial projections on market research estimates of purchasing intentions, trial rate, and so on.

Further, screening procedures were considerably thorough in financial institutions, compared to other service companies. Easingwood argued that this result might have been due in part to the difficulty of withdrawing new financial products. Discussions with many managers suggested that the elimination of a service that have not met its objectives, while it still has many loyal customers, it is not the right strategy to follow. It is better to cut down any promotional back of the product and to make it unavailable to new customers.

Concept development and testing

An important stage of the new product development process is the concept development and testing. The Product Development Management Association defines product concept as 'a clearly written and possibly visual description of the new product idea that includes its primary features and consumer benefits, combined with a broad understanding of the technology needed' (Rosenau, 1996).

An example of a new product concept for a new digital cordless phone is as follows:

> This digital cordless telephone will have a standby time of up to 265 hours and a talk time of up to nineteen hours. Its dimensions will be 105 × 55mm, while its weight will be 97g. The telephone will have a digital screen that will display call time, caller ID (if already stored in the phonebook), battery level, and in range/out of range indication. The telephone (both handset and base) will be silver, and it will be priced at 83 euros. It will be sold in a package containing handset, base, battery pack NiMh, telecom line cord, power adapter, user manual and warranty leaflet. The telephone will be available in most electrical appliance shops.

After the concept is developed, a concept test follows which ensures that the product under development is what the target market needs. During concept testing information is collected about:

- the degree to which the customers perceive the appropriateness of the new product idea for satisfying their needs;
- their intention to buy (or try) the new product.

This information reflect the reactions of potential customers and it can either be used to permit the developer to estimate the sales value of the concept or to make changes to the concept to enhance its potential sales value (Rosenau, 1996).

The product concept is verbally described or visually presented to potential customers who are asked for their reactions to it. For example, there is discussion of whether the product's benefits are well perceived, whether they think that the product can satisfy their needs and if yes, how much they are willing to pay, what quantity to buy and how often.

Concept testing is usually conducted through personal interviews with the respondents either at their home (for consumer products) or at their place of work (for industrial products).

Further down, we provide a sample of questions, which are asked during a concept test for a new drinking chocolate.

- How would you describe your first reaction from this new drinking chocolate? (totally negative, somewhat negative, somewhat positive, totally positive)
- How different would you find this new drinking chocolate compared to other competitive products? (Very different, somewhat different, not particularly different, not different at all).
- How likely is it that you would buy this new drinking chocolate at the price of xxx? (definitely not buy, probably not buy, maybe buy/maybe not buy, probably buy, definitely buy)

As far as the way the questions can be addressed, concept testing can take the following forms (Lodish et al., 2001):

1 *Monadic testing*: the respondent is exposed to only one product concept. It is appropriate when direct competitors are hard to identify or there is little external customer search for an alternative offering prior to purchasing.
2 *Paired comparison testing*: the respondent gets exposed to a pair of product concepts, one of the new products and another of its main competitor's product and the following question is usually posed: 'Which would you prefer to purchase, product A or product B?' To answer this question the following scale can be used: definitely prefer A, moderately prefer A, toss-up, moderately prefer B, definitely prefer B.

Although, concept testing is a useful tool for evaluating the customer's initial reaction to a new product, its results must be analysed with caution, as it provides an indication of likely product acceptance and there is no guarantee that the opinions expressed (either positive, or negative) will be translated into relevant action (purchase or no purchase, respectively).

Actually, it has been argued that, for most new products, particularly concepts in categories familiar to the customer, concept tests are likely to overstate the market acceptance, while for concepts in categories new or unfamiliar to the customer the concept tests may understate the product's acceptance (Cooper, 1993).

In order to reach a more accurate estimate about the purchase intention of potential customers, it is usually recommended to consider some 75 per cent of those who would 'definitely buy' the product plus some 35 per cent of those who would 'probably buy' the product.

For products that will be sold through the Internet the so-called *dry test* can be used (Lodish et al., 2001). In this case, product descriptions are provided and when the potential customer actually starts the order process he/she is informed that the product is in development and that the company is testing market place reaction. As an expression of thanks and apology, the company could send these potential customers a gift and put their name on the list of those who will get the chance to buy the product when it is ready at a special price.

Marketing strategy

Concept development and testing is followed by the marketing strategy for the new product/service. It should be noted, though, that the marketing strategy neither starts, nor is concluded at this stage. In fact, it extends throughout the new product development process from the moment the company decides to develop a new product until it is finally launched in the market.

More specifically, during the initial stages of new product development (namely, idea generation and screening, concept development and testing) the company gathers marketing information and makes preliminary estimates for various market-related variables (for example, market size, marketing resources requirements, target market, competitive products). In the marketing strategy stage, this kind of information is gathered more systematically in order to allow making accurate estimates about market conditions, customer needs and market potential. As the process proceeds to the development and further to testing, the company continues to collect marketing information (for example, degree of new product acceptance from the customers). This information needs to be incorporated into the marketing strategy which will be finalized during the commercialization/launching stage.

The marketing strategy of a new product/service is depicted in the marketing plan (Figure 6.2). This plan consists of the following elements:

1 Introduction. The marketing plan begins with:

   - description of the new product (characteristics, benefits);
   - reference to the marketing plan's time frame;
   - the marketing plan's relation to other corporate plans (for example, business plan);
   - obligations and responsibilities of company's executives.

2 Analysis of external environment. In this section the following elements are provided:

   - size of the market;
   - market growth rate;
   - customer analysis (characteristics, needs, buying behaviour);
   - competitor analysis (products, prices, distribution channels, promotional activities, market shares, profitability);
   - description of market trends (social, demographic, economic);
   - opportunities and threats of the external environment.

3 Analysis of internal environment. In this section the following elements are provided:

   - marketing audit (description of marketing activities and outcomes);
   - strengths and weaknesses of the company.

4 Marketing objectives. The objectives set for the new product may be:

   - quantitative (for example, sales and profits for the first year);
   - qualitative (for example, improvement in the company's image).

5 Marketing strategy. This section includes the following:

   - target market;
   - product strategy[1] (positioning, quality specifications, branding, packaging, sizes, variants, product services);
   - pricing strategy (higher than, lower than, equal to competition);
   - distribution strategy (distribution channels, geographical coverage);
   - promotion strategy (advertising, personal selling, sales promotion, public relations).

Figure 6.2   **Marketing planning for new products/services**

6 Action plan. In this section the following are included:

- pricing activities;
- distribution activities;
- promotion activities;
- action plan monitoring mechanism;
- budget (forecasted revenues and costs);[2]
- time schedule and assignment of responsibilities.

Business analysis

Business analysis is the next npd stage in which the new product idea is more thoroughly evaluated taking into consideration the respective financial facts. In this set of npd activities, a cost-benefit analysis is conducted, where the expected sales and profits are estimated and compared to the costs of developing and nurturing the new product. It is obvious that business analysis is strongly related to the marketing strategy. This is why in most cases these two stages are undertaken concurrently. The results of the business analysis are incorporated in the new product budget, which is part of the new product's marketing plan.

Business analysis is based on a number of projections regarding:

- the life of the new product and market demand over the product's life cycle;
- the development, production and launching costs;
- the investments needed in assets, equipment, working capital and market development;
- the selling price;
- the sales revenue, profitability[3] and return on investment.

A number of economic financial evaluation models have been proposed in the literature. Two such models are DEMON (Decision Mapping via Optimum go-no go Networks) (Charnes et al., 1966, 1968) and SPRINTER (Specification of Profits with Interaction under Trial and Error Response) (Urban, 1968).[4]

In order for new product evaluations to be correct, irrespective of the model used, they must be based on accurate forecasts about market demand and sales. A variety of new product forecasting models are available in the literature. These models can be classified into the following three categories (Wind, 1982):

1 Subjective models, including the Delphi method, the Analytic Hierarchy Process, the Chain Ratio Model, which companies use to incorporate the judgements of experts and other relevant past experience in order to make forecasting judgements. This approach is useful when the company is introducing a fundamentally new product, bearing little resemblance to previous ones.

2 Analogue models, which consider the historical performance of similar products and assume that the way a new product is accepted in the market place will be close to the way similar products are accepted. Needless to say that these models require careful identification of the similarities between the new product and the products, which serve as the base for comparison. Choffray and Lilien (1986) used the analogue approach to develop a microcomputer marketing decision support system (MMDSS) for forecasting sales and evaluating launch strategies prior to new industrial product introduction. The key objective of this project was to identify and quantify the determinants of sales growth for new industrial products. Considering the historical performance of 112 industrial products, the authors identified the determinants of their initial rate of penetration, and their speed of diffusion, which were then incorporated into the MMDSS. According to the authors' results, the industrial products with high initial penetration rates were reformulated products (modified) without major internal demand and had first, a short development process with a high level of personal involvement, secondly, few competitors of importance and thirdly, lower price relative to competition. Regarding their speed of diffusion, it was found that this is greater when first, the sales force pressure is higher than for competitive products; secondly, the price in the long-run is lower than competitive products; thirdly, the R&D effort after launch as a percentage of sales is low; fourthly, no new competitors enter the market; fifthly, the pricing strategy is free of restriction; and lastly, the customers are not highly satisfied with existing products.

3 Analytical first purchase (diffusion type) models which are used for describing and forecasting the diffusion of an innovation among a given set of prospective adopters over time. The underlying behavioural concept of these models is the adoption-imitation process, which implies that the new product is first adopted by the 'innovators' who, in turn, influence others to adopt it through word of mouth communication and demonstrated product usage. It must be noted that the main impetus underlying these contributions is the new product growth model suggested by Bass (1969).

Summary

- Pre-development stages include new product strategy development, idea generation, idea screening, concept development and testing, marketing strategy, and business analysis.
- New product strategy development sets the strategic requirements to be satisfied by the new product/service. There are internally driven and externally driven new product strategic roles/objectives.
- New product strategy objectives for service firms tend to be specific to particular sectors.
- About 6.6 ideas are required to generate one successful product, while the largest number of new product ideas is weeded out at the idea screening stage, that is, much earlier in the npd process, mainly because clearer strategic objectives exist that guide the development process. Hence, fewer resources are wasted on unsuccessful products.
- An idea for a new product or service can derive from a variety of sources, both internal and external to the company. Customer involvement in idea generation is critical for both manufactured goods and services.

- Idea generation techniques can be grouped in the following two categories: the creative techniques and the analytical techniques.
- The most important idea screening criteria are: economic performance/financial potential, corporate/internal synergy, technological synergy/production-design synergy, product differential advantage.
- Product concept is a clearly written and possibly visual description of the new product idea that includes its primary features and consumer benefits, combined with a broad understanding of the technology needed. Concept testing aims at identifying customer reactions prior to development.
- The marketing strategy stage involves the development of a marketing plan for the new product/service.
- Business analysis refers to a cost-benefit analysis where the expected sales and profits are estimated and compared to the costs of developing and nurturing the new product.
- Accurate forecasts about market demand and sales are imperative for business analysis. There are three types of product forecasting models, namely subjective, analogue and analytical first purchase (diffusion type) models

Questions

1 Select three internally driven strategic roles/objectives for a hotel chain and provide three new service ideas that could satisfy each of these objectives.
2 Describe the product concept for a new baby formula and write down five criteria for evaluating its marketability.
3 Provide a list of information needed for preparing the marketing plan of a new face cream for men.
4 Identify the appropriate sources inside and outside the company for collecting the information you provided in question 3.

Notes

1 In the case of services, this strategy includes: positioning, branding, core and supplementary services, and service quality.

2 In the appendix, we provide the basic concepts and an example of a new product's budget.

3 Break-even analysis can be used in calculating profitability of a new product. Break-even analysis identifies the sales level of the new product (in number of units) at which neither a profit nor a loss is made. Above this level or break-even point the product is profitable, while below this point it is suffering a loss. The break-even point formula is as follows:

break-even point (units) = total fixed costs/unit contribution

where unit contribution = selling price per unit – variable cost per unit

4 An extensive overview of these models can be found in Wind (1982).

References

Abraham, D. and Pickett, S.E. (2002) 'Refining the innovation process at Texaco', *Perspectives on Business Innovation*, 8. The Cap Gemini Ernst & Young Center for Business Innovation.

Alam, I. (2002) 'An exploratory investigation of user involvement in new service development', *Journal of the Academy of Marketing Science*, 30(3): 250–61.

Bass, F. (1969) 'A new product growth model for consumer durables', *Management Science*, 15: 215–27.

Booz, Allen and Hamilton (1968) *Management of New Products*. New York: Booz, Allen and Hamilton, Inc.

Booz, Allen and Hamilton, (1982) *New Products Management for the 1980s.* New York: Booz, Allen and Hamilton, Inc.

Charnes, A., Cooper, W., DeVoe, J.K. and Learner, D.B. (1966) 'DEMON: decision making via optimum go-no go networks – a model for marketing new products', *Management Science,* 12 (July): 865–87.

Charnes, A., Cooper, W., DeVoe, J.K. and Learner, D.B. (1968) 'DEMON Mark II: external equations solution and approximation', *Management Science,* 14 (July): 682–91.

Choffray, J. and Lilien, G. (1986) 'A decision-support system for evaluating sales prospects and launch strategies for new products', *Industrial Marketing Management,* 15: 75–85.

Cooper, R. (1993) *Winning at New Products.* Reading, MA: Perseus Books Publishing.

Cooper, R. and de Brentani, U. (1984) 'Criteria for screening new industrial product', *Industrial Marketing Management,* 13: 149–56.

Cooper R. and Kleinschmidt, E. (1986) 'An investigation into the new product process: Steps, deficiencies, and impact', *Journal of Product Innovation Management,* 3:71–85.

Davison, H., Watkins, T. and Wright, M. (1989) 'Developing new personal financial products – some evidence on the role of market research', *International Journal of Bank Marketing,* 7(1): 8–15.

Easingwood, C. (1986) 'New product development for service companies', *Journal of Product Innovation Management,* 4: 264–75.

Foxall, G. (1989) 'User initiated product innovations', *Industrial Marketing Management,* 18: 95–104.

Griffin, A. (1997) 'PDMA research on new product development practices: updating trends and benchmarking best practices', *Journal of Product Innovation Management,* 14: 429–58.

Gruner, K. and Homburg, C. (2000) 'Does customer interaction enhance new product success?', *Journal of Business Research,* 49(1): 1–14.

Hubka, V. (1983) 'Design tactics = methods + working principles for design engineers', *Design Studies* 4(3): 188–95.

Lilien, G., Morrison, P., Searls, K., Sonnack, M. and von Hippel, E. (2002) 'Performance assessment of the lead user idea-generation process for new product development', *Management Science,* 48(8): 1042–59.

Lodish, L., Morgan, H.L. and Kallianpur, A. (2001) *Entrepreneurial Marketing: Lessons from Wharton's Pioneering MBA Course.* Chichester: John Wiley & Sons, Inc.

Mahajan, V. and Wind, J. (1992) 'New product models: practice, shortcomings and desired improvement', *Journal of Product Innovation Management,* 9: 128–139.

Neal, M. and Corkendale, D. (1998) 'Codeveloping products: involving customers earlier and more deeply', *Long Range Planning,* 31(3): 418–25.

O' Meara, J. T., Jr. (1961) 'Selecting profitable products', *Harvard Business Review,* 39: 83–9.

Rosenau, M. (1996) *The PDMA Handbook of New Product Development.* John Wiley & Sons.

Sanchez, A. and Elola, L. (1991) 'Product innovation in Spain', *Journal of Product Innovation Management,* 8: 49–56.

Seidel, M., Niederlaender, F. and Gabriel, S. (2003) 'The BMW group cultivates worldwide "passion for innovation" in product development (part 1)', *Visions Magazine,* XXVII (1).

Teixeira, D. and Ziskin, J. (1993) 'Achieving quality with customer in mind', *Bankers Magazine,* January/February: 29–35.

Urban, G.L. (1968) 'A new product analysis and decision model', *Management Science,* 14 (April): 490–517.

Von Hippel, E. (1978) 'Successful industrial products from customer ideas', *Journal of Marketing,* 42: 39–49.

Von Hippel, E. (1986) 'Lead users: a source of novel product concepts', *Management Science,* 32(7): 791–805.

Von Hippel, E., Thomke, S. and Sonnack, M. (1999) 'Creating breakthoughs at 3m', *Harvard Business, Review* 77(5): 47–57.

Wind, Y. (1982) *Product Policy: Concepts, Methods and Strategy.* Reading, MA: Addison-Wesley Publishing Company.

Further reading

Cooper, R. (1985) 'Selecting winning new product projects: using the Newprod system', *Journal of Product Innovation Management,* 2: 34–44.

Cooper, R. (1987) 'Defining the new product strategy', *IEEE Transactions on Engineering Management,* 34(3): 184–93.

Cooper, R. (1988). 'Pre-development activities determine new product success', *Industrial Marketing Management,* 17(3): 237–47.

7 Development, Testing and Launching New Products and Services

Introduction

In this chapter we continue the presentation of the remaining new product/service development stages. More specifically, the stages to be analysed include technical development, testing and introduction to the market or launching. Further, we discuss the cycle times by npd stage and the allocation of resources during the new product development process.

This chapter provides answers to the following questions:

- Which particular activities are undertaken during the stages of technical development, testing and launching?
- What is the cycle time for different product development stages, and
- Which factors are associated with shorter product development cycle times?

Development of new products and services

After the new product idea has passed the business analysis stage successfully, the next stage refers to its actual development. During this stage, the idea will be translated in concrete and tangible terms. According to Cooper and Kleinschmidt (1988) the development stage absorbs the largest part of the innovation budget. A number of design and production engineers, and marketers should work together and by taking into consideration market and technical requirements should be able to turn an idea presented on paper into a final product. A product prototype is usually developed and is operationally tested as a way to examine the technical feasibility of a new product. However, in the development of services, prototyping is not easy to develop due to its intangible nature. Usually, the development stage is the longest in the whole process. The study by Cooper and Kleinschmidt (1988) has shown that the product development stage accounts for 419 person-days, almost 2 person-years, out of the 905 person-days spent on average on the entire new product project.

This stage is not only long but also critical. It actually involves bringing two separate elements into accord: customer satisfaction and technical feasibility. In order to facilitate this accord, Crawford (1984) advocates the development of a new product protocol. The protocol is an agreement between three departments (marketing, technical, and

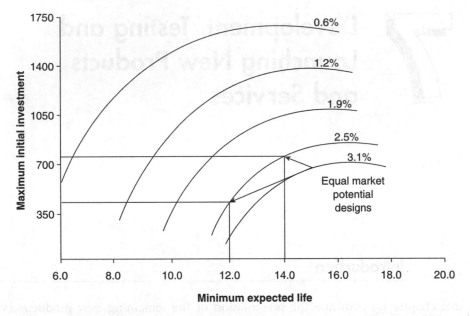

Figure 7.1   **Sample trade-off curves for the acceptance submodel of the industrial market response model**

Source: Choffray and Lilien (1978)

general management) on what the product will be and it defines the objectives for the R&D effort. Agreement must be reached on:

1   the definition of the target market;
2   the product's concept;
3   the benefits the product will deliver;
4   how the product will be positioned in the market; and
5   the product's features, attributes, design specifications and requirements.

A number of approaches have been developed in the literature to provide marketing-based information and guidelines for the design of industrial products and services. It is true that unless the new product has the specifications required by the target market segments, it will not be accepted by the market. In 1978, Choffray and Lilien presented a model for evaluating product design scenarios and designing new product strategy. Their approach, the *industrial market response model*, has four submodels each directly relating organizational buying behaviour to a key product strategy area: the awareness model, the acceptance model, the individual evaluation model and the group decision model. It is the product acceptance submodel, which provides insight into product design trade-offs and allows prediction of the rate of market acceptance for a product with a given design. Using data from their industrial cooling systems study, the authors show how the acceptance model assesses design trade-offs in terms of market potential. Figure 7.1 shows ISO acceptance curves of trade-offs between maximum initial investment cost (price) and minimum system life expectancy for industrial cooling systems. It is clear that a system life expectancy of twelve years and cost of $450 a ton of cooling lead to the same level of market acceptance (2.5 per cent) as fourteen years and $700 a ton.

Further development of the industrial market response model led to *Designor*, a decision support procedure for industrial product design (Choffray and Lilien, 1982). This procedure can be used not only to evaluate the impact of alternative product designs on market share and sales, but also to isolate segments that are inadequately served by comparing competitive product designs to the specifications preferred by key market segments.

Wind et al. (1978) presented an application of conjoint analysis to the study of the most desirable features of an industrial type new product scientific and technical information (STI) services. The methodology can be briefly described as follows: conjoint analysis was utilized to assess the utilities of respondents/organizational members (274 scientists, information specialists and managers of 163 companies) for various features and attributes of an STI system. The utility function for the entire sample provided initial guidelines for the design of a system that would have had a wide appeal. However, given that the market for STI was quite heterogeneous in its preferences for system attributes, a utility segmentation (analogous to benefit segmentation) was undertaken, using cluster analysis, resulting in five utility segments. To gain insights into the nature of the segments, a series of multiple discriminant analyses was conducted against the STI usage data and the personal and organizational demographic characteristics of the respondents. The utility functions (of each segment) provided system designers with a tool against which to evaluate various system options (any possible combination of features) and a source of ideas for new system configurations. According to the authors, the resulting utilities by segment not only reduced considerably the R&D guesswork, but also provided vigorous answers to questions dealing with what the buyers' and users' reaction would be if certain changes were made.

Further adaptations of conjoint analysis based methods to optimal product design, resulted in approaches such as the *Posse* (product optimization and selected segment evaluation) methodology, which has been implemented in the design of a number of industrial products such as telecommunications and office equipment (Green et al., 1981).

Quality function deployment (QFD) is an alternative managerial technique for product development which has its origins in Japan, and it was first applied in 1972 at Mitsubishi's Kobe shipyard. QFD is claimed to reduce design time by 40 per cent and design costs by 60 per cent while maintaining and even enhancing product design quality (Hauser and Clausing, 1988). It manages across individual functional aspects of new product development (for example, marketing, engineering), providing mechanisms that bind the individual functional tasks into a coherent process. As described in the work of Sullivan (1986) cross-functional teams use a series of interaction matrices in order to transform the customer needs into product specifications (Figure 7.2). The first matrix is called 'house of quality'. It relates data generated from market research on customer needs and wants to propose performance characteristics of the product (engineering design inputs). The second QFD matrix relates potential product features to the delivery of performance characteristics. The third and fourth matrices bring process characteristics and production requirements into the engineering and marketing relationships.

In a study of thirty-five new product development teams using QFD within US firms, Griffin (1992) identified the factors leading to QFD application success and failure. The project characteristics associated with producing more successful applications of QFD involved less complex, service projects that implied an incremental change. Similarly, QFD implementation success is related to the following factors: treat QFD as an investment; a high commitment to QFD; project members champion QFD use; team members familiar with each other; QFD as a means to achieving an end; goals that stretch capabilities; high cross-functional integration.

In the case of intangible products (namely, services), a process is what is actually developed. Shostack (1984) claims that for process design purposes a 'blueprint' should be prepared. *Blueprinting*, also called flowcharting, describes all process steps that customers and service employees must follow in a given service environment. Figure 7.3 provides an example of blueprinting for a savings account.

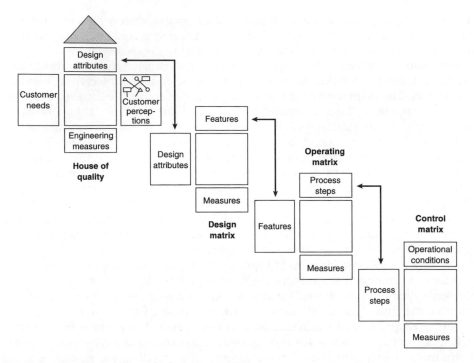

Figure 7.2   **Quality function deployment matrices**
Source: Sullivan (1986)

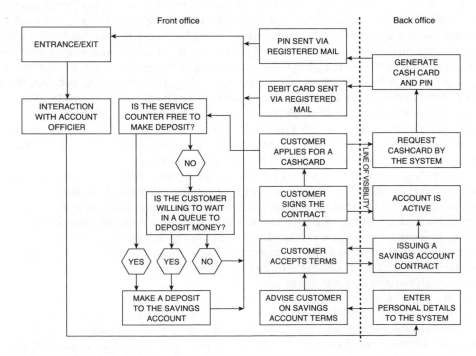

Figure 7.3   **Blueprinting of a savings account**

Testing of new products

Testing the new product is the next step in the new product development process during which the company can yield valuable information about customer reactions to a product prototype. There are two types of testing:

- Product use testing which examines possible product/operating problems, and
- Market testing which identifies possible market-related pitfalls.

Product use testing

Product use testing means use under normal operating conditions (Crawford, 1997). In the case of manufactured goods, this testing allows the developing company to obtain valuable reactions to product features and characteristics such as durability, technical performance, energy consumption, materials tolerance. As far as services are concerned, characteristics such as speed of delivery, service homogeneity, customer responsiveness are important.

There are two types of product testing, namely alpha testing and beta testing (Crawford, 1997):

- *Alpha testing* is conducted in-house, in a laboratory setting or some part of the developing firm's regular operations.
- *Beta testing* takes place on the premises of the intended market users. It is quite common in the software market where beta versions of new software are provided to computer experts for testing.

Alpha and beta testing: the case of Gillette

The Gillette Company, which began its operation in 1901, is well known for its ability to meet consumers' needs and launch successful new products in the market. Gillette's success can largely be attributed to the extensive alpha and beta tests conducted to its new products. Alpha tests are done with the participation of approximately 200 volunteer employees from throughout the company. These people begin their workday at the South Boston R&D operations with a shave, in small booths with a sink and a mirror, using a variety of razors, shaving creams and aftershave lotions. Afterwards, these volunteers respond to a number of questions relating to the performance of each product.

In addition to alpha tests, Gillette conducts beta tests of the products with actual users. For example, more than 5,000 men tested the Sensor before entering the market.

Source: Thomas (1995)

Market testing

Product tests are undoubtedly important in obtaining reactions to product features and characteristics. However, the results of a product test may not be sufficient for identifying customers' preference, as other influences may affect the customer's decision. These influences include brand image, price, easy access to the points of sale to name a few. Therefore, when the product is finally in its expected market form and as a last-stage check prior to full-scale introduction, market testing may be undertaken to evaluate the product and its marketability under selected field conditions.

How can a product test lead to the wrong decision: the case of New Coke

The Coca-Cola company was suffering from shrinking market share for decades from 60 per cent just after World War II to under 24 per cent in 1983. The sweeter taste of Pepsi was increasingly preferred, so Coca-Cola marketers decided to test a new formula comparable to the formula of Diet Coke sweetened with high fructose corn syrup instead of aspartame.

Double blind taste tests were conducted with the participation of 190,000 consumers in thirty-five US cities. These tests revealed that most consumers preferred the taste of New Coke to Old Coke (55 per cent vs. 45 per cent), and Pepsi (56 per cent vs. 44 per cent). On the basis of these product test results New Coke was introduced on 23 April 1985 with the slogan 'The best just got better' while the production of the original formula ended that same week.

Hundreds of angry letters were sent to the company. The Old Coke Drinkers of America organization was founded and attempted to sue the company, while it lobbied for the return of the old formula in the market. Under this great pressure exerted by the nostalgia for the old formula, the company announced its return in the market under the name Coca-Cola Classic on 10 July 1985.

It is apparent that product tests focusing solely on taste could not reveal the deep and abiding emotional attachment to the Coca-Cola brand name.

There are different market testing methods depending on the type of the market, namely, consumer (B2C) or industrial (B2B).

The main methods of market testing for consumer products are the following:

1 *Simulated test marketing*: a number of 30–40 potential consumers are tracked down (in the street or a shopping mall) and are invited to participate in the test. This market testing method comprises the following steps: first, potential consumers who agree to participate provide information about their buying behaviour in relation to the category of the product under investigation (for example, how often they purchase products from this category, how much, and which brands they prefer, and so on). Next, the participating consumers are exposed to print advertisements and/or TV commercials of various products in the category, including the company's new product. Then, they receive a small amount of money and are asked to make purchases in a specific store (simulated or real). Afterwards, consumers are asked to discuss the reasons for their buying behaviour (purchases, non purchases), and what would make them change their behaviour. This discussion aims at unveiling the reasons for selecting (or not selecting) the company's new product (for example, how advertising or other marketing mix elements influenced their buying decision).

2 *Test marketing*: this is the most frequently used market testing method of consumer products. Test marketing is conducted in a few representative cities. The selected cities represent the country's average in terms of demographic and psychographic characteristics. In this sense, the results of test marketing in these cities would be representative of the population. In this method, the new product is placed on the stores' shelves, while a full promotional campaign is also carried out. The company monitors sales figures and reaches useful conclusions regarding market acceptance and competitive reactions.

3 *Consumer panels*: a number of potential consumers agree to use the new product repetitively and provide their opinion and purchase intention.

As far as industrial (B2B) products are concerned, there are four main methods for their market testing (de Brentani, 2000; Kotler, 2003):

1 The new product is tested in a limited *geographical area*. Sales people attempt to make an actual sale as part of a regular sales call.

2 The new product is tested in *distributor and dealer display rooms*. This method reflects the product's normal selling situation.

3 The new product is tested in a *trade show*. This method has the advantage of testing the new product to a large number of potential buyers, but is also has the disadvantage of revealing the product to competitors. Therefore, the vendor must be ready to launch the product to the market shortly after the trade show.

5 The new product is tested through *speculative sale*. Sales people approach the potential customer and pretend to make a sale using prepared selling materials, a real product and a veritable price list. Here, the objective is not test whether an actual sale can be accomplished, but rather to test the customer's level of interest and excitement willingness to ask for a sample, or purchase intention if the product was available.

Market test can be viewed an acceptance test, which, when feasible, can provide useful information as it involves: first, the identification of key purchasing influences; secondly, the testing of user reaction to the product and its features; thirdly, the testing of price possibilities and an assessment of users' reaction to various price levels; fourthly, the determination of the most effective sales approach; and lastly, the testing of the effectiveness of promotional materials and plans.

However, little is still done regarding the development of market test models for products and services and the quantitative estimation of new product market acceptance. One useful model that has been developed and tested empirically by Scott and Keiser (1984) includes estimates of variations in likely market response as a function of price, product attributes, and environmental factors. Their model provides estimates about first, the likelihood of adopting a new product and secondly, how this likelihood of adoption varies as attributes of the product, supplier or decision environment are changed. Their approach consists of the following seven steps:

1 The product adoption decision-making process and the decision-making environment are analysed descriptively to identify first, steps in the process, secondly, key influences involved at each step and their choice criteria, thirdly, the dynamics of how various decisions which lead to final choice are reached, fourthly, characteristics of substitute products, fifthly, barriers to acceptance of the innovation, and sixthly, positive factors leading to adoption. This exploratory phase is quite revealing in itself and serves to enrich and to support (or question) the modelling results.

2 Attributes of the product, potential suppliers, and the decision-making environment, which are believed to influence judgement and decision at various stages in the adoption process are identified.

3 Alternative product offerings are described in terms of combinations of levels of the attributes (for example, price, product features, financing arrangements). These offerings referred to as product concepts, are usually complete or fractional orthogonal designs to facilitate unambiguous estimation of parameters of the judgement process. For example, an offering described by two attributes, each with three levels, would have nine concepts for a complete orthogonal design.

4 An appropriate sample or set of samples of potential adopters representing target markets of interest is selected for modelling.

5 Members of the sample are carefully educated in the choices to be made, in order to make the conditions of the judgement modelling episode roughly equivalent to the actual decision-making situation that is likely to occur.

6 Decision-makers are asked to make judgements on the product concepts. These judgements may be quantitative, ordinal (namely, rank orders) or discrete choices.

7 The judgements are analysed quantitatively to estimate the judgement functions.

Woodside et al. (1988) have applied Scott and Keiser's model in a new wool testing service among customers located in three different channel levels of the wool manufacturing market in New Zealand. The central strategic marketing implications for this study are first, modelling of customer acceptance of new industrial services is likely to be helpful in planning specific marketing strategies for customers at different channel positions and secondly, gaining customer acceptance of a new industrial service among customers located at different channel levels is likely to require adjusting features of the service to meet the requirements of customers at each channel level.

There is no doubt that testing is an important new product development stage. However, there are certain situations that this stage is not considered necessary. For instance, in the cases whereby:

*   neither the product, nor the market are new to the company;
*   the investment cost and projected sales are low;
*   it is quite possible that sensitive product or market information will be revealed to the competitors, who may rush to launch their rival products or follow an aggressive marketing strategy for their existing products (for example, increase promotion, reduce prices);
*   the nature of the product makes testing quite difficult; for example, in the fashion industry, designs, colours and types of clothes are decided by a limited number of designers.

Launching of new products and services

The final stage of new product development refers to product launching or product introduction in the market. At this stage, costs increase dramatically, as considerable investments are made in production facilities, training and the launch programmes. Booz et al. (1982) revealed that of the total amount of money spent on the commercialization stage, as much as 67 per cent was spent on successful projects. Further, Cooper and Kleinschmidt (1988) have found that the launching stage absorbs the second largest part of the innovation budget after product development and that compared to failed products, successful ones had significantly more time devoted to them in terms of person-days during the market launch stage.

During this stage, the company finalizes and implements:

*   the production (or service operations) plan, and
*   the marketing plan.

The production (or service operations) plan is the responsibility of the production department (or service operations department). By contrast, the marketing plan is prepared and executed by the marketing department. We will turn our attention to this plan in the remainder of the chapter.

New product preannouncement

Preannouncement is a formal, deliberate communication directed to one or more audiences such as customers, competitors, or distributors. The timing of preannouncements usually takes the form of 'teaser' ads and may range from a few days to many weeks before the new product is actually introduced in the market.

A teaser ad campaign for Gillette's Sensor shaving system

The Sensor shaving system is one of the enduring innovation successes of Gillette, which was introduced in January 1990 in sixteen countries, marking the company's first pan-Atlantic product launch. The company has successfully undertaken a 'teaser' ad campaign, which has been on the air for a number of weeks before the introduction of its Sensor shaving system with the slogan: 'Gillette is about to change the way men shave forever'.

In their seminal study of market signalling, Eliashberg and Robertson (1988) specified that preannouncing may be prevalent when: first, the new product will require the customer to undertake considerable learning before adoption, and product trial is not necessary; secondly, the competitive environment is non-combative, and therefore competitive retaliation is unlikely; thirdly, the firm has low market dominance in the product category because of low cannibalization risks; fourthly, the firm is small in the number of total sales and number of employees, and as such it tends not to be susceptible to 'market overhanging' allegations (namely, deliberate intent of injuring competitors' sales).

The same researchers also found that:

- In 51 per cent of new product introductions an announcement of the launch had been made.
- These announcements were directed towards sales personnel (in 84 per cent of the cases), customers (97 per cent), and distributors (55 per cent).
- The time of announcement varied from 1 to 24 months before the actual launch of the product.

Rabino and Moore (1989) also researched preannouncing within the mainframe computer market in Northern America. Their main results are as follows:

- The formal announcement of a new-product introduction is not an isolated communication, but rather, the culmination of a multifaceted process, comprising informal as well as formal components, co-ordinated and formalized under the management of corporate executives.
- The nature and length of the announcement process is determined by product-related variables and may vary not only from company to company, but from product to product within the same company.

- An announcement may be targeted to any of a number of different constituencies in keeping with specific strategic objectives.
- The exact content of an announcement, as well as the medium and timing of its communication, is determined in keeping with the target audience.

Moreover, a mail survey of 346 marketing managers of British and US companies focused on the incumbent reactions on new product announcement (NPA) signals (Robertson et al. (1995). According to this study:

- About 40 per cent of the firms surveyed acknowledged receiving an NPA signal from competitors. Of those who received a signal, 50.4 per cent reacted; while of those reacting, 63.7 per cent reacted with the introduction of a new product, and 36.2 per cent reacted by utilizing an alternative marketing mix instrument (for example, lowered price or increased advertising).
- Press announcements (23.1 per cent) and trade journals (26.1 per cent) were the most popular media where the signals appeared.

New product launch strategies

There are two different launch strategies, namely a full market launch and a rollout strategy:

- *Full market launch*: this means that the new product is launched to all target markets simultaneously. This strategy is preferred when competition is not far behind and the company can benefit from the first mover advantage. Being first in the market, usually translates into getting the best distributors, an image as an innovator and a larger long-term market share (Robinson and Fornell, 1985; Robinson, 1988). However, a full market launch involves considerable risk and cost and has often led to failure when inadequate resources were assigned to the effort (de Brentani, 2000).
- *Rollout strategy*: this means that the launching efforts roll out or are progressively undertaken, in the sense that the new product is introduced one segment at a time. The rollout strategy is frequently used as quasi test marketing in an attempt to learn from the mistakes made in one segment, thus increasing the possibilities of success in the next segment. For example at the end of 2004, Coca-Cola Great Britain introduced its Diet Coke brand in a 250ml. 'mini-break' can, initially in an exclusive deal with Boots around the country.

One of the most cited studies about new product launch strategies has been conducted by Chris Easingwood and Charles Beard (1989). The two researchers identified four new product launch strategies of high technology companies, which can accelerate their initial rate of adoption. These strategies are presented below in the order in which they would normally be considered by management.

Strategy 1: cooperate with other producers

Working with other producers in the production and/or marketing of the new product, may take the form of technology sharing or embarking on an education programme. This strategy aims at increasing the total market impact achieved. Two approaches can be used.

Share the technology The technology may be licensed to other producers, even competitors at least for two reasons: first, for raising total demand and secondly, for preventing users being confronted with competing and incompatible technologies. This strategy was used by Sony when licensing out its 8mm camcorder technology.

Embark on an education programme   This strategy, which aims at educating a target audience about the benefits of the new technology, can establish a degree of technological leadership and further accelerate early adoption. Market education must be distinguished from promotion because the product itself is not so much the subject of attention as the technology incorporated into it. The educated audience can be other producers of similar technologies, as well as those in a target market. This strategy, which was the second most popular, was used by Intel Corp., which educated the market about potential microprocessor units.

Strategy 2: position the product in the market

This strategy aims at positioning the new product in the market so as to win early market acceptance. Three main approaches can be used.

Approach innovative adopters   Innovative adopters are those early buyers of new products who are undeterred by the risks of early adoption because innovators are promising target customers for major new product launches. This strategy was the most popular of all. Here, it must be pointed out that there are two problems with approaching innovators, first, innovators may be hard to identify and reach, and/or secondly, innovators may be too few. Manufacturers of minicomputer peripheral equipment when approaching university scientists and engineers to promote their new products practically use such a strategic approach.

Approach heavy users of the product category   Research has shown that early adopters of a new product are likely to be heavy users of the general product category from which the product comes. In that respect, an effective strategy could be to concentrate marketing efforts on heavy product category users. Not surprisingly, this strategy was a fairly popular one. Pharmaceutical companies use this approach when promoting new drugs to heavy users of the drug category (namely, hospital specialists).

Approach heavy users of the preceding technology   The above approach can sometimes be focused on users of the technology that the new product is intended to replace. This strategy was explained as being an attempt to consciously position the product in such a way that it is seen as completely superseding a preceding technology. This strategy was pursued to some degree. For example, Apricot (advanced IBM compatible personal computers) used this approach by positioning its product to users of Amstrad personal computers (basic IBM compatibles).

Strategy 3: directly reduce the risk of adoption

The purpose of this strategy is to increase adoption by directly reducing the risk of early adoption. There are two forms of risk reduction:

Trial without purchase   At least two methods can be used for implementing this strategy as a way to reduce the risk of adoption incorporated in high technology new products, namely an introductory trial and leasing.

A common characteristic of early adopters is that they are not price sensitive, but rather they foster quality and superiority. Therefore, it would not be effective to reduce the price of the product. Alternatively, it might well be helpful to reduce the price of trying the product, or even to offer a free introductory trial. By so doing, the potential adopter has a relatively risk-free opportunity to self-assess the product's performance. Uniroyal usually offers ninetey-day in factory free trial of its tyres.

The second way of implementing the strategy of 'trial with purchase' is by leasing the product to potential adopters. This approach is particularly appropriate for a company with many customers, some of which need the latest technology and are willing to pay for it, while others do not need the latest technology and expect to pay less. Products that are no longer leading-edge technology can then be passed down to users who do not need the very latest technology. This strategy was found to be rather unpopular.

Absorb the risk   A novel approach to risk reduction is for the producer to absorb the risk of adoption. The client pays for the installation and operating costs, but enjoys most of the expected benefits of the technology without the associated risks. This strategy was found to be the least used.

Strategy 4: win market support

This strategy aims at encouraging good 'word-of-mouth' for the new product. Market support can be achieved through the following two approaches:

Win the endorsement of opinion leaders   Opinion leaders are people who exercise high influence over the target market. The researchers give an illustrative example from the personal computer industry, where those influential constituents between the manufacturer and the customer are called the infrastructure and include the business and new press, the trade press, financial analysts, dealers and software producers and vendors. Companies must develop a systematic plan for influencing opinion leaders and gain their support. Prior to the Macintosh launch, Apple has worked with the computer press as part of this strategy.

Establish a 'winner' image   It is generally stated that successful products receive the market's acceptance more easily. Hence, some companies attempt to create for their products a success image. Although effective, this strategy seems to be quite expensive. Microsoft spends heavily on the launch of its new software programmes.

'Legitimize' the product   Another way of winning market support is to publicize the names of the organizations that have already adopted the product. Alternative methods for achieving that are direct word-of-mouth communication from the adopter to potential adopters, or beta tests by the early adopter.

New product launch tactics

Another empirical investigation from Beard and Easingwood (1996) complements the research described earlier in the area of new product launch (Easingwood and Beard, 1989). Their survey aimed to investigate the use of four new product launch tactics, namely market preparation, targeting, positioning and market attack (Table 7.1).

The process of launch tactics development starts with the market preparation launch tactics, which comprise the actions taken to prepare the market for the launch (for

Table 7.1   **Launch tactics and examples of associated actions for high technology products in the UK**

1 Market preparation tactics	2 Targeting tactics
1 Licensing the product technology (e.g. licensing to inaccessible markets)	1 Target innovators (e.g. target customers quick to adopt new products)
2 Supply to other equipment manufacturers (OEMs) (e.g. supplying OEMs to access new markets)	2 Target early adopters (e.g. concentrate on good product support services)
3 Provide pre-launch information (e.g. give pre-launch demonstrations of the product)	3 Target late adopters (e.g. research market expectations of the product)
4 Create special distribution arrangements (e.g. look for new dealers in new markets)	4 Target existing customers (e.g. meet the needs of existing customers)
	5 Target competitors' customers (e.g. emphasize improvements over competitors' products)

3 Positioning tactics	4 Market attack tactics
1 Appeal to heavy users (e.g. concentrate on the needs of heavy users)	1 Use opinion leaders (e.g. put high profile stories in the trade press)
2 Emphasize exclusivity (e.g. concentrate on the quality of the product)	2 Use reference sites (e.g. use beta test sites as reference sites)
3 Emphasize a low price (e.g. undercut the dominant competitor's price)	3 Use educating methods (e.g. create awareness of the product technology)
4 Emphasize technological superiority (e.g. emphasize the new technology in the product)	4 Use a winner image (e.g. promote the success of the company)
5 Emphasize a special application (e.g. research the needs of one application)	5 Promote the product to dealers (e.g. give assistance to dealers with presentations)
6 Emphasize a safe bet (customer protection) (e.g. stress the credibility of the company)	6 Lend or lease the product (e.g. lend the product for trial)
	7 Promote to one special customer (e.g. persuade certain influential customers to adopt)

The actions presented as examples in each tactic exhibited the highest importance among all actions associated with the same tactic.

Source: adapted from Beard and Easingwood (1996)

example, provide pre-launch information). The second set of tactics considered during launch refers to targeting marketing actions to the most appropriate group of potential customers (namely, innovators, early or late adopters, existing customers, competitors' customers). Next, decisions must be made regarding product positioning. The researchers provide a list of six different positioning tactics, which could be used. The final step of the launch process is to develop and implement tactics aimed at attacking the market (for example, use of opinion dealers).

The researchers were particularly interested in when marketers actually use these tactics. It was hypothesized that this might depend on the degree of market newness and technological maturity. Table 7.2 summarizes their results.

According to their findings, products that are launched in new markets, have either given less attention to preparation and targeting or use other forms of preparation and targeting than those provided in the study. On the contrary, the positioning and attack tactics showed a very strong importance to the launch. Among the most important positioning tactics was emphasis on technological superiority and a special application. The

Table 7.2 **New product launch tactics/actions by the degree of market newness and technological maturity**

Established market	• Targeting: competitors' customers, late adopters • Positioning: low prices • Attack: dealer focus
New market	• Market preparation: pre-launch information • Targeting: innovators • Positioning: special application, technical superiority • Attack: opinion leaders, reference sites, educating methods, lend or lease
Established technology	• Targeting: competitors' customers • Positioning: low prices • Attack: dealer focus, lend or lease
New technology	• Market preparation: pre-launch information • Targeting: innovators, early adopters • Positioning: technical superiority, special application, 'safe bet' • Attack: educating methods, opinion leaders, reference sites, winner image, single customer

Source: adapted from Beard and Easingwood (1996)

attack tactics for new markets comprised the use of opinion leaders, reference sites, education methods, and lending or leasing. The use of the launch tactics for established markets is limited, proving that the launch tactics studied tend to be used less in established markets than in new markets.

As far as technological maturity is concerned, the emphasis for products based on new technologies is placed on targeting innovators and early adopters. The market is prepared by releasing pre-launch information on the product, to give the market time to absorb the new benefits gained by adopting the new technology. Technologically new products are positioned heavily on the basis of their technological superiority, with some focus on special applications, and a safe bet image. Almost all the attack tactics play a positive role in the launch of a new technology, especially the use of educating methods. Despite the high risk, most producers that have developed a new technology, do not consider sharing the technology through licensing or OEMs to be important. New products incorporating established technologies mainly focus on targeting customers of competitive products and to some extent attacking the market through promotion to dealers, and the provision of lend or lease schemes.

Additionally, the researchers investigated whether the launch tactics differed among products with varying degrees of innovativeness. For the analysis, a market-technology matrix of four quadrants was prepared, each representing a distinct type of innovation, namely normal innovation, technological innovation, market innovation, and revolutionary innovation.

Normal innovations refer to incremental extensions of the marketing and technological possibilities, such as the improvement of process technology to reduce costs, the addition of features to the product, or sub segmentation of the market. Products that fall into this category are marketed on the basis of competing for market share and on price.

Technological innovations describe a new technological product that has been introduced to an established market. Targeting actions are directed to existing customers, in order to keep them from being won over by the competition, as well as late adopters to generate new sales.

In market innovations, the technology is known. It has been already launched in the market and now it is introduced to a new market. Thus, the customers in the new market are not familiar with the technology. Launch tactics aim at reducing customer uncertainties such as confusion over the benefits offered or lack of information. The tactics identified here are particularly concerned with market preparation and include licensing and using OEMs.

In launching revolutionary innovations, that is new technological products introduced to new markets, the following tactics are used. These products are usually targeted at early adopters. They are positioned to emphasize technological superiority, a special application or some form of exclusivity. Further, methods of education and/or reference sites are used to attack markets of revolutionary innovations. All in all, these tactics suggest that revolutionary innovations are marketed on a small-scale basis where the intention is to raise awareness of the new technology and its new applications to a small group of well-informed customers.

The relationship between strategic and tactical decisions in new product launching

As we discussed earlier in this chapter, new product launch decisions can either be strategic or tactical. Recognizing the fact that the strategic launch decisions made early in the npd process affect the tactical decisions made later in the process, Hultink et al. (1997) examined the associations between various sets of strategic and tactical decisions in *new industrial product* launching. The strategic decisions examined were the following:

- product strategy (product innovativeness, npd cycle time, product newness);
- market strategy (market growth rate, stage of the PLC, targeting strategy);
- competitive stance (number of competitors, product advantage);
- firm strategy (driver of npd, innovation strategy).

The tactical decision that these researchers examined were as follows:

- product (branding decisions, breadth of assortment);
- distribution (distribution channels, distribution expenditures, distribution intensity);
- pricing (price level, pricing policy);
- promotion (promotion expenditures, salesforce intensity).

By analysing 221 new industrial products, Hultink et al. (1997) found that the way in which managers make strategic decisions on the basis of product innovativeness (*product strategy*), market targeting (*market strategy*), the number of competitors (*competitive stance*), and whether the project is marketing – or technology – driven (*firm strategy*) are associated with later tactical decisions about branding (*product*), distribution expenditure and intensity (*distribution*), and pricing tactics (*pricing*). In this sense, more innovative products which are developed as a result of combining technological possibilities with a market need are targeted into niche markets with fewer competitors, and are launched using exclusive distribution, high distribution expenditures and skimming pricing with a company name as the brand name.

By contrast, strategic decisions made regarding product newness (*product strategy*) and the firm's innovation strategy (*firm strategy*) are associated with tactical launch decisions regarding the breadth of product assortment (*product*), the distribution channels (*distribution*), the pricing policy (*pricing*), and the intensity of the salesforce (*promotion*). For example, firms that develop newer-to-the-firm products using less innovative strategies (namely, follower instead of innovator), launch only a small range of them at once with low sales force intensity through new channels with penetration pricing.

In a second series of analyses, Hultink et al. (1997) developed a typology of industrial product launch strategies, which is based on different combinations of strategic and tactical launch decisions. Four launch strategies were identified, namely niche followers, niche innovators, mass marketers, and would-be me-toos. These strategies have differential impacts on the performance of new industrial products.

Products launched using a *niche innovators* strategy were the most successful ones. These products are developed in companies whose basic innovation strategy is to pioneer new products and lines, which are driven by both technology and market needs. The strategic aspects of their launches use a niche focus to target relatively more innovative products into markets where the number of competitors is low. Tactical launch decisions associated with this strategy are exclusive distribution with higher distribution expenditures, a skimming price strategy, and a broad product assortment.

Products launched using a *niche followers* strategy were the second most successful ones. Niche followers combine both market and technology drivers in their development processes to produce rather innovative new products. Their new product strategies target new products and product lines to markets where there are few incumbent competitors. As far as the tactical launch decisions are concerned, niche followers launch a moderately broad product assortment branded with the company name and distributed through new, exclusive distribution channels. They exhibit no particular preference in relation to pricing, while their basic new product strategy is that of the niche player with a preference for fast imitation.

Mass marketers, which are moderately successful, use new product strategies targeting equally innovative reformulated products, intensively marketed by the sales force to mass markets in which there are numerous competitive offerings. Products in this group, are offered as a broad assortment at a price to rapidly penetrate the market. Branded after another of the company's product groups, they are intensively distributed but with lower overall distribution expenses than competition, through the firm's current marketing channels.

Would-be me-toos, which are largely unsuccessful, comprise market-driven less innovative new products launched into a wide range of highly-competitive markets. The small assortment of such new products are selectively distributed through new distribution channels with the moderate assistance of the sales force and with equal to competition's distribution expenses. The low performance of such products reflects the mismatch between the strategic and tactical launch decisions.

In another investigation of the launch strategies of 208 *new consumer products*, four distinct clusters of new consumer product introductions were identified (Hultink et al., 1997). These clusters are characterized by different combinations of strategic and tactical launch decisions, as well as different performance outcomes.

More specifically, the first cluster consists of consumer products, which are developed by technologically driven companies that have relatively long cycle times. These products, which are innovative and exhibit higher levels of product advantage, are launched into markets with a considerable number of competitors and use a new brand name as a way of differentiation. Distribution is selective, promotion expenditures are lower than those of competitors, and the pricing strategy is competitive. Products in this cluster were the least successful of all.

The second cluster comprises new consumer products that are developed through a mix of technology and market drivers over a one to three year period. These products are more innovative than the competitive ones, and they are launched into niche markets where there are no competitors. Distribution is intensive, promotion is higher than competitors' and skimming pricing is used. There are some similarities between the strategic launch profiles of clusters 1 and 2. Both clusters contain products, which are considered to be more innovative and of higher advantage but in cluster 2, the development cycle time is shorter and the companies are driven by a mix of both market and technological perspectives. At the tactical level of the launch, products in cluster 2 are distributed intensively, have higher promotion expenditures, and use a skimming pricing strategy. There is no clear indication regarding branding strategy. This cluster is the most successful one.

The third cluster characterizes new products launched into selective segments where the number of competitors is between one to three. Regarding the strategic launch decisions, there are no clear indications as to whether the launches are technologically or market driven, nor on their innovativeness. The tactical launch decisions are also unclear, with the exception of pricing strategy, which is regarded as a penetration pricing strategy for a low advantage product compared to competition.

Finally, the fourth cluster describes consumer products which are mass marketed, market driven and of low advantage. The development of such products lasts less than 1 year and they are introduced into mass markets where there are already between one to three competitors. The tactical launch decisions include use of company name, equal promotional expenditure to that of the competitors, intensive distribution and penetration pricing. This cluster consists of moderately successful products.

In an attempt to provide a more in-depth investigation of the launching decisions that lead to new product success, Hultink et al. (2000) included in their analyses additional variables relating to strategic and tactical launch decisions and compared successful and unsuccessful new consumer and industrial products. Their analysis was based on a sample of 1,018 new product introductions from the Netherlands, the UK, and the USA. This study revealed that there are differences in the strategic and tactical launch decisions for successful and unsuccessful products launched in consumer and industrial markets (Table 7.3).

Table 7.3   **Strategic and tactical launch decisions for successful consumer and industrial products**

Successful consumer products are	Successful industrial products are
• More innovative than competitive products	• More innovative than competitive products
• Developed in 6 months to 3 years	• Developed in 6 months to 1 year
• More often improvements	• More often improvements
• Introduced in markets growing 5%–10%	• Introduced in markets growing >10%
• Introduced more often with the following objectives: enter an existing market; improve company image; use of excess capacity; put up barriers to competitors	• Introduced more often with the following objectives: enter an existing market; improve company image; increase penetration; lower costs
• Introduced in a broader range	• Introduced in a broader range
• More often a brand extension	
• Introduced with relatively higher distribution expenditures as competitors	• Introduced with relatively similar distribution expenditures as competitors
	• Introduced in existing channels of distribution
• Introduced at similar prices as competitors	
• Introduced with penetration pricing	
• Introduced with relatively higher promotion expenditures as competitors	• Introduced with relatively similar promotion expenditures as competitors
• Introduced more often with print, TV, radio advertising and public relations	• Introduced more often with direct marketing

Source: adapted from Hultink et al. (2000)

As far as the strategic launching strategies are concerned, both product innovativeness and newness are associated with higher levels of performance independent of market type (namely, consumer and industrial). However, successful consumer products more often than unsuccessful ones are developed in short to moderate cycle times and introduced into moderately growing markets (5–10 per cent growth rate) to utilize excess capacity and raise barriers to competition. In contrast, successful industrial products are more likely to be developed in shorter cycle times and introduced into markets with higher growth rates (over 10 per cent) and fewer competitors in order to increase market penetration through producing existing products at lower costs.

Regarding the tactical launch decisions, launching a broader assortment of products using print advertising is associated with higher success, independent of market type. Despite these similarities, successful consumer products are more often (than unsuccessful products) offered as part of a broader range of brand extensions introduced with higher relative distribution and promotion expenditures, priced similar to the competition in order to penetrate the market. Further, promotion budgets are spent on print, TV, and radio advertising. On the other hand, successful industrial products do not feature high-intensity actions or investments. More specifically, they are more likely to be introduced with distribution and promotion expenses similar to competitors, with promotion budget spent on direct marketing and print advertising. Successful industrial products are offered in a broader assortment. Finally, brand and pricing decisions are not associated with the performance of new industrial products.

Benecol: the launching of a new functional margarine

Nutritional habits in advanced countries have raised the level of cholesterol at alarming levels. The increase of cholesterol levels may be attributed to a number of factors. More specifically, the westernization of lifestyle, during the 1980s, created a rather more speedy and complex daily life. This life style resulted into less physical action, less attention to daily diet, more anxiety over personal professional issues and the need for more convenience and taste. The combination of all these factors has led to the increase of the cholesterol levels and has set this as the most important health-problem among the population of the northern countries.

In the 1980s the University of Helsinki in Finland found an ingredient called plant stanols ester, which reduces cholesterol in a natural way. Stanols occur naturally in small amounts in corn, wheat, rye and other plants such as pine trees and have been known to lower cholesterol for some time. Combining stanols with rape seed oil extracts resulted in plant stanols ester, which in turn is easily blended into foods without changing their taste or quality. As part of a major public health initiative to lower the nation's cholesterol, in late 1980s, the University of Helsinki asked the Finnish food manufacturer Raisio to produce a food that would include this specific ingredient. Raisio used plant stanols ester in a spread (namely, margarine) that was branded 'Benecol' (bene colesterol).

'Benecol' is included among the so-called functional food products as it provides health benefits beyond basic nutrition by leading to reduced risk for cholesterol. More specifically, the unique ingredient in 'Benecol' foods, affects the cholesterol that humans eat and it is naturally produced in the body. It works by blocking the absorption of cholesterol into the body. 'Benecol' can actually reduce LDL (bad) cholesterol levels by up to 15 per cent as part of a healthy diet and lifestyle. More than 40 clinical studies prove its effectiveness in lowering cholesterol. Benecol was first launched in Finland in 1995, while today it is present in various markets in Europe and elsewhere, including Sweden, Belgium, Spain, Greece, UK, Ireland, Germany, Austria, Poland, and the USA. Apart from margarine, the 'Benecol' brand has been extended to other product categories, like yoghurt drink, cheese spread, milk, and low fat bio yoghurt.

In Greece, 'Benecol' functional margarine is produced and distributed by Minerva SA, which is the oldest edible oil company in Greece. The company was founded in 1904 dealing exclusively in olive oil. Today, Minerva is one of the two largest edible oil companies in Greece. It is a member of the international group of companies Paterson-Zochonis (PZ) and, it markets, besides Minerva olive oil, a wide range of well-known and successful food products: oils (for example, 'Mountain Regions', 'Elaionas', 'Horio Koloneiki Variety'), margarine ('Fast') and related cooking products ('Mivervini'). There should be a reference to the fact the that Minerva Company has been producing margarine since late 1970s, therefore the company has more than 30 years of experience in producing margarine. Apart from the opportunities found in the functional margarine sub-market, a strong point of the company was the ability to produce margarine of high quality.

The decision to launch 'Benecol' in the Greek market was based on a number of market facts and figures. More specifically, by analysing consumer behaviour data Minerva identified an increasing interest in Mediterranean diet with a particular preference to functional food products. Given the rising concern of Greeks about increased cholesterol levels, the company explored the possibility of entering the functional margarine sub-market with 'Benecol'. An examination of the market size and competition in this market revealed first, the domination of soft margarine (75 per cent of the market share, compared to 'brick' type 22 per cent and the 'liquid' type 3 per cent); secondly, the stagnation of total market sales; thirdly, the steady increase in the sales of functional margarine, representing one-third of the total margarine market (in value); fourthly, the existence of only one competitor in the functional margarine market, namely Elais (a Unilever company) with 'Becel pro activ' brand and lastly, the lack of new players. The lack of new players can be either a positive or a negative factor in the decision-making process for entering a market. That depends on who the players are. In the Minerva case, the existence only of Unilever-Elais was a factor that embraced its decision with more risk. This is because Unilever-Elais is a company with more resources than Minerva and had already established the brand Becel pro activ as the generic brand of the functional margarine market. Therefore, Minerva had to take sales (and therefore market share) from a very powerful and competitive company.

In 2003, Minerva took the strategic decision to enforce its presence in the margarine market by entering the functional margarine segment. In this way, it was expected that the company would further reinforce its corporate image as a company of high quality and healthy food products.

'Benecol' was targeted to persons with cholesterol problems. After extensive market research, two target markets were selected. The first target market was called the 'harmonies' and included persons that live a well-balanced life; they are involved in athletic activities and possess a high social status. For these people, nutrition is synonymous with health and pleasure. They are well informed, but not hysterical about what constitutes good health. They consider cholesterol as something that will affect their health and they want to control and prevent it. The second target market, which is called 'neurotics', comprises persons that are traditional, introverted, lacking in knowledge, and easily persuaded. These

(Continued)

(Continued)

people are particularly interested in the functional benefits of nutrition, but although they have an obsession with good health, they are superficially informed. They want to find a safe, reassuring solution to their cholesterol problem.

After the development of alternative product concepts, a number of qualitative consumer concept tests were conducted using eighteen focus groups. On the basis of these tests, the company decided the following product's positioning statement: 'Benecol is the effective spread in the reduction of cholesterol while it functions in a totally natural way'.

In late March 2004, Minerva launched 'Benecol' in a 250g. pack while in late November 2004 it also introduced a pack of 500g. The product's packaging emphasizes first, the 'natural way' (it uses a green colour in the form of a leaf and it refers to plant stanols from oily seeds), secondly, the more friendly, more 'food', tasty product (image of lump of margarine on a knife, ready to spread), and thirdly, the healthy solution with 'no salt' (important for persons that are afraid of or have high blood pressure).

A dynamic plan of promotion was also prepared for both doctors and consumers. Communication to doctors aimed at increasing product credibility, recommendation and ultimately word-of-mouth. The promotion tools that were used included: visits to doctors by trained medical visitors, direct mail of leaflets that presented the main published findings of clinical studies that has proved the effectiveness of the product; participation in medical or relevant conferences. In the context of its launching plan, the company used a distinguished pathologist, a specialist in atherosclerosis, as a consultant. His role was to consult Minerva in related medical issues (cholesterol, heart effects, and so on), to indicate medical conferences and relevant events for participation, to monitor packaging claims, information texts and promotional leaflets and to train the medical visitors.

Communication to consumers included TV advertisements, magazine and newspaper advertisements and in-store promotion that included a consumers' information leaflet provided by trained promoters and discount coupons (0.50€ for Benecol 250gr. and 1€ for Benecol 500g.) This promotion took place selectively in major stores of the largest supermarket chains (for example, Carrefour-Champion, AB Vassilopoulos-Delhaize group, Sklavenitis, and Massoutis). Further, the product's price was set at the same level as competition, and distribution was intensive, while the shelf policy was to be next to the competitive leading brand.

The launching strategy followed by Minerva was considered as successful since the first year's market share achieved for 'Benecol' was 7.2 per cent, which is very close to the targeted market share of 8.0 per cent.

New service launching

The use of marketing communications tools in new service launching

The launching activities of new services have not been extensively researched. In a recent study, the authors of this book revealed the extent of use of twenty-seven marketing communications tools used in the launching of 100 new retail financial services (Avlonitis and Papastathopoulou, 2000). On the basis of their degree of use, the top ten tools are as follows:

1 detailed product manuals for the sales force (for example, on product specifications, target-market, product's operating mode);
2 point of purchase (POP) promotion;

3 training seminars for the sales force;
4 use of pamphlets, leaflets;
5 use of indoor advertising;
6 intensive efforts by the sales force;
7 product promotion through 'cross-selling';

8 extensive publicity (for example, articles about the product were written in the business press);
9 promotion at customer sites;
10 use of newspaper advertising.

Obviously, the marketing communications tools that are more frequently used refer mainly to personal selling and also to below-the-line advertising at the points of sales through pamphlets and leaflets, sales manuals and indoor advertisement in support of the sales effort. Clearly, companies operating in the retail financial market seem to follow a rather traditional branch-based approach in communicating their new products to the public. Above-the-line advertising (for example, TV, radio advertisements), public relations (for example, press releases and editorials) and sales promotion (for example, gifts, contests) are of limited use.

Additional analyses revealed that, the most frequently used marketing communications tools for non-innovative products are selling efforts at the points of sales, detailed product manuals for the sales force, training seminars for the sales force, pamphlets and leaflets, indoor advertising, and intensive selling efforts. On the other hand, innovative products base their communication strategy on the following nine tools: detailed product manuals for the salesforce, pamphlets and leaflets, training seminars for the sales force, selling efforts at the points of sale, indoor advertising, articles about the product in the business press, intensive selling efforts, selling efforts through 'cross-selling', and newspaper advertising.

In general, innovative products compared to non-innovative products, are launched using more above-the-line and below-the-line advertising, direct mail, selling efforts at customer sites and training seminars for the sales force.

Impact of marketing communications tools on new service performance

As part of the same study, Avlonitis and Papastathopoulou (2000) also attempted to identify whether different marketing communications tools are used by four different groups of products, namely innovative successful, innovative unsuccessful, non-innovative successful and non-innovative unsuccessful products. Most of the tools tend to show significant differences in use between these four product groups. In fact, we observe a continuum of use from innovative successful products (highest use), through non-innovative successful, to innovative unsuccessful and finally, to non-innovative unsuccessful products (lowest use). More specifically, innovative successful products appear to have the most integrated communications package consisting of print advertising, press coverage, intensive selling from well trained direct sales force and also branch sales force with the support of indoor advertising. Further, marketing communications for non-innovative successful products is based on a lower number of promotional tools that refer to press coverage and intensive branch selling by trained staff with the support of indoor promotional material. The marketing communications mix of the innovative unsuccessful products, on the other hand, is limited to selling efforts from a branch based and well trained sales force with the support of pamphlets/leaflets. Finally, non-innovative unsuccessful products appear to be the group with the minimum use of any of the promotional tools examined in our study. These products, barely, receive any communication support during their launch.

These results suggest that, compared to non-innovative retail financial products, innovative ones tend to follow a more complete as well as an aggressive marketing communications strategy. What is even more interesting is that such a strategy is found to be really meritorious in terms of performance, in the sense that innovative products that are promoted extensively have higher possibilities to succeed in the market than similar products that are not given a decent communications support during their launch.

In addition, the study revealed that three marketing communications factors have been found to discriminate between successful and unsuccessful new retail financial products irrespective of their degree of innovativeness.

- *Intensive selling* is the most important marketing communications factor leading new retail financial products to success. Products that were strong in this factor were presented at fairs and trade shows, had extensive indoor advertising presence and were promoted indirectly in conjunction with other company products (namely, cross-selling techniques). This finding clearly underscores the profound importance of personal selling in launching new retail financial products successfully. Further, it is consistent with previous research, which has shown that intensive sales force efforts lead to higher new product performance. Meidan (1996) provides a number of reasons why personal selling is perhaps the most important element in the communications process in the financial services industry. These include creating financial product awareness, developing financial product preference, negotiating prices and other terms, closing a sale and providing after sales reinforcement and reassurance to the customer.
- *Below-the-line advertising* is second in the success list of promotional tools for launching new financial products targeted to the retail market. Products that used below-the-line advertising heavily were communicated through the extensive use of pamphlets, leaflets, sales manuals and press coverage. As we already mentioned, these promotional tools are supportive to the main selling effort.
- *Telemarketing* also plays a critical role in leading retail financial products to high performance outcomes. Projects that were strong in this factor were those using the telephone for selling the product as well as for direct response advertising such as a telephone hotline for potential customers. Apparently, telemarketing is a highly efficient way of differentiating retail financial products in terms of their delivery process.

New product development cycle time

It is argued that firms, which succeed in developing and marketing new products faster than competitors can obtain first mover advantages (Kuczmarksi, 1992; Carmel, 1995; Gupta et al., 1992). Firms such as 3M, Compaq and Xerox are often cited as examples of firms that compete on time to market. In this respect, considerable research has been undertaken in the last two decades in the area of new product development cycle time, and particularly the duration of the new product development process and the factors associated with reduced new product development times, so that as new product introduction is accelerated.

Average cycle time

In a recent study, Griffin (2002) found that industrial firms have been taking on average twenty-seven months to develop their more innovative products. Taking a closer look at the innovative nature of new products, it was revealed that new-to-the-world products required 53.2 months and new product lines needed thirty-six months. Next generation

improvements had an average cycle time of twenty-two months, while incremental improvements required 8.6 months to develop.

As far as innovative industrial products are concerned in general, the stage of development is the longest one, averaging over eight months to complete. What follows is the test and validation stage (4.8 months), the commercialization/launch stage (4.5 months) and the manufacturing development stage (4.2 months).

Griffin (2002) also found that first, services take about half the time of manufactured goods to develop; secondly, consumer goods take less time to develop than B2B goods; thirdly, there is no difference between cycle times for consumer versus B2B services.

Factors and methods of reducing the new product development cycle time

A number of factors have been found to be associated with reduced product development cycle time, including:

- clear project goals (Kessler and Chakrabarti, 1999; Lynn et al., 1999);
- process concurrency (Kessler and Chakrabarti, 1999);
- increased dedication of team members (Adler et al., 1995; Zirger and Hartley, 1996);
- cross-functional teams (Griffin, 1997; Dröge et al., 2000);
- more participatory management style, for complex projects (Clift and Vandenbosch, 1999);
- computer aided design and engineering (Dröge et al., 2000).

Murmann (1994) studied a sample of German mechanical engineering companies and provides the following ten project-specific activities, which can reduce the cycle time and the cost of new product development:

1   define clearer project objectives;
2   concentrate the resources on fewer development projects;
3   use pre-development tools to reduce technical uncertainty;
4   improve project planning;
5   improve paralleling and overlapping of development tasks;
6   increase the competence and success responsibility of the project manager;
7   improve expert and cross-functional knowledge;
8   insure early manufacturability of the design concept;
9   improve communication and communication behaviour of employees;
10   intensify time and cost controlling in development.

Millson et al. (1992) suggested that companies seeking to speed up their new product development processes must take a hierarchical approach to implementing the following npd acceleration techniques:

Simplify any action that makes managerial processes and communication more simple and easier to perform. New product development simplification may be achieved by integrating tasks into more meaningful groups.

Eliminate delays: all tasks must be monitored for unused time between and within activities.

Eliminate steps: evaluate each task on the basis of the 'added value' that contributes to customer satisfaction in order to shorten or completely eliminate unnecessary npd operations.

Speed-up operations: certain npd tasks must be performed more rapidly. Process acceleration can apply to every task from idea generation to new product launch. In this framework, several well-established manufacturing and design automation processes may be employed, including computer aided design/computer aided manufacturing (CAD/CAM).

Parallel processing: paralleling specific activities can accelerate npd process as it involves performing two or more npd tasks simultaneously. Parallel processing may be achieved using critical path methodologies (CPM) such as program evaluation and review technique (PERT).

A survey of Dutch companies found that the hierarchy of acceleration techniques proposed by Millson et al. (1992) has a positive effect on npd speed (Nijssen et al., 1995). In the same study, it was also reported that implementing these acceleration methods more carefully helps to safeguard and improve the financial performance of the company.

Recently, Langerak and Hultink (2005) moved the research field forward by empirically testing the impact of the npd acceleration approaches on development speed and product profitability. First, they grouped fifty individual techniques which have been identified in the literature into nine npd acceleration approaches, namely:

- supplier involvement;
- lead user involvement;
- speeding up activities and tasks;
- reduction of parts and components;
- training and rewarding of employees;
- implementation of support systems and techniques;
- stimulating inter-functional cooperation;
- emphasis on the customer, and
- simplification of organizational structure.

Next, the researchers examined the impact of these approaches on development speed and new product profitability. They found that lead user involvement and training/ rewarding of employees increase both development speed and profitability. Supplier involvement, speeding up activities and tasks, and a simplification of the organizational structure also enhance development speed while an emphasis on the customer has an additional positive impact on new product profitability. Both new product speed and profitability increase firm performance.

Further, the same study revealed that innovators and fast followers should not select the same npd acceleration approaches as the speed and profitability impact of the majority of the acceleration approaches depends on the innovation strategy of the firm. More specifically, innovators can use only two npd acceleration approaches (namely, implementation of support systems and techniques, and emphasis on the customer) to improve profitability, while fast followers can implement five approaches (for example, lead user involvement, reduction of parts and components, training and rewarding of employees, stimulating inter-functional coordination and emphasis on the customer).

Summary

- During the product development stage, a product prototype is usually developed and is operationally tested as a way to examine the technical feasibility of a new product.
- Several techniques are available for optimal product design such as Designor and Posse and quality function deployment.
- There are two types of testing: product use testing, which examines possible product/ operating problems and market testing that identifies possible market-related pitfalls.
- There are different market testing methods depending on the type of the market, namely, consumer (B2C) or industrial (B2B).

- Types of market testing for consumer products include simulated test marketing, test marketing, consumer panels. Industrial (B2B) products can be market tested in a limited set of geographical areas, distributor and dealer display rooms, a trade show and through speculative sales.
- During launching, the production plan and the marketing plan are finalized. In marketing terms, there are two different launch strategies, namely a full market launch and a roll-out strategy.
- Effective launch strategies differ depending on the degree of product and market newness.
- The launching tactics that lead to success differ between innovative and less innovative new services.
- There are various factors that accelerate new product development cycle times, for example, cross-functional development, clear new product objectives, supplier and lead user involvement.
- The speed and profitability impact of the majority of the acceleration approaches depends on the innovation strategy of the firm.

Questions

1 Select one banking service and prepare a blueprint including the necessary customer activities, front-office activities, and back-office activities.
2 Think of a recent new consumer product that has been launched in the market and discuss the alternative ways of product and market testing.
3 What launch strategies could you use for new software?
4 What factors would you consider in order to decide upon the launching strategy of a new electronic game?

References

Adler, P., Mandelbaum, A., Nguyen, V. and Schwerer, E. (1995) 'From project to process management: an empirical framework for analyzing product development time', *Management Science*, 41(3): 458–84.

Avlonitis, G. and Papastathopoulou, P. (2000) 'Marketing communications and product performance: innovative vs. non-innovative new retail financial products', *International Journal of Bank Marketing*, 18(1): 27–41.

Beard C. and Easingwood C. (1996) 'New product launch: marketing action and launch tactics for the high-technology products', *Industrial Marketing Management*, 25: 87–103.

Booz, Allen and Hamilton (1982) *New Products Management for the 1980s*. New York: Booz, Allen and Hamilton.

Bowers, M. (1989) 'Developing new services: improving the process makes it better', *The Journal of Services Marketing*, 3(1): 15–20.

Carmel, E. (1995) 'Cycle time in packages software firms', *Journal of Product Innovation Management*, 12(2): 110–123.

Choffray, J.M. and Lilien, G. (1978) 'Assessing response to industrial marketing strategy', *Journal of Marketing*, 42: 20–31.

Choffray, J.M. and Lilien, G. (1982) 'DESIGNOR: a decision support procedure for industrial product design', *Journal of Business Research*, 10: 185–97.

Clift, T. and Vandenbosch, M. (1999) 'Project complexity and efforts to reduce product development cycle time', *Journal of Business Research*, 45: 187–98.

Cooper, R. and Kleinschmidt, E. (1988) 'Resource allocation in new product process', *Industrial Marketing Management*, 17: 249–62.

Crawford, M. (1983) *New Products Management.* Homewood, IL: Richard D. Irwin, Inc.

Crawford, M. (1997) *New Products Management.* 5th edition. Homewood, IL: Irwin McGraw Hill.

Crawford, M. (1984) 'Protocol: New tool for product innovation', *Journal of Product Innovation Management,* 2: 85–91.

de Brentani, U. (2000) 'Designing and marketing new products and services', in Keith Blois (ed.) *The Oxford Textbook of Marketing,* Oxford University Press.

Dröge, C., Jayaram, J. and Vickery, S. (2000) 'The ability to minimize the timing of new product development and introduction: an examination of antecedent factors in the North American automobile supplier industry', *Journal of Product Innovation Management,* 17(1): 24–40.

Easingwood, C. and Beard, C. (1989) 'High technology launch strategies in the UK', *Industrial Marketing Management,* 18: 125–38.

Eliashberg, J. and Robertson, T. (1988) 'New product preannouncing behavior: a market signaling study', *Journal of Marketing Research,* 25: 282–92.

Green, P., Caroll, J. and Goldberg, S. (1981) 'A general approach to product design optimisation via conjoint analysis', *Journal of Marketing* 45: 17–37.

Griffin, A. (1992) 'Evaluating QFD's use in US firms as a process for developing products', *Journal of Product Innovation Management,* 9: 171–187.

Griffin, A. (1997) 'PDMA research on new product development practices: updating trends and benchmarking best practices', *Journal of Product Innovation Management,* 14: 429–58.

Griffin, A. (2002) 'Product development cycle time for business-to-business products', *Industrial Marketing Management,* 31: 291–304.

Gupta, A.K., Brockhoff, K. and Weisenfeld, U. (1992) 'Making trade-offs in the new product development process: a German/US comparison', *Journal of Product Innovation Management* 9(1): 11–18.

Hauser, J.R. and Clausing, D. (1988) 'The house of quality', *Harvard Business Review* (May–June): 63–73.

Hultink, E., Griffin, A., Hart, S. and Robben, H. (1997) 'Industrial new product launch strategies and product development performance', *Journal of Product Innovation Management,* 14: 243–57.

Hultink, E., Hart, S., Robben, H. and Griffin, A. (2000) 'Launch decisions and new product success: an empirical comparison of consumer and industrial products', *Journal of Product Innovation Management,* 17(1): 5–23.

Kessler, E. and Chakrabarti, A. (1999) 'Speeding up the pace of new product development', *Journal of Product Innovation Management,* 16(3): 231–47.

Kotler, P. (2003) *Marketing Management: Analysis, Planning, Implementation and Control.* 11th edition. Englewood Cliffs, NJ: Prentice Hall.

Kuczmarksi, T.D. (1992) *Managing New Products.* Englewood Cliffs, NJ: Prentice Hall.

Langerak, F. and Hultink, E.J. (2005) 'The impact of new product development acceleration approaches on speed and profitability: lessons for innovators and fast followers', *IEEE Transaction on Engineering Management,* 52(1).

Lynn, G., Abel, K., Valentine, W. and Wright, R. (1999) 'Key factors in increasing speed to market and improving new product success rates', *Industrial Marketing Management,* 28: 319–26.

Meidan, A. (1996) *Marketing Financial Services.* London: Macmillan.

Millson, M., Raj, S. and Wilemon, D. (1992) 'A survey of major approaches for accelerating new product development', *Journal of Product Innovation Management* 9: 53–69.

Murmann, P. (1994) 'Expected development time reductions in the German mechanical engineering industry', *Journal of Product Innovation Management,* 11: 236–252.

Nijssen, E., Arbouw, R. and Commandeur, H. (1995) 'Accelerating new product development: a preliminary empirical test of a hierarchy of implementation', *Journal of Product Innovation Management,* 12: 99–109.

Rabino, S. and Moore, T. (1989) 'Managing new-product announcement in the computer industry', *Industrial Marketing Management,* 18: 35–43.

Robertson, T., Eliasberg, J. and Rymon, T. (1995) 'New product announcement signals and incumbent reactions', *Journal of Marketing* 59: 1–15.

Robinson, W.T. (1988) 'Sources of market pioneer advantage: The case of industrial goods industries', *Journal of Marketing Research,* 25(1): 87–94.

Robinson, W.T. and Fornell, C. (1985) 'The sources of market pioneer advantages in consumer goods industries', *Journal of Marketing Research,* 22(3): 207–304.

Scott, J. and Keiser, S. (1984) 'Forecasting acceptance of new industrial products with judgement modelling', *Journal of Marketing,* 48(2).

Shostack, L. (1984) 'Designing services that deliver', *Harvard Business Review,* 62 (January–February): 133–9.

Sullivan, L.P. (1986) 'Quality function deployment', *Quality Progress,* 19(6): 39–50.

Thomas, R. (1995) *New Product Success Stories.* Chichester. John Wiley & Sons.

Wind, Y., Grashof, J. and Goldhar, J. (1978) 'Market based guidelines for design of industrial products', *Journal of Marketing,* 24: 27–37.

Woodside, A., Sanderson, H. and Brodie, R. (1988) 'Testing acceptance of a new industrial service', *Industrial Marketing Management,* 17(1): 65–71.

Zirger, B. and Hartley, J. (1996) 'The effect of acceleration techniques on product development time', *IEEE Transactions on Engineering Management,* 43(2): 143–52.

Further reading

Shostack, G.L. (1981) 'How to design a service', *European Journal of Marketing,* 16(1): 49–63.

Wilson, E. (2005) 'The nose knows: new product development at Yankee Candle Company', *Journal of Business Research,* 58(7): 989–94.

8 Successful Adoption and Diffusion of New Products and Services

Introduction

New product/service success is an issue of strategic importance for companies that aim at surviving and sustaining a differential advantage in highly competitive markets. As customer needs and wants tend to change over time, companies must accommodate their offerings to satisfy the changing customer preferences. The ultimate objective should be to accelerate the adoption and diffusion of their products/services in the market.

The studies about new products and services focus either on their development process, or their adoption and diffusion in the market. The first set of studies examines the factors that the company must consider when developing new products and services, while the second research stream investigates the factors that speed up the adoption/ diffusion of new products and services in the market.

In an attempt to present the relevant literature in this important issue, as part of the present book, the following questions will be addressed:

- How can we define success/failure of new products and services?
- Which are the success factors of new products and services?
- What is the role of innovativeness in the success of new products and services?
- Which is the adoption process of innovations?
- Which factors affect the adoption of innovations by consumers?
- Which factors affect the adoption of innovations by organizations?

Defining new product/service success

An important, yet quite difficult new product development task, is to measure the performance of a new product or service. There are several ways of measuring performance. Cooper and Kleinschmidt (1987) identified the following three main new product performance dimensions, namely:

- financial performance (for example, sales, profits, pay back period);
- opportunity window (for example, degree to which the new product opened up new business opportunities to the company in terms of a new product category or new markets);
- market impact (for example, market share in domestic and foreign markets).

It is important to note that, depending on the criteria used and the time at which performance is measured, a new product or service may be characterized as successful and unsuccessful at the same time. There are several examples of simultaneous product success and failure. Three such cases are provided below.

Three simultaneous product successes and failures

The Ford Taurus was considered as a 'technical failure' due to the very high rates of long-term defects in the early production years of the model. However, this car has also been considered as commercially successful because customers liked its styling and driving performance. Ford managed to correct the technical problems and the Taurus was thereafter even better received by the market.

Xerox mouse was a technical and customer success, but a financial failure as well. It was the first computer mouse, but Xerox did not commercialize it, because it resulted in an inadequate financial return on the investment.

Kodak's instant picture is difficult to be characterized as either successful or unsuccessful. If performance had been measured one to two years after the product's launch, then it would have been classified as a success (the product had achieved nearly a 35 per cent share while simultaneously expanding significantly the volume of the whole category). However, if performance had been measured in the long run, the product would have been characterized as unsuccessful because of the large financial cost of infringing on Polaroid's patents.

Source: Griffin and Page (1996)

Further, it has been found that what constitutes an appropriate performance measure, depends on the product's degree of innovativeness. In a study by Griffin and Page (1996) six types of new products reflecting different degrees of innovation were examined, namely new-to-the-world, new-to-the-company, product improvements, additions to existing product lines, cost reductions, and product repositionings, as well as their association with performance measures. The degree to which the product met profit goals is the most useful measure of financial success for all innovative types of products, except for new-to-the-world and cost reduction products. Further, for new-to-the-company, additions to existing lines, improvements/revisions, and repositionings, profit is most useful performance measure, while margin seems to be most useful for cost reductions. Customer satisfaction is found as the most useful performance measure for product improvements/revisions and cost reductions, whereas customer acceptance is most useful for product repositionings. Finally, market share is the most useful performance measure for new-to-the-company and product line extensions.

Success factors of new products

Despite the strategic importance of new products, empirical evidence put forward in the last forty years, indicates that the percentage of new product failure reached 40–60 per cent (Booz et al., 1982; Lin, 1986; Griffin, 1997). The scientific community has well recognized that such percentages are very alarming for the prosperity and growth of organizations.

Therefore, a significant number of studies have been undertaken during the last decades providing insights into the determinants of new product success. Three research approaches have been followed in these studies, which usually looked at the new product development process and the characteristics of the market and the product itself. These approaches are presented below.

Examination of successful new products

The first approach attempted to investigate new product success with the hope of uncovering the common ingredients of high performance. Research on critical success factors was initiated by Myers and Marquis's (1969) landmark study of 567 successful products and processes in 121 companies in five industries. The most important determinants of new product success were found to be: identifying and understanding user's needs and focus on R&D activities for satisfying them, appropriate internal and external communication, and considerable commitment of financial resources.

Similar success factors have been uncovered from other studies in the United States such as the work of Globe et al. (1973) and the work of Roberts and Burke (1974), which involved the examination of six successful products conducted in the laboratories of General Electric. Extensive market inputs including market studies and marketing research, especially at the beginning of the project, and proficient R&D management targeted at satisfying market needs, played a central role in shaping the success of the industrial innovations studied.

Booz et al. (1982) also identified seven factors leading to high new product performance. These are: fit to market needs, fit to the functional strengths of the company, technological superiority, top management support, use of proper development process, suitable competitive environment and proper organizational arrangements for product development.

Examination of unsuccessful new products

The second research approach is premised on the argument that it is easier to diagnose 'what went wrong' than it is to identify 'what went right', and that a critical analysis of past failures is the first step towards prescriptive solutions.

A number of National Industrial Conference Board studies in the United States have used this approach. More specifically, Hopkins and Baileys (1971) found that new product failure is the result of eight distinct factors: inadequate market analysis, product defects (technical or in quality), higher cost than estimated, bad timing in product introduction, competitors' reaction, inadequate marketing effort and efficiency, inadequate sales force, inadequate product distribution. Some years later, Hopkins (1980) shortened this list of eight failure factors to the following five, namely ineffective product marketing, poor market research, inadequate assessment of market potential, poor understanding of competitor's strengths and weaknesses, and inaccurate product pricing.

In the late 1970s, Calantone and Cooper (1979) examined eighty-nine industrial market failures and developed the following six scenarios of product failures:

The better mousetrap no one wanted (28 per cent of failures)

Products in this scenario were innovative and unique, but were rejected by the market. There has been an overestimation of the number of potential customers who might buy and use the product. However, technical problems were absent in development, and there was no strong competitive market reaction. Their selling effort as well as launch timing were appropriate.

The me-too product meeting a competitive brick wall (24 per cent of failures)

These cases were products which were very similar to products already on an established market, meeting the same customers' needs These products tended to be product modifications of the company's existing product line that were targeted at new markets for the company. Little new technology was required by the company in their development. Poor financial analysis and an inadequate selling effort characterized the development of these products.

Competitive one upmanship (13 per cent of failures)

Failure products in this group were typical 'me too' products introduced into the market the same time as similar competitive products. Detailed market research, product development and market testing as well as market launch activities tended to be poorly carried out.

Environmental ignorance (7 per cent of failures)

These products had ignored customer's needs, and therefore they were deemed inappropriate for the market. Competitive products were introduced at about the same time, while competitors themselves were already firmly entrenched in the market. The selling and promotional effort was both inadequate and misdirected. These products were characterized by a number of low performed activities: market studies, financial analysis, test markets, production start-up, and product launch. The lack of resources allocated to marketing research and selling efforts were thought to contribute to these failures.

The technical dog product (15 per cent of failures)

These products were unique and innovative products, but they had technical problems. Engineering and production flaws and deficiencies doomed the project to failure. More, preliminary technical assessment and product development activities were poorly executed.

The price crunch (13 per cent of cases)

Although products in this scenario were well suited to customer needs, they were introduced at prices higher than customers were willing to pay, in a market where competitors tended to react to their introduction by cutting prices. Furthermore, market studies, market testing, and product launch were poorly undertaken.

Comparative examination of successful and unsuccessful new products

The third approach has taken the stance that only through a direct comparison of successful and unsuccessful products will the keys to success be uncovered. Roy Rothwell and his colleagues at the University of Sussex were the first to follow this approach.

Their study was entitled 'The Scientific Activity Predictor from Patterns of Heuristic Origins' (SAPPHO).

The SAPPHO study was conducted in two phases. In phase 1, twenty-nine pairs of new products were investigated (Rothwell, 1972). Product success was primarily related to the following five factors:

1 understanding of user needs;
2 attention to marketing and publicity;
3 efficiency of development;
4 effective use of outside technology and external scientific communication; and
5 seniority and authority of the managers responsible for the development of the product.

In phase 2, the project has been extended to include a new total of forty-three pairs of new products, thirty-two in chemical processes and twenty-one in scientific instruments (Rothwell et al., 1974). The key success factors relate to need satisfaction. That is to say, user needs must be identified and met, and it is important that these needs are monitored throughout the course of the innovation since they are in constant change. The importance of good communications and efficient market intelligence is also underscored. It seems very important to achieve integration throughout the innovation process between the marketing and R&D functions.

Other studies of success and failure products in European markets followed SAPPHO. A study of Hungarian electronics products confirmed the SAPPHO findings and emphasized communication, technical competence and proficiency market understanding and synergy, product planning and management support (Szakasits, 1974). Kulvik's (1977) study in Finland also led to similar conclusions.

In the other side of the Atlantic and specifically in Canada, Robert Cooper is considered to be one the main contributors in the area of critical success factors in product innovation. This research has conducted two extensive studies, namely NewProd I and II and provided a thorough examination of the factors affecting the post-launch performance of new products

In the NewProd I study, Cooper (1979) examined 102 successful and ninety-three failed products within 103 industrial firms in Canada. A total of eleven factors appeared to differentiate between new product successes and failures. In order of importance, these were:

- introducing a unique but superior product;
- having market knowledge and marketing proficiency;
- having technical and production synergy and proficiency;
- avoiding dynamic markets with many new product introductions;
- being in a large, high need, growth market;
- avoiding introducing a high-priced product with no economic advantage;
- having a good 'product/company fit' with respect to managerial and marketing resources;
- avoiding a competitive market with satisfied customers;
- avoiding products new to the firm;
- having a strong marketing communications and launch effort;
- having a market-derived idea with considerable investment involved.

In the NewProd II study, Cooper and Kleinschmidt (1986) investigated the new product development process of 203 projects and have drawn the following results. The completeness of the new product process (for example, the number of activities carried out) is strongly related to performance. Further, preliminary market assessment and the formal market launch stage were much more prevalent in successful projects than in the unsuccessful ones. These two activities showed the most significant differences between successes and failures. Further, successful projects consistently featured a higher frequency of nine out of thirteen activities. Three of these activities were particularly strongly related to project outcomes:

- initial screening;
- preliminary technical assessment, and
- product development

Cooper and Kleinschmidt (1987) reported additional results of the NewProd II study. They concluded that product advantage, pre-development marketing activities (namely, market study, concept testing), and product synergy are the most important factors discriminating product successes from failures.

In a later study of 103 new chemical products, Cooper and Kleinschmidt (1993) examined six key areas for each new product project that are related to new product performance. According to the findings, product differentiation is the number one factor discriminating successful from unsuccessful new products in the chemical industry, whereas, synergy and familiarity are moderately important to success. Moreover, following a 'low price' strategy does not seem to be effective in increasing new product performance. Market attractiveness has an impact on new product performance and so do product innovativeness, entry order and the stage of product life cycle, in a rather moderate degree, though.

Extending the work of Cooper outside the boundaries of Canada, Mark Parry and Michael Song (1994) examined the new product development practices of 129 state-owned enterprises in the People's Republic of China (PRC). The analysis of 258 new product successes and failures indicated that relative product advantage and collection of marketing information were highly correlated with new product success, just as it was the case in Canada. Additionally, a number of factors which has not been significantly correlated with success in Canadian firms emerged as significant correlates of success in the PRC. These included the level of competitive activity, the timing of the product launch, and the level of proficiency in executing activities in the early stages of the product development process.

The issue of what separates new products winners and losers has also been addressed in a study 788 new product introductions from 404 Japanese firms (Song and Parry, 1996). Overall, results revealed the critical role of product advantage, project definition and predevelopment proficiencies, marketing and technological synergy.

Moreover, two surveys have also been conducted at researchers at the Stanford Innovation Project in United States examining over 330 new products (Maidique and Zirger, 1984, 1985; Zirger and Maidique, 1990). These studies suggest that the following key factors positively affect product outcome: quality of the R&D organization; technical performance of the product; the product's value to the customer; synergy of the new product with the firm's existing competence; and management support during the product development and introduction processes.

How Starbucks developed one of its most successful products:
Frappuccino® Ice Blended Coffee

Frappuccino® ice blended coffee is an icy blend of dark-roasted coffee and low-fat milk that turned out to be an extraordinary success for Starbucks. The original idea came from Dina Campion who managed a district of about ten Starbucks outlets in and around Santa Monica, California. Nearby coffee bars were very successful in offering granitas, namely, sugary, blended, cold coffee drinks. Although Starbucks was serving iced lattes and iced mochas with ice cubes, it started losing customers who were were asking for a blended drink.

(Continued)

(Continued)

At first, Starbucks owner Howard Schultz did not support the idea at all. By contrast, California store managers strongly believed that this could be a winning idea, so they had asked the company's headquarters many times to develop such a blended beverage. In September 1993, Dina Campion persuaded the company's retail operations to purchase a blender for her. Without asking permission, Dina started experimenting with different blends in a Starbucks outlet in the dry San Fernando Valley, where blended drinks were very popular during summertime. The initial results were presented to the food and beverage department, which then agreed to develop a proprietary blended drink for further testing.

In May 1994, the product was tested in the Third Street Promenade Store in Santa Monica, which is located in a crowded outdoor mall. The store's manager and assistant managers disliked the new drink. But instead of complaining about it, they tried to improve it. Both had previously worked for a California company that invented variations of fruit shakes, smoothies, and yogurt drinks, so they knew what they were doing. After using various combinations of ingredients, changing the ratio of ice to liquid, lengthening the blending time from ten to twenty-five seconds, and conducting extensive sampling to customers, they came up with their final version of the drink. The recipe was further refined by a team of food consultants.

In autumn 1994, the new blended coffee was tested at twelve southern California stores, followed by formal research in three cities to get broader customer feedback. The results of all these tests revealed that the market simply loved the product.

By the end of 1994, Starbucks decided to launch the product nationwide under the 'Frappuccino' brand. The name was used for a cold drink that was offered in Coffee Connection in Boston. Starbucks acquired this company in the summer of 1994. So, Starbucks was able use this name, which seemed perfect as it evoked both the coldness of a frappé and the coffee in a cappuccino.

Soon after the North American Coffee Partnership (NACP) was formed which is a joint venture between Starbucks Coffee Co. and PepsiCo, Inc., This partnership developed a bottled version of Frappuccino. This ready-to-drink (RTD) coffee was tested in West Coast supermarkets in the summer of 1996. Positive consumer response was beyond any expectation. On the basis of this result the partnership took the decision to launch it in the market. This turned out to be a very wise decision. The product that now comes in seven flavours is the leader in the RTD market in the USA.

Source: adapted from Schultz and Yang (1997)

Recently, Henard and Szymanski (2001) synthesized this growing body of evidence about the factors associated with new product success/failure by conducting a meta-analysis of the existing empirical findings. Their study revealed that the dominant drivers of new product success are the following eleven factors: market potential, dedicated human resources, marketing task proficiency, product meeting customer needs, product advantage, predevelopment task proficiency, dedicated R&D resources, technological proficiency, launch proficiency, order of entry, and the technological sophistication of the product. From this analysis, it becomes apparent that new product success is strongly associated with the detailed study and evaluation of market attractiveness and the implementation of the appropriate marketing strategies for satisfying customer needs.

iPod: A smashing success from Apple

In November 2001, Apple Computer released a small, stylish, silver-coloured digital music player for Macs and PCs which is called the iPod. In this device, music can be imported in a variety of formats like MP3 and AAC from the owner's collection of CDs or the iTunes Music Store.

The major advantage of iPod over competitive products is that it offers the largest number of songs in the smallest physical space. iPod's basic version weighs only 5.6 ounces, holds up to 5,000 songs and allows up to twelve hours listening to music non-stop. Further, it plays games, keeps text notes, appointments (using the alarm clock/sleep timer), contacts, calendars and to-do lists.

The 'Apple click wheel' placed at the centre of the device is one of iPod's strongest points. The owner can spin it with his/her thumb to navigate the long list of songs (or artists). He/she can touch a button to pick a track and use the wheel again to adjust the volume. The white headphones are also unique and they have become a status symbol.

The product now comes in four more versions, iPod mini, iPod shuffle, iPod photo and iPod U2 special edition:

iPod mini

It weighs just 3.6 ounces and holds up to 1,500 songs, up to eighteen hours of listening.

iPod shuffle

It can be autofilled with up to 240 songs either from iTunes or the owner's CD collection. It allows twelve hours of continuous playback time, and it weighs only 0.78 of an ounce.

iPod photo

It carries up to 15,000 songs and full-colour album cover art or 25,000 photos.

iPod U2 special edition

It has a bold, black case with a unique red Apple click wheel. On the flip side, there are autographs from all four U2 band members. It brings together an amazing 400 U2 tracks plus 4,600 other songs.

iPod nano

This pencil-thin device plays for up to 14 hours between battery charges. It comes in two models, 2GB (500 songs) and 4GB (1,000 songs). It also carries photos, podcasts and audio books.

Since its introduction, Apple has sold approximately 10 million iPods around the world. Only in the last quarter of 2004, Apple has sold 4.5 times more devices than in 2003 (4.58 million compared to 939,000). iPod covers some 70 per cent of the MP3 player market. Not surprisingly, industry experts characterize it as one of the most successful products ever launched in this market.

Success factors of new services

In late 1980s, Ulricke de Brentani laid the keystones of critical success factors research in business-to-business services and especially financial services (de Brentani, 1989, 1991,

1993, 1995a, b; de Brentani and Cooper, 1992; Cooper and de Brentani, 1991; de Brentani and Ragot, 1996). Her studies are based on dyadic comparisons between successful and unsuccessful new services.

In her first study, de Brentani (1989, 1991) examined a sample of 276 new industrial services (150 successful and 126 unsuccessful services) and identified four types of performance measures that companies use to evaluate their new services, namely sales and market share performance, competitive performance (namely, service uniqueness, competitive advantage), 'other booster' or performance of other company services, and cost performance. According to this study, each type of performance is associated with different success factors.

New services that score high in the first performance measure, sales and market share seem to have a clear market orientation – satisfaction of well recognized customer needs/wants, high growth market, consistency with existing customer values/operating systems. Marketing orientation within the firm (namely, pre-selling a new service to front line personnel) is also essential. Further, marketing synergy in terms of choosing projects which fit in with the firm's usual business and benefit from its marketing proficiencies, are also significant determinants of sales and market share success.

As far as competitive performance is concerned, service innovativeness, service quality, satisfaction of a certain customer problem/need, and effective marketing activities, underscore success in this particular performance dimension.

For the third performance indicator, 'Other Booster', the dominant success variables are expertise and provision of auxiliary services aimed at the company's existing customer base. More than that, successful projects with respect to this performance measure are usually introduced for trial to one or two individual customers. The new services are highly synergistic with the firm's management skills, reputation and financial resources and take advantage of available expert and customer contact personnel.

A high cost performance indicator is achieved in projects that are improvements or modifications of existing services. These services also tend to fit well with available resources, including production and marketing, financial and managerial expertise, producing important cost efficiencies. Further, other projects that improve this performance dimension are new services that respond to peaks or troughs in customer demand, and feature good internal communications and employee involvement.

In 1992, de Brentani and Cooper report on a study in 106 new industrial financial services, in an attempt to identify factors that discriminate between successful and unsuccessful new services. The dominant factors are as follows:

Synergy refers to the degree of fit between the needs of the new service project and the resources, skills and experiences (human, financial, marketing, managerial) of the company, as well as the existing, behind-the-scenes production or operations facilities.

Product/market fit refers to the degree to which the service meets customer needs/wants and responds to important changes in these customer needs/wants, and also it is consistent with existing customer values and operating systems.

Quality of execution of the launch includes the following:

- the service had been fully tested prior to launch – there were no bugs in the production;
- the launch programme or plan was highly detailed and well documented;
- service personnel had received extensive training;
- a formal promotional programme was designed and implemented; and
- internal marketing had been done – the service was well promoted to front line personnel.

The characteristics of *unique/superior* products are the following:

- it delivered unique and superior benefits to users (versus competitive services);
- it provided better value than previously available services;

- it featured a better service outcome (or end result) than competitors;
- it had higher quality and was faster or more efficient;
- it was more reliable (fewer fail points), and
- it had a higher quality image developed for it.

Quality of execution of marketing activities refer to the following:

- the new service had concept descriptions that were carefully researched with potential customers prior to product design (a concept test);
- the new service built in a detailed and in-depth market study as input to product design, and
- the new service featured a well-executed market launch.

In 1995, de Brentani had also reported five new service development scenarios associated with different levels of performance. The most important scenario refers to the 'customized expert services', which fully exploit the firm's expert capabilities and resources, especially human resources in providing a customized, high quality service to the clients. In contrast, the most unsuccessful scenario referred to the 'poorly planned "industrialized" clone services'. These services are me-too equipment based services that are introduced to the market long after competitive offerings. They lack customer orientation, service quality and fit poorly with the company's resources and capabilities and they do not follow a proficient development process.

A number of success/failure studies for new services have also been conducted in the UK. For example, Easingwood and Storey (1991) examined seventy-seven new consumer financial services and concluded that the factors that are positively correlated with success are overall quality (for example, quality of the service itself compared to competitive services, quality of the service delivery system, and quality of the after-sales service), development of a differentiated product, product fit and internal marketing, and the use of technology.

In a later study, Easingwood and Storey (1993) found that the most significant discriminating factors between successful and unsuccessful new service were total quality, consistency in communications, direct mail strength, and unique product.

Edgett and Parkinson (1994) and Edgett (1994) provide insights into the performance correlates within the British building societies industries. The researchers examined data from sixty-two successful and fifty-six unsuccessful new services. Three appeared to be the critical success determinants, namely market synergy, organizational arrangements and the use of market research.

Product innovativeness and new product/service performance

As it has been shown in the previous sections, the studies pertaining to success/failure of new products are more general in nature and they do not take into consideration any contingencies that could affect the importance of new product/service success factors. One of the most cited contingency factors is the degree of innovativeness of the new product/service (Cowell, 1988; Rochford and Rudelius 1992; Urban and Hauser 1993; Crawford 1997; Veryzer, 1998). A number of studies have investigated the role of product innovativeness in the success of new industrial products, new industrial services and new consumer services. These studies are presented below.

Table 8.1 **Relative ranking of development activities according to their impact on** performance for innovative and non-innovative industrial products

New product development activities	Innovative industrial products	Non-innovative industrial products
Strategic planning	Second highest positive impact	Negative impact
Idea development and screening	No significant impact	No significant impact
Business and market opportunity analysis	Negative impact	Highest positive impact
Technical development	Third highest positive impact	Third highest positive impact
Product testing	No significant impact	No significant impact
Product commercialization	Highest positive impact	Second highest positive impact

Source: adapted from Song and Montoya-Weiss (1998)

The role of product innovativeness in the success of new industrial products

Song and Montoya-Weiss (1998) have investigated the moderating role of product innnovativeness in the relationship between new product development (npd) activities and new product performance. Six general sets of npd activities were identified, namely strategic planning, idea development and screening, business and market opportunity analysis, technical development, product testing, and product commercialization. Performance was measured in terms of achieving profit objectives. In Table 8.1 we present the npd activities that affect the success of really new products and incremental innovations.

The results indicate that the proficiency levels of strategic planning, market analysis, technical development and product commercialization are significant determinants of new product success positively or negatively for both really new and incremental products, while idea development and screening and product testing activities are not significant determinants of success for either really new or incremental products.

It is also interesting to note that business and market opportunity analysis should be given most attention when incremental products are developed, while this activity is negatively related to the performance of really new products. These results may be attributed, to the fact that in the case of 'me-too' offerings the company capitalizes on prior knowledge regarding targeted markets and technology. Extensive market study is important for identifying market trends, analysis of customer needs and competitive strategies. On the contrary, for really innovative offerings, customer needs are often unspecified, while competition is usually non-existent. Thus, potential users cannot compare the new offering with something similar in the market, and they are often unable to envision the potential entailed in a highly innovative new offering (Veryzer, 1998). Consequently, emphasis in business and market opportunity analysis could be ineffective and thus, undesirable (Lynn et al., 1996).

In a similar vein, the proficiency of strategic planning is one of the success factors of really new products, while it is negatively related with the performance of incremental products. According to the researchers, strategic planning sets the guidelines and the objectives of the

Table 8.2 Success factors of innovative and non-innovative new business services

Factor	Rank Non-innovative business services	Innovative business services
Client/need fit	1	2
Strategy and resource fit	2	7
Front line expertise	3	3
Formal testing and launch	4	4
Low complexity/cost	5	–
Innovation culture and management	6	1
Formal evaluation and design	7	–
Service quality evidence	8	5
Market potential	–	6

Source: de Brentani (2001)

new product helping to reduce uncertainty and risk inherent in an innovative offering. Conversely, when a rather 'me-too' product is developed, the company does not run any particular risk/uncertainty, so strategic planning may increase cycle time, allowing competitors to enter the market and establish a winning market position.

The role of product innovativeness in the success of new business services

The role that product innovativeness plays in the performance of new products has also been examined in the business services market. For example, de Brentani (2001) studied twelve factors that covered four dimensions/factors, namely product-related, market-related, company-related and new service development (nsd) process-related dimensions, and found that nine of these dimensions play a role in the performance of new business services, depending on their degree of innovativeness. These factors are presented in Table 8.2.

Client need/fit, frontline expertise and formal testing and launch are among the factors that lead to success regardless of the service's level of newness. However, other factors were found to have a unique performance impact depending on whether the new business service was an innovative or non-innovative offering. For example, as far as non-innovative business services are concerned, their success is also based on strategy and resource fit, formal evaluation and design, service quality evidence (namely, tangible features to help customer define and evaluate it), while successful innovative business services also base their success on an innovative culture and management within the company (for example, visionary new product championing, expert and frontline involvement in nsd, cross-functional teams with excellent internal communications).

The role of product innovativeness in the success of new consumer services

The development activities that are related to success differ between innovative and non-innovative consumer service as well. The authors of the present book have investigated the role of innovativeness in the development of successful new retail financial services (Avlonitis and Papastathopoulou, 2001). The relevant results are presented in Table 8.3

Table 8.3 **Relative ranking of development activities according to their impact on performance for really new and incremental consumer services**

New service development activities	Innovative consumer services	Non-innovative consumer services
Idea generation and screening	Highest positive impact	No significant impact
Technical development	Fourth highest positive impact	Second highest positive impact
Market testing	No significant impact	No significant impact
Operational testing	Negative impact	No significant impact
Internal marketing and training	Second highest positive impact	No significant impact
Marketing strategy and commercialization (+)	Third highest positive impact	Highest positive impact

Source: adapted from Avlonitis and Papastathopoulou (2001)

More specifically, the results indicate that two development activities positively influence the performance of both innovative and non-innovative new retail financial services, namely marketing strategy and commercialization, and technical development. Although, it would be normally expected that technical development, during which the service blueprinting is designed, would be more critical for innovative compared to non-innovative services, the opposite stands. This result is consistent with other research studies suggesting that, when financial service providers develop innovative offerings, the main concern should not be on the seamless operation of a set of established procedures (de Brentani, 2001). It is known that such discontinuous innovations are targeted to innovators and early adopters who, most likely, are more willing to make a trade-off between receiving an innovative service and accepting minor deficiencies in its delivery process. By contrast, when the degree of innovativeness of the new service diminishes, potential buyers perceive no scope for compromising between the features of the new service offered and drawbacks in the delivery process. In fact, it is very likely that, for 'me-too' offerings the only significant benefits perceived by the market are the improvements in their delivery process. Thus, financial service providers must concentrate their efforts on minimizing any fail points that could occur in the operating/delivery systems of non-innovative service offerings.

Moreover, market testing is not related to the performance of neither innovative nor non-innovative retail financial services. Given the competitive conditions that characterize the retail financial industry, reluctance in testing new services that are really new to the local market could be, at least partly, explained by the fact that information regarding these products would be readily available to competitors. In a market where significant proportion of new product introductions can be easily imitated, it is imperative to reduce the advance warning to competitors of the new offerings (Harrison, 2000). Thus, in order to keep the new project confidential and subsequently minimize the risk of imitation, financial service providers try to avoid any pre-launching market exposure.

Further, the two most important success determinants of the innovative services refer to the idea generation and screening and internal marketing and training activities. Given the plethora of offerings witnessed in the financial industry, mainly as a result of deregulation, developers have to devote considerable time and effort in generating and evaluating alternative product ideas, before a really innovative product can be

Table 8.4   Impact of development activities on the success of different types of service innovativeness

Development activities	Idea generation and screening	Business analysis and marketing strategy	Technical development	Testing	Launching
Type of service innovation					
New to the market					
New to the company					
New delivery process					
Service modification					
Service line extension					
Service repositioning					

Overall performance

Financial performance

Non-Financial performance

Source: Gounaris et al. (2003)

developed. Also, promoting the new service to frontline personnel and organizing training sessions for these people has been repetitively found as an important correlate of new service success (de Brentani, 1989, 1993, 2001; Cooper and de Brentani, 1991; Easingwood and Storey, 1991; de Brentani and Cooper, 1992; Storey and Easingwood, 1993). When it comes to really new services in particular, it seems that such new offerings that incorporate new features to market and an innovative technology need an extra effort on behalf of the customer-contact staff in order to be fully understood and promoted effectively to the target market.

Finally, it seems that the marketing strategy and commercialization activities positively influence performance for both types of service innovations. During this stage, market opportunity analysis is performed, enabling financial companies to identify market characteristics and trends, select target markets for the new service and prepare a marketing plan to adequately meet the needs of the selected markets. The proliferation of new services coupled with the increasing competitive pressures witnessed in the financial industry can account for the importance of this stage. Service providers have to make quite explicit which new services they have introduced (either really new or imitations) through extensive promotional efforts in order to increase product awareness and attract more customers and sales than competition. In fact, the analysis has shown that, marketing strategy and commercialization is relatively more effective for non-innovative products, as it ranked first in importance in this group, while it is ranked third in the group of innovative products. Non-innovative offerings have to face existing competitors' offerings and potential customers that are more experienced and demanding. Financial service providers who are successful in this type of endeavour monitor closely the needs, wants and priorities of the potential customers and respond to these with selling propositions that are perceived by the market as different from competitive offerings (Urban and Hauser, 1993; Crawford, 1997; Song and Montoya-Weiss, 1998; de Brentani, 2001).

In an attempt to shed more light on the role of innovativeness on the success of new consumer financial services, Gounaris et al. (2003) examined the importance of five development activities for the performance of six different types of service innovativeness. Researchers measured overall, financial and non-financial performance. Their results, which are summarized in Table 8.4, indicate that depending on the type of innovativeness, the impact of each development stage on performance varies. For example, idea generation is found as a determinant of financial success in the case of new delivery processes, while this stage does not have any significant impact on the performance of service modifications or service line extension. Likewise, technical development is positively related to the overall as well as financial performance of certain innovative types of services, namely new delivery process, service modifications and service line extension.

Adoption and diffusion of innovation

Adoption and diffusion of innovation can be examined in the context of both business-to-business (B2B), and consumer (B2C) market. Irrespective of the market, the adoption of innovation refers to the decision of a company or consumer to adopt an innovation on a systematic basis, while the diffusion of innovation refers to the spread of the innovation from its source of development to the adopters' community.

The adoption process

The process of adopting an innovation occurs over time and includes six stages, which differ in the amount of information and the interest that the potential adopter has for the innovation (Rogers, 1995). These stages are as follows:

1 Unawareness: the individual or company is not aware of the existence of the innovation.
2 Awareness: gradually, the individual or company becomes aware of the existence of the innovation, but is insufficiently motivated to seek further information about it.
3 Interest: the individual or company expresses an interest for the innovation and searches for further information in order to have a more complete picture about the innovation and its characteristics.

4   Evaluation: the individual or company identifies the advantages and disadvantages of the innovation according to their needs and wants.
5   Trial: if the evaluation is positive, the individual or company uses the innovation on a limited basis to further evaluate its usefulness.
6   Adoption: if the individual or company is satisfied by the trial use of the innovation, then it is adopted for systematic use.

The objective of the innovation's supplier is to reduce the time the potential adopter spends in each stage, so as the adoption process is speeded up and the number of adopters increases.

Individual adopter categories

On the basis of the length of time required for the adoption of an innovation, Rogers (1982, 1995) has developed what he has called the 'individual innovativeness theory'. According to this theory, there are five different individual adopter categories (Figure 8.1). These are as follows:

The first category refers to innovators representing the first 2.5 per cent of the individuals who ultimately adopt the innovation. They require less time to adopt compared to the other adopter types. They have higher incomes, which reduce the uncertainty risk inherent in the innovation.

The second category refers to early adopters (13.5 per cent). These individuals can serve as opinion leaders for other individuals, and they participate in community organizations more than late adopters.

The third category is early majority (34 per cent). These individuals tend to adopt innovations sooner than the average person. They do not like taking unnecessary risks and tend to be active in community affairs.

The fourth category is called late majority (34 per cent). Individuals that belong in this category tend to adopt because of economic or social reasons.

Finally, the fifth category refers to laggards who represent the last 16 per cent of adopters. Individuals in this category adopt innovations with considerable time lag. In some cases by the time they adopt the innovation, it is already replaced in the market by a more recent innovation.

Factors affecting the rate of innovation adoption by individuals

The rate of adoption of an innovation depends on various factors. These factors can be grouped in the following three categories: innovation characteristics, adopter characteristics, and supplier's marketing activities.

Seven innovation characteristics have been found to influence the rate of innovation adoption in the consumer market (Fliegel and Kivlin 1966; Ostlund, 1974; LaBay and Kinnear 1981; Rogers 1983, 1995). These are as follows:

- *Relative advantage*: when the innovation appears superior to existing products/services, it tends to be adopted more quickly. For example, the diffusion of mobile telephony in the developed countries around the world can be, at least partly, attributed to the advantage of independence offered to the user relative to traditional telephony.
- *Compatibility*: when an innovation is compatible with the values and experiences of individuals, then its rate of adoption is accelerated. For example, mobile telephony is compatible with the contemporary way of living.

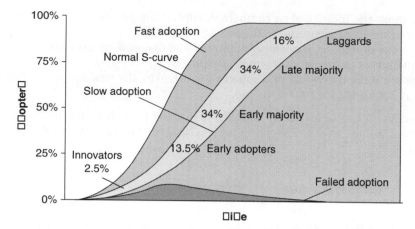

Figure 8.1   **Diffusion curve and innovativeness**

Source: H. Bouman, B. van den Hooff, L. van de Wijngaert, J. van Dijk (2005), *Information and Communication Technology in Organization*. London: Sage. Reprinted with permission.

- *Low perceived risk*: innovations that are characterized by low functional, economic, or physical risk are adopted more quickly.
- *Low complexity*: innovations that are not considered complex and difficult to use are also adopted more quickly.
- *Divisibility, trialability*: when an innovation can be tried on a limited basis, then its rate of adoption increases more easily (for example, the use of third generation – (3G) services like video calling, music downloads, which are provided free of charge for a trial period).
- *Observability/communicability*: when an innovation's benefits can be observed prior to purchase, it can be adopted more quickly. For example, the public use of mobile phones by innovators positively influenced the adoption of this innovation by other individuals who could observe the advantages of mobile phones.
- *Low switching cost*: when the monetary or psychological cost of switching from an existing product/service to an innovation is low, its adoption occurs more quickly.

Once marketers identify which of the aforementioned characteristics may hinder the diffusion of a particular innovation, a number of different marketing strategies and tactics are available to address this problem. For example, if consumers perceive a high risk in adopting the innovation, money-back guarantees and an 'easy-return' policy may be used.

As far as the individual characteristics are concerned, according to the literature, (Feldman and Armstrong 1975; Taylor, 1977; Hirschman, 1980; LaBay and Kinnear, 1981; Rogers, 1983; Dickerson and Gentry, 1983) innovators normally have:

- higher income;
- higher education;
- higher social presence;
- higher risk taking;
- greater exposure to media, and tend to be younger.

Finally, apart from the innovation and individual characteristics, the rate of adoption and diffusion of innovation can be accelerated by the extensive support in terms of distribution, communication and pricing provided by the supplier of the innovation (Gatignon and Robertson, 1989). More specifically, the innovation needs considerable advertising, acceptance and support from the distribution channels and appropriate pricing to appeal to innovators.

Factors affecting the rate of innovation adoption by organizations

The literature on the adoption and diffusion of innovations in the industrial markets has examined a host of variables, which might explain why some firms tend to be innovators adopting a new industrial/technological product or process ahead of others. There are four rather distinct research traditions in the study of adoption and diffusion of innovations by organizations.

The first research tradition addresses the issue of determining the economic, organizational and managerial characteristics of organizations that influence the rate with which organizations adopt innovations. For example, it has been found that early adopters tend to be larger firms, with increased profitability and market share (Moch and Morse, 1977; Kimberly and Evanisko, 1981; Kennedy, 1983; Fritz, 1989; Ali, 1994; Frambach et al., 1998), while they have a more positive attitude towards new ideas (Baldwin and Scott, 1987; Morrison, 1996; Han et al., 1998; Hurley and Hult 1998; Srinivasan et al., 1999). Furthermore, the less centralized and formal the companies, the easier is the initiation of the adoption process while for the final acceptance of an innovation, higher levels of centralization and formalization are required (Sapolsky, 1967, Zaltman et al., 1973).

Another research tradition focuses on the innovation characteristics associated with the rate of adoption. More specifically, it has been reported that adoption is positively related with relative advantage (Tornatzky and Klein, 1982; Rogers, 1983, 1995; Onkvisit and Shaw, 1989; Robinson, 1990; Mansfield, 1993; Frambach et al., 1998), compatibility with existing company systems (Tornatzky and Klein, 1982; Rogers, 1982, 1995; Holak 1988), lack of complexity (Tornatzky and Klein, 1982; Rogers 1982, 1995; Frambach et al. 1998), trialability (Tornatzky and Klein, 1982; Rogers, 1982, 1995; Mathur, 1998), observability (Rogers 1982, 1995) and lack of uncertainty (Nooteboom, 1989).

The third research tradition refers to the marketing activities of the supplier of the innovation. All in all, existing research suggests that the more targeted and intensive the marketing activities of the supplier, the more rapid is the adoption and diffusion of a technological innovation (Gatignon and Robertson, 1989; Ram and Jung, 1994; Frambach et al., 1998). A detailed investigation of such activities has been made by Easingwood & Beard (1989) for high tech products (see Chapter 7). Frambach et al. (1998) have studied the adoption of electronic banking in the Dutch business market and concluded that the adoption of this new technology is accelerated, when: first, the supplier of such an innovation targets innovators, emphasizing the product characteristics of the innovation, the price level, the integration possibilities, the use friendliness, and so on, and secondly, the supplier's marketing activities aim at reducing the perceived risk from the adoption of the innovation (for example, low introduction price, free trial period).

As one of the basic parameters of adoption and diffusion of innovations is the communication of the supplier with the market, a fourth research tradition is concerned with the different information sources used by the members of the adopting/buying organization at the different stages of the adoption process, such as awareness, interest, evaluation and adoption. Understanding these information sources allows the supplier to use the most appropriate communication vehicles to provide these information that will allow potential adopters (for example, innovators, early adopters) to move from one stage of the adoption process to the next.

The major research findings stemming from this kind of research may be summarized as follows:

- Impersonal commercial sources, for example, advertising in trade journals, tend to be significant information sources in triggering awareness of a new industrial product (Urban and Churchill, 1968).
- Other impersonal commercial sources, like, for instance, direct mail and catalogues are important sources throughout the buying decision process (Moriarty and Spekman, 1984; Bunn and Clopton, 1993).
- Impersonal non-commercial sources, like internal confidential notes and reports of the purchasing department, are particularly important when there is considerable uncertainty and long duration in the buying process (Bunn and Clopton, 1993).
- Personal commercial sources, for example, sales staff, are important (Frambach et al., 1998), particularly at the evaluation and adoption stages, where personal demonstration and application as well as persuasion and order writing may be required (Webster, 1971).

Models for organizational adoption and diffusion of innovation

A number of models have been developed in the literature examining the adoption of innovations by organizations. In the following sections we present three of these models, which have been put forward by Baker (1983), Robertson and Gatignon (1986) and Frambach and Schillewaert (2002).

Baker's model of industrial adoption process

A useful model that describes the factors that impact on the adoption process of an industrial product has been put forward by Professor Michael Baker in 1971 and reformulated in 1983. The notation describing this model may be expressed as follows:

$$P = f[SP (PC, EC, (T_A - T_D), (E_A - E_D), BR]$$

where:

P = purchase (adoption)
f = a function (unspecified) of
SP = selective perception
PC = precipitating circumstances
EC = enabling conditions
T_A = technological advantages
T_D = technological disadvantages
E_A = economic advantages
E_D = economic disadvantages
BR = behavioural response

According to this model, an organization's adoption decision can be seen in terms of a sequence of factors each of which is described below.

Selective perception: the awareness of an organization of different innovations and its subsequent reactions will be conditioned by the characteristics of the organization including the education, skills, and motivation of its management and workforce, the degree of 'openness' of the organization as a whole in terms of its relationships with other organizations, including suppliers, and so on. These characteristics influence management's perception of the issues raised during the adoption process, from initial awareness of the potential innovation to final acceptance and implementation or rejection.

Precipitating circumstances: these factors cause a company to begin to evaluate an innovation for the first time. For example, deteriorating performance of an existing machine tool with increasing running costs might force management to consider its replacement. New competitors or new markets might similarly precipitate consideration of new investment. Perhaps, less obviously, the appointment of new senior management or most obviously the actions of the supplier of the innovation may also precipitate consideration of new investment.

Enabling conditions: they refer to the conditions that must be present if the innovation is to fit into the organization, like for instance, adequate finance to purchase the innovation and adequately trained personnel, compatibility with existing investment, and so on.

Technical/economic advantages/disadvantages: these factors which refer to the advantages/disadvantages of the innovation compared to competitive innovations are taken into consideration when evaluating alternative suppliers and establishing the changes, if any, that are necessary for the innovation to fit into the organization's needs.

Behavioural response: refers to all those factors that influence the decision process as it develops, like for example, the decision-making procedures and the management's attitude to technical change.

How UK and German companies adopt flexible manufacturing systems

Professor M. Baker's model has been used by one of the authors of this book in examining the process of adopting the flexible manufacturing systems (FMS) technology by UK and German companies (Avlonitis and Parkinson, 1986). An FMS is a highly customized manufacturing system that consists of several machine tools controlled by a central computer, and linked by automated material handling (also computer controlled).

In the companies surveyed, the adoption process of FMS has been found to include the following stages: awareness of the FMS concept, specific interest in FMS, technical evaluation of FMS, economic evaluation of FMS and finally, adoption or rejection.

The companies that are receptive to FMS share a number of characteristics, which influence their selective perception: they are large, typically employing more than 1,500 people. They enjoy large market shares both in the domestic as well as export markets. Further, the senior management of these companies, particularly the German ones, tend to have had a formal technical education. This fosters receptiveness to new technical developments. They are also outward looking, establishing personal contacts with FMS suppliers and users (particularly the Germans), and regularly consult reports, trade journals and other sources of information.

(Continued)

(Continued)

As far as the *precipitating circumstances* are concerned, these include the unpredictable and fragmented demand, the severe price competition, and the rising costs of labour. These factors seem to create a pressure on companies to 'streamline' their manufacturing facilities, making them more cost effective and at the same time more flexible in terms of volume and quality of output.

Moreover, this study revealed a number of *enabling conditions*, which make a company seriously evaluate the adoption of the flexible manufacturing system technology. More specifically, the compatibility of this technology with the companies' existing human and technical infrastructure is one of the most important factors that help to overcome the individual's psychological resistance to FMS technology. Another important enabling condition is the existence in the company of a 'process champion' who is able to 'sell' the FMS concept internally and achieve the necessary high level of coordination between all those involved. A third crucial enabling condition that contributes to the evaluation of the FMS technology is the external support from suppliers, universities, and the government. These bodies can offer technical support (universities), feasibility studies (suppliers) and grants (government).

The *technical advantages* that are considered as important criteria for technical evaluation include the supplier's technical capabilities and reputation, as well as the supplier's knowledge of the customer's manufacturing problems. Similarly, the *technical risk* that can lead to the rejection of the FMS technology refers to the 'lost output' in case something goes wrong with the FMS. The perception of risk is increased considerably when the company lacks confidence in the potential supplier's ability to meet specifications. The *economic risks* that are considered during the economic evaluation of the FMS include the high initial cost of investment and the long payback period. The *economic advantage* of the FMS is that it may receive financial assistance or credit guarantees from the government.

Finally, the companies that tend to adopt the FMS technology have management teams that are willing to take calculated risks (*behavioural response*). In fact, the 'essentiality' of FMS, as perceived by management, is one of the main factors that enhance the relative advantage of the FMS technology to the adopting companies, and consequently, their ability to tolerate the technical and economic risks involved in its adoption.

Factors affecting the organizational adoption of information and communication technologies (ICT)

In today's highly competitive markets the use of information and communication technologies (ICT) by organizations (for example, LAN, WAN, Internet, ERP, CRM) seems an imperative for reducing the uncertainties surrounding production and administrative processes and, consequently, for sustaining their competitive advantage. According to the studies that have been published in the literature, the ICT characteristics and the organizational characteristics that influence the adoption of such new technologies are as follows:

ICT characteristics

- *Relative advantage*: the higher is the relative advantage of the Internet (Mehrtens et al., 2001) and electronic data interchange systems (EDI) (Bouchard, 1993; Premkumar et al., 1994; Iacovou et al., 1995) over competitive offerings, the more likely are their adoption.

- *Compatibility*: The higher the compatibility of a new technology with existing company systems, the more likely is their adoption. This finding refers to enterprise resource planning (ERP) software (Waarts et al., 2002) EDI (Bouchard, 1993, Premkumar et al., 1994) and the Internet (LaRose and Hoag, 1996).
- *Security*: the higher the perceived security of transactions, the more likely is the adoption of the Internet by organizations (Kalakota and Whinston, 1996, Wang et al., 1998; Min and Galle, 1999).
- *Cost*: the buying firm's perceived concern over the high cost of investment has a negative effect on the adoption of EDI (Premkumar et al., 1994 and Carbone, 1996).

Organizational characteristics

- *Size*: the larger the size of a company, the more likely it is to adopt ICT tools like EDI (Premkumar et al., 1994), the Internet (LaRose and Hoag, 1996), E-purchasing (Min and Galle, 2003) and ERP (Kara, 1999).
- *Attitude towards IT innovation*: the more positive is the attitude of a company towards ERP, the earlier is its adoption (Waarts et al., 2002).
- *Existence of an adoption 'champion'*: companies that adopt the Internet are more likely to have a 'champion' for this ICT tool. In small companies this role is usually played by the owner (LaRose and Hoag, 1996, Mehrtens et al., 2001).
- *Level of IT use in the organization*: companies that have high levels of IT use are more likely to adopt the Internet (Mehrtens et al., 2001).
- *Level of IT knowledge among employees*: the Internet is adopted by organizations that have employees with increased IT knowledge (Mehrtens et al., 2001).
- *Intensity of competition*: the more competitive the environment in which the company operates, the earlier is the adoption of information and communication technologies like ERP (Waarts et al., 2002), EDI (Iacovou et al., 1995) and the Internet (Klein, 1998).

Robertson and Gatignon's model of organizational adoption and diffusion of innovation

One of the most cited models in the organizational diffusion literature has been developed by Robertson and Gatignon (1986). This model focuses on the competitive factors that influence the diffusion of new technologies. More specifically, the adoption/diffusion process is influenced by the innovation characteristics, the organization's characteristics, as well as the supply side competitive environment and the adopter industry competitive environment. The supply side competitive environment includes structural factors (namely industry competitiveness, supplier reputation, technology standardization and vertical coordination with customers) and resource commitments (namely, R&D allocation and marketing support).

The hypothesized relationship between each structural factor of the supply side competitive environment and the adoption/diffusion of a technological innovation is as follows:

- Industry competitiveness: the greater the competitive intensity of the supplier group, the more aggressive pricing policies are used, thus encouraging more rapid diffusion.
- Supplier reputation: the more favourable the reputation of the supplier group, the less the uncertainty about the innovation's performance, thus the more rapid the initial diffusion.

- Technology standardization: the more standardized the technology, the less the prices and the uncertainty about the use of the innovation, and thus the more rapid the diffusion.
- Vertical coordination with customers: when there is a high degree of vertical dependence and coordination between supplier and customer, there is a increase in the flow of information as well as the customer's involvement in the development of the innovation. In such a case, not only do these customers adopt the innovation more rapidly, but they can also provide opinion leadership for late adopters.

Furthermore, supply side resource commitments to ongoing R&D and marketing programmes may positively affect the diffusion of a new technology, as they contribute to the development of enhanced technologies which meet the needs of the company's customers.

Moreover, the adopter industry competitive environment generally affects receptivity to innovation. In fact, the willingness to innovate seems to be a function of specific structural and communication factors. The structural factors include industry heterogeneity, competitive intensity and demand uncertainty. The communication factors include signal frequency and clarity, level of professionalism and cosmopolitanism of the industry.

Factors affecting the adoption of laptop computers by US companies

A study of the adoption of laptop computers by US companies revealed the following results:

The greater the vertical coordination between suppliers and customers, and the more the supplier incentives (for example, discounts, seminars and manufacturer visits, trials), the more likely is the adoption of laptops. Also, the greater the concentration ratio of an industry (excluding monopoly) is, the more rapid the adoption of laptops, as companies provide the necessary resources to innovate in order to create and maintain competitive advantage. In contrast, the greater the price competition the less likely is the adoption of laptops, because the industry's financial resources are depleted. Finally, companies with individuals that have a preference for negative information (in order to make a more informed decision) are more likely to adopt laptop computers.

Source: Gatignon and Robertson (1989)

The relationship between each of the structural factors of the adopter industry competitive environment and the adoption/diffusion of a technological innovation is as follows:

- Industry heterogeneity: the speed of diffusion will be maximized at an intermediate level of industry heterogeneity. In such industrial conditions the transmission of information is likely to be lower in innovation content than information transmitted within a heterogeneous industry.
- Competitive intensity: when competitive intensity is low, that is under monopolistic conditions, the interest of organizations in adopting an innovation is low. In contrast, when the industry is highly competitive, the financial resources of the industry are depleted and the acceptance of innovation is stifled. In cases of oligopolistic competition, the adoption/diffusion of innovation is encouraged.

- Demand uncertainty: in industries where there is difficulty in forecasting demand accurately, receptivity to innovation is most pronounced if the strategy for pre-empting new entry requires new technologies for cost reduction or for gaining new market segments.

The relationship between each of the communication factors of the adopter industry competitive environment and the adoption/diffusion of new technological innovations is described below:

- Signal frequency and clarity: such signals may be announced intentions of competitors about new investments, production processes, pricing systems or product introductions. The more frequent and clear these signals are, the more the available information about the adoption of an innovation from competitors is and therefore, the more rapid is the adoption of the innovation by other companies in the industry.
- Level of professionalism: the higher the level of professionalism of an industry in terms of professionals with technical expertise, the more rapid is the diffusion of an innovation, as such professionals may better evaluate the necessity of adopting the innovation.
- Cosmopolitanism of the industry: this means the greater the external (rather than local) orientation of an industry, the greater the exposure to new ideas about innovative technologies and the more rapid the adoption/diffusion of technological innovations.

The adoption of electronic banking in the Dutch business market

Electronic banking in the business market allows companies to process banking transactions electronically. The first electronic banking system was introduced in the Dutch business market in 1985. Since then, an increasing number of companies have adopted this service innovation. In an attempt to unveil the factors that influence the adoption of this service innovation in the Dutch business market, a study has been conducted in 247 organizations (101 adopters and 146 non-adopters of electronic banking).

According to this study, the perceived relative advantage of this innovation had a significant positive effect on its adoption, while the perceived complexity of electronic banking, defined as the degree to which the product is perceived as difficult to handle, had a significantly negative effect on its adoption. Furthermore, the supplier's marketing strategy was another important determinant of electronic banking's adoption in the business market. In more detail, the likelihood of adopting electronic banking increases the more times the potential adopter is exposed to a marketing strategy with the aim of positioning the innovation in the market or reducing the risk of adoption. Similarly, the adoption decision of the company (namely, potential adopter) seems to be influenced positively by the number of meetings with the supplier, the number of brochures on electronic banking read, and the number of exhibitions visited where electronic banking is demonstrated.

These results have clear managerial implications. The suppliers of electronic banking should focus on positioning their innovation in the marketplace by making potential adopters more familiar with the innovation and by facilitating adoption. Effective tools include a free trial period of the innovation or a low introduction price. Suppliers should also bear in mind the necessity of creating and explicitly communicating the relative advantage of the innovation and reducing its perceived complexity, if they seek to increase the adoption of their innovation in the business market.

Source: Frambach et al. (1998)

Frambach and Schillewaert's model of organizational innovation adoption

Frambach and Schillewaert (2002) have recently published a model that enhances our understanding of the factors that influence adoption, as it examines the adoption decision not only at the organizational level as previous studies did, but also at the level of the individual adopter within the organization.

As far as the organizational factors are concerned, the adoption of an innovation is influenced by three factors: adopter characteristics, namely size, structure, organizational innovativeness or strategic posture; environmental influences like network externalities and competitive pressures; and perceived innovation characteristics (namely, relative advantage, compatibility, complexity, trialability, observability and uncertainty), which in turn are influenced by the supplier's marketing efforts (namely, effective targeting, communication strategy and risk reduction) and the social network (namely, interconnectedness and network participation).

In order to have a more compete picture of the factors that influence the organizational adoption of innovations, it is also important to examine the acceptance of these innovations within organizations. There are five factors that explain individual acceptance, namely: attitude towards the innovation; organizational facilitators/ internal marketing, namely, training, social persuasion, and organizational support; personal innovativeness; social influences towards the adoption/rejection of the innovation; personal characteristics, like demographics, tenure, product experience and personal values.

Summary

- Different measures of new product/service performance can be used, for example, sales, profits, market share, impact on the performance of other company products.
- Depending on the criteria used and the time at which performance is measured, a new product or service may be characterized as successful and unsuccessful at the same time.
- What constitutes an appropriate performance measure depends on the product's degree of innovativeness.
- The most frequently cited success factors of new products and services include product synergy, product/market fit, unique/superior product, and quality of execution of launch.
- The degree of product innovativeness moderates the relationship of various process-related, product-related, market-related, and company-related factors with the performance of new products and services.
- The adoption process of innovations comprises six stages, namely unawareness, awareness, interest, evaluation, trial, adoption.
- On the basis of the length of time required for the adoption of an innovation, there are five different individual adopter categories, namely innovators, early adopters, early majority, late majority, laggards.
- The rate of adoption of an innovation depends on three sets of factors: innovation characteristics, adopter characteristics and supplier's marketing activities
- A number of models have been developed in the literature examining the adoption of innovations by enterprises.

Questions

1 Select a new industrial product in your country, identify its degree of innovativeness and discuss the factors that are critical to its success in the market.
2 Identify two factors/attributes that may be considered important for the success of an innovative mortgage scheme in the market and discuss the relevant NSD process activities/ stages that should be emphasized.
3 Write down how a service marketer can help overcome the low observability problem of a new transatlantic air route.
4 Discuss the marketing activities that a supplier of production robots may use in order to increase the rate of their adoption in the market.

References

Ali, A. (1994) 'Pioneering versus incremental innovation: review and research propositions', *Journal of Product Innovation Management*, 11: 46–61.
Avlonitis, G. and Papastathopoulou, P. (2001) 'The development activities of innovative and non-innovative new retail financial products: implications for success', *Journal of Marketing Management*, 17: 705–38.
Avlonitis, G. and Parkinson, S. (1986) 'The adoption of flexible manufacturing systems in British and German companies', *Industrial Marketing Management*, 15: 97–108.
Baker, M. (1983) *Market Development*. Hamondsworth: Penguin Books.
Baldwin, W. and Scott, J. (1987) *Market Structure and Technological Change*. Chur, Switzerland: Harwood Academic Publishers.
Booz, Allen and Hamilton (1982) *New Products Management for the 1980s*. New York: Booz, Allen and Hamilton, Inc.
Bouchard, L. (1993) 'Decision criteria in the adoption of EDI', *Proceedings of the 14th ICIS*: 365–76.
Bunn, W. and Clopton, S. (1993) 'Patterns of information source use across industrial purchase situations', *Decision Science*, 24: 437–78.
Calantone, R. and Cooper, R. (1979) 'A discriminant model for identifying scenarios of industrial new product failure', *Journal of the Academy of Marketing Science*, 7(3): 163–83.
Carbone, J. (1996) 'Distributors see growing EDI interest', *Purchasing* 120(8): 59–60.
Cooper R. (1979) 'The dimensions of industrial new product success and failure', *Journal of Marketing*, 43(3): 93–103.
Cooper, R. and de Brentani, U. (1991) 'New industrial financial services: what distinguishes the winners', *Journal of Product Innovation Management*, 8: 75–90.
Cooper, R. and Kleinschmidt, E. (1986) 'An investigation into the new product process: steps, deficiencies and impact'. *Journal of Product Innovation Management*, 3: 71–85.
Cooper, R. and Kleinschmidt, E. (1987) 'Success factors in product innovation', *Industrial Marketing Management*, 16(3): 215–23.
Cooper, R. and Kleinschmidt, E. (1993) 'Major new products: what distinguishes the winners in the chemical industry?', *Journal of Product Innovation Management*, 10: 90–111.
Cowell, D.W. (1988) 'New service development', *Journal of Marketing Management* 3(3): 296–312.
Crawford, M. (1997) *New Products Management*. Homewood. IL: Richard D. Irwin, Inc.
de Brentani, U. (1989) 'Success and failure in new industrial services', *Journal of Product Innovation Management*, 6(4): 239–58.
de Brentani, U. (1991) 'Success factors in developing new business services', *European Journal of Marketing*, 25(2): 33–59.
de Brentani, U. (1993) 'The new product process in financial services: strategy for success', *International Journal of Bank Marketing*, 11(3): 15–22.
de Brentani, U. (1995a) 'New industrial service development: scenarios for success and failure', *Journal of Business Research* 32: 93-103.
de Brentani, U. (1995b) 'Firm size: implications for achieving success in new industrial services', *Journal of Marketing Management*, 11: 207–25.

de Brentani, U. (2001) 'Innovative versus incremental new business services: different keys for achieving success', *Journal of Product Innovation Management*, 18: 169–87.

de Brentani, U. and Cooper, R. (1992) 'Developing successful new financial services for businesses', *Industrial Marketing Management*, 21: 231–41.

de Brentani, U. and Ragot, E. (1996) 'Developing new business-to-business professional services: what factors impact performance?', *Industrial Marketing Management*, 25: 517–30.

Dickerson, M.D. and Gentry, J.W. (1983) 'Characteristics of adopters and non-adopters of home computers', *Journal of Consumer Research*, 10: 225–35.

Easingwood, C. and Beard, C. (1989) 'High technology launch strategies in the UK', *Industrial Marketing Management*, 18: 125–38.

Easingwood, C. and Storey, C. (1991) 'Success factors of new consumer financial services', *International Journal of Bank Marketing*, 7(1): 41–54.

Easingwood, C. and Storey, C. (1993) 'Marketplace success factors for new financial services', *Journal of Services Marketing*, 7(1): 41–54.

Edgett, S. (1994) 'The traits of successful new service development', *Journal of Services Marketing*, 8(3): 40–9.

Edgett, S. and Parkinson, S. (1994) 'The development of new financial services: identifying determinants of success and failure', *International Journal of Service Industry Management*, 5(4): 24–38.

Feldman, L. and Armstrong, G. (1975) 'Identifying buyers of a major automotive innovation', *Journal of Marketing*, 39: 47–53.

Fliegel, F. and Kivlin, J. (1966) 'Attributes of innovation as factors in diffusion', *American Journal of Sociology*, 72: 234–48.

Frambach, R. and Schillewaert, N. (2002) 'Organizational innovation adoption: a multi-level framework of determinants and opportunities for future research', *Journal of Business Research*, 55: 163–76.

Frambach, R., Barkema, H., Nooteboom, B., and Wedel, M. (1998) 'Adoption of a service innovation in the business market: an empirical test of supply-side variables', *Journal of Business Research*, 41: 161–74.

Fritz, W. (1989) 'Determinants of product innovation activities', *European Journal of Marketing*, 23(10): 32–43.

Gatignon, H. and Robertson, T. (1989) 'Technology diffusion: an empirical test of competitive effects', *Journal of Marketing*, 53 (January): 35–49.

Globe, G. et al. (1973) 'Key factors and events in the innovation process', *Research Management*, 8–15.

Gounaris, S., Papastathopoulou, P. and Avlonitis, G. (2003) 'Assessing the importance of the development activities for successful new services: does innovativeness matter?', *International Journal of Bank Marketing*, 21(5): 266–79.

Griffin, A. (1997) 'PDMA research on new product development practices: updating trends and benchmarking best practices', *Journal of Product Innovation Management*, 14: 429–58.

Griffin, A. and Page, A. (1996) 'PDMA success measurement project: recommended measures for product development success and failure', *Journal of Product Innovation Management*, 13: 478–96.

Han, J., Namwoon, K. and Srivastava, R. (1998) 'Market orientation and organizational performance: is innovation a missing link?', *Journal of Marketing*, 62: 30–45.

Harrison, T. (2000) *Financial Services Marketing*. Harlow, Essex: Pearson Education Ltd.

Henard, D. and Szymanski, D. (2001) 'Why some new products are more successful than others', *Journal of Marketing Research*, XXXVIII: 362–75.

Hirschman, E. (1980) 'Innovativeness, novelty seeking and consumer creativity', *Journal of Consumer Research*, 7: 289–95.

Holak, S. (1988) 'Determinants of innovative durables adoption: an empirical study with implications for early product screening', *Journal of Product Innovation Management*, 5: 50–69.

Hopkins, D. (1980) 'New product winners and losers', Conference Board Report, No. 773.

Hopkins, D. and Baileys, L. (1971) 'New product pressures', *Conference Board Report*.

Hurley, R. and Hult, T. (1998) 'Innovation, market orientation and organizational learning: an integration and empirical examination', *Journal of Marketing*, 62: 42–54.

Iacovou, C., Benbasat, I. and Dexter, A. (1995) 'Electronic data interchange and small organizations: adoption and impact of technology', *MIS Quarterly*, 19(4): 466–85.

Kalakota, R. and Whinston, A. (1996) *Frontiers of Electronic Commerce*. Reading, MA: Addison-Wesley.

Kara, D. (1999) 'ERP integration', *Information Week*, 8: 1a–6a.

Kennedy, A. (1983) 'The adoption and diffusion of new industrial products: a literature review', *European Journal of Marketing*, 17: 31–88.

Kimberly, J. and Evanisko, M. (1981) 'Organizational innovation: the influence of individual, organizational, and contextual factors on hospital adoption of technological and administrative innovations', *Academy of Management Journal*, 24: 689–713.

Klein, M. (1998) 'Small business grows online', *American Demographics*, 20(2): 30.

Kulvik, H. (1977) 'Factors underlying the success or failure of new products', *Helsinki: University of Technology*, Report No. 29.

LaBay, D.G. and Kinnear, T.C., (1981) 'Exploring the consumer decision process in the adoption of solar energy systems', *Journal of Consumer Research*, 8: 271–8.

LaRose, R. and Hoag, A. (1996) 'Organizational adoption of Internet and the clustering of innovations', *Telematics and Informatics*, 13(1): 49–61.

Lin, L. (1986) 'Tangible and intangible reasons for new product failure rate', in P. Krausher (ed.), *New Product Development*. ESOMAR Monograph Series 1.

Lynn, G.S., J.P. Morone, and A.S. Paulson (1996) 'Marketing and discontinuous innovation: the probe and learn process', *California Management Review*, 38(3): 3–37.

Maidique, M. and Zirger, B.J. (1984) 'A study of success and failure in product innovation: the case of the US electronics industry', *IEEE Transactions in Engineering Management*, 4: 192–203.

Maidique, M. and Zirger, B.J. (1985) 'The new product learning cycle', *Research Policy*, 14: 299–313.

Mansfield, E. (1993) 'The diffusion of flexible manufacturing systems in Japan, Europe and the United States', *Management Science*, 39: 149–59.

Mathur, A. (1998) 'Examining trying as a mediator and control as a moderator of intention-behavior relationship', *Psychology in Marketing*, 15: 241–59.

Mehrtens, J., Cragg, P. and Mills, A. (2001) 'A model of Internet adoption by SMEs', *Information & Management*, 39: 165–76.

Min, H. and Galle, W. (1999) 'Electronic commerce usage in business-to-business purchasing', *International Journal of Operations and Product Management*, 19(9): 909–21.

Min, H. and Galle, W. (2003) 'E-purchasing: profiles of adopters and nonadopters', *Industrial Marketing Management*, 32(3).

Moch, M. and Morse, E. (1977) 'Size, centralization and organizational adoption of innovations', *American Sociological Review*, 42(5): 716–25.

Moriarty, R. and Spekman, R. (1984) 'An empirical investigation of the information sources used during the industrial adoption process', *Journal of Marketing Research*, 21: 137–47.

Morrison, P. (1996) 'Testing a framework for the adoption of technological innovations by organizations and the role of leading edge users', *Inst Study of Business Marketing*: 1–17.

Myers, S. and Marquis, D. (1969) *Successful Industrial Innovations*. (NSF 69-17) Washington, DC: National Science Foundation.

Nooteboom, B. (1989) 'Diffusion, uncertainty and firm size', *International Journal of Research in Marketing*, 6: 109–128.

Onkvisit, S. and Shaw, J. (1989) 'The diffusion of innovations theory: some research questions and ideas', *Akron Business and Economic Review*, 20: 46–55.

Ostlund, L. (1974) 'Perceived innovation attributes as predictors of innovativeness', *Journal of Consumer Research*, (1): 23–9.

Parry, M. and Song, M. (1994) 'Identifying new product successes in China', *Journal of Product Innovation Management*, 11: 15–30.

Premkumar, G., Ramamurthy, K. and Nilakanta, S. (1994) 'Implememtation of electronic data interchange: an innovation diffusion perspective', *Journal of Management Information Systems*, 11(2): 157–86.

Ram, S. and Jung, H. (1994) 'Innovativeness in product usage: a comparison of early adopters and early majority', *Psychology in Marketing*: 11: 57–67.

Roberts, W. and Burke, E. (1974) 'Six new products – what makes them successful', *Research Management*, 16: 21–4.

Robertson, T. and Gatignon, H. (1986) 'Competitive effects on technology diffusion', *Journal of Marketing*, 50: 1–12.

Robinson, W. (1990) 'Product innovation and start-up business market share performance', *Management Science*, 36: 1279–89.

Rochford, L. and Rudelius, W. (1992) 'How involving more functional areas within a firm affects the new product process', *Journal of Product Innovation Management* 9: 287–99.

Rogers, E. (1983) *Diffusion of Innovations*, 3rd edition. New York: The Free Press.

Rogers, E. (1995) *Diffusion of Innovations*, 4th edition. New York: The Free Press.

Rothwell, R. (1972) *Factors for Success in Industrial Innovations from Project SAPPHO – A Comparative Study of Success and Failure in Industrial Innovation*. Brighton, Sussex, England: S.P.R.U.

Rothwell, R., Freeman C., Horsley A., Jervis V. T. P., Robertson A. B. and Townsend J. (1974) 'SAPPHO Updated-Project SAPPHO Phase II', *Research Policy*, 3: 258–91.

Sapolsky, H. (1967) 'Organizational structure and innovation', *Journal of Business* 40(4): 497–510.

Schultz, H. and, D.J. Yang (1997) *Pour Your Heart into It: How STARBUCKS Built a Company One cup at a Time*. New York: Hyperion.

Song, M. and Montoya-Weiss, M. (1998) 'Critical development activities for really new versus incremental products', *Journal of Product Innovation Management*, 15: 124–35.

Song, M. and Parry, M. (1996) 'What separates Japanese new product winners from losers', *Journal of Product Innovation Management*, 13(5): 422–39.

Srinivasan, R., Lilien, G. and Rangaswami, A. (1999) 'The role of technological opportunism in the adoption of radical technologies by firms: an application to e-business', *Institute for the Study of Business Marketing*, 26.

Storey, C. and Easingwood, C. (1993) 'The impact of the new product development project on the success of financial services', *The Service Industries Journal*, 13(3): 40–54.

Szakasits, D. (1974) 'The adoption of the SAPPHO method in the Hungarian electronics industry', *Research Policy* 3: 18–28.

Taylor, J.W., (1977) 'A striking characteristic of innovators', *Journal of Marketing Research*, 14: 104–7.

Tornatzky, L. and Klein, K. (1982) 'Innovation characteristics and innovation adoption-implementation: a meta-analysis of findings', *IEEE Transactions on Engineering Management*, 29: 28–45.

Urban, G. and Hauser, J. (1993) *Design and Marketing of New Products*. Englewood Cliffs, NJ: Prentice Hall.

Urban, O. and Churchill, G. (1968) 'Adoption research: information sources in the industrial purchasing decision' in Robert L. King (ed.), *Marketing and the New Science of Planning*. Chicago: American Marketing Association. pp. 352–9.

Veryzer, R.W. (1998) 'Discontinuous innovation and the new product development process', *Journal of Product Innovation Management*, 15: 304–21.

Waarts, E., van Everdingen, Y. and van Hillegersberg, J. (2002) 'The dynamics of factors affecting the adoption of innovations', *Journal of Product Innovation Management*, 19: 412–23.

Wang, H., Lee, M. and Wang, C. (1998) 'Consumer privacy concerns about Internet marketing', *Communications ACM*, 41(3): 63–70.

Webster, F. (1971) 'Informal communication in industrial markets', *Journal of Marketing Research*, 7: 186–9.

Zaltman, G., Duncan, R. and Holbek, J. (1973) *Innovations and Organizations*. New York: John Wiley.

Zirger, B. and Maidique, M. (1990) 'A model of new product development: an empirical test', *Management Science*, 36(7): 867–83.

Further reading

Cooper, R. (1993) *Winning at New Products*. Reading, MA: Perseus Books Publishing.

Debackere, K., Van Looy, B. and Papastathopoulou, P. (1998) 'Managing innovation in a service environment, in B. Van Looy, R. Van Dierdonck and P. Gemmel (eds). *Services Management: An Integrated Approach*, London: Financial Times Pitman Publishing.

9 Identification and Revitalization of Weak Products and Services

Introduction

As has already been discussed in Chapter 4, one of the main marketing activities of a company is the evaluation of its existing products/services. Such an evaluation can be done using different approaches like the multidimensional 'screening' approach, the 'index' approach, and the product portfolio classification/matrix approach.

Among the outcomes of product portfolio evaluation is the identification of weak products and services. Such offerings should be either changed or deleted in order to allow for a more productive utilization of corporate resources. As Wind (1982) has pointed out, 'Explicit attention should be given to the product change/deletion decisions, since the potential profit contributions of such decisions are, in many cases, significantly larger (especially in the short run) than the profit contribution of the new product activities of the firm.'

The product revitalization/elimination decision-making process comprises four stages, which are depicted in Figure 9.1. The identification of candidates for elimination is the first stage of the process, followed by the analysis and revitalization of weak products and services. The third stage refers to the evaluation of weak products/services and the elimination decision-making, while the final stage of the process refers to the implementation of the elimination decision.

In this chapter, we turn our attention to the first two stages of the revitalization/elimination process. In order to examine these stages in more detail, we address the following questions:

- Which process do companies follow to identify weak products and services?
- Which audit criteria do companies use and what is their relevant importance?
- What factors of the internal and external environment influence the importance of alternative audit criteria?
- How do companies diagnose what is wrong with the product/service that has failed to meet management expectations?
- What alternative corrective actions are generally considered and evaluated by management to revitalize a weak product/service?
- To what extent is the consideration of alternative corrective actions influenced by the company's idiosyncratic internal and external environment conditions?
- What kind of evaluation practices do companies use to select or reject alternative corrective actions?
- Which alternative corrective actions are actually used by companies?

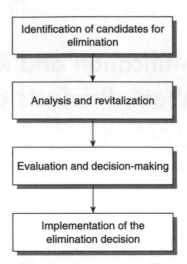

Figure 9.1   **The product revitalization/elimination decision-making process**
Source: Hurst (1959); Alexander (1964); Kotler (1965); Worthing (1971); Hamelman and Mazze (1972); McSurely and Wilemon (1973)

The weak product identification process

In a study, which has been undertaken in UK by one of the authors of this book investigating the weak product identification process in 114 engineering companies, it has been found that no formal system existed by which weak products were brought to the attention of management (Avlonitis, 1986). Only a small proportion among the companies studied carried out regular reviews of the product line. The majority of companies generally considered a set of unwritten performance dimensions/criteria to evaluate product performance.

In general, two broad patterns of weak product identification activities were uncovered, namely:

- Management-cycle activities: weak products were identified during management meetings, which brought together departmental heads under a chief executive and which dealt with a variety of management topics in addition to product issues.
- Product planning-cycle activities: weak products were identified during committee meetings whose main responsibility was the evaluation of existing and new products and/or the selection of the company's product-mix for the future.

These patterns of weak product identification activities exhibited basic differences not only in the way that weak products were identified, but also in the revitalization/elimination process that followed.

Management-cycle activities: the meeting patterns observed were board meetings, sales meetings, executive meetings, and so on. These meetings were held on a regular basis and provided the occasion for a review of the state of the company as was reflected in the management accounts (profit and loss accounts, balance sheet, and so on).

In the companies where management-cycle activities were the dominant mode of product decision making, the weak product identification activity was neither a continuous process nor an integral part of the company's product planning process. The performance of products was evaluated in a fragmented form as part of the normal operational duties of functional departments. These companies had established product goals as part of their budgeting and operational planning, mainly in terms of sales volume and profit margins, against which the actual performance was compared. No systematic market-share analysis was observed in these companies. However, the evaluation of products in terms of sales volume and profit margins was supported, in many cases, by departmental reports, sales analysis reports, reports of orders behind schedule and semi-annual inventories. The accumulation of such data assisted management to identify 'performance discrepancies' with respect to the company as a whole and/or a specific product.

However, given the historical nature of these data, the 'discrepancy' identification of a weak product did not come out of observing trends and predicting or planning strategies to handle future problems. Instead, the identification of a weak product was in response to a stimulus where a real problem had been created in the past and had been allowed to grow to an significant size either through a failure to fully recognize and appreciate the problem or through a failure to define properly the nature of the problem. This could be partly attributed to the fact that none of these companies had explicitly established minimum standards of product performance serving as 'warning signals' and indicating acceptable levels of product performance below which action on the product was called for.

Product planning-cycle activities: these activities were observed dealing with a variety of product issues, while they were mainly undertaken in larger companies. For example, some companies, in addition to a product development committee which was concerned with project management of new products from research to market launch, had set up a product range review committee. This committee was primarily concerned with the evaluation of existing products as well with the evaluation of new product proposals submitted by the new product development committee. The product range review committee meeting was conducted semi-annually, and was normally attended by the managing director and other executive directors as well as by senior departmental managers. For each meeting, the participants submitted reports dealing with financial and market evaluations of the product line. These covered past sales and profits, market shares, changes in competitive activities and general behaviour of products in the market.

The historical analysis of the products' performance was restricted to a single previous period (one year) except for those products, which displayed significant deviations from the pre-established targets (product goals). However, given the absence of minimum standards of product performance in these companies, the products whose performance had not been consistent with company expectations were recognized through a subjective analysis, which allowed the participants to tailor their judgement to each product's situation.

In some very large companies, the weak products were identified during product-planning committee meetings. During the product-planning committee meetings, which were attended by executive managers, product managers and R&D personnel, the need for new product development and/or range extension to meet market demand and competition was evaluated; and the suitability of the existing products for the market was assessed. The product managers were generally entrusted with the responsibility of gathering and maintaining the necessary information about their products, including profit margins, market share and sales trends. In the light of this information, the product-planning committee determined which products were experiencing either incipient problems or serious 'weaknesses'.

In some companies, the identification of weak products was an integral part of the company's new product planning activity. In these companies, the product/marketing managers working closely with the R&D managers, were generally entrusted with the responsibility for first, the collection, development and evaluation of ideas for potential products; and secondly, the maintenance of current knowledge on competitive products and their effects on the company's market share; and thirdly, the development of detailed statistics and graphs with respect to the company's existing products and markets including profit margins and sales and market trends. The information provided by the product/ marketing managers enabled the company's top management to identify the current phase of the company's products in their respective life cycles and, consequently, to initiate the development work to replace the products that had reached their stage of maturity.

Finally, another approach which was used by a limited number of companies, though, refers to the product life cycle (PLC) concept as a means of monitoring the individual product profits and formulating product plans and marketing strategies.

> It (i.e. the PLC concept) highlights gaps in the product range, which could arise in the future due to reduction in profit margins as the products enter their maturity and decline stages. R&D resources can be specifically directed towards either formulating new products or redesigning the existing ones, which will generate the profits at the required time in the future, and compensate for the decline arising from current products.
>
> General Manager of a company using the PLC concept

The weak service identification process

Despite the importance of weak service identification, the marketing literature is quite salient on this topic. The study by Argouslidis and McLean (2004) of the UK financial services industry, revealed that an auditing mechanism exists with which most financial institutions periodically screen their range of financial services. In larger financial institutions there is some kind of documentation, ranging from standardized checklists with pre-defined audit criteria to sophisticated computerized auditing mechanisms. Given the extensive use of computers in business operations, financial organizations can monitor the performance of their services on a daily basis. However, the systematic audits are conducted annually in order to make sure that every service in the range generated satisfactory sales volume and profitability and that all financial services were delivered in a way that satisfied the needs of customers.

The audit criteria for identifying weak products

The investigation of the weak product identification process provides insights into the product performance dimensions/criteria generally considered by companies in order to identify weak products.

In Table 9.1, we present the weak product identification/audit criteria which have been uncovered by a number of studies in the USA, for example, Rothe (1970), Eckles (1971), Pletcher (1973) and Hise and McGinnis (1975), and in the UK, for example, Avlonitis and Hart (1985) and Avlonitis (1986).

As shown in Table 9.1, profitability is extremely important in identifying weak products as candidates for revitalization/elimination in both industrial and consumer products' companies.

Table 9.1   **Audit criteria for identifying weak products**

Study	Audit criteria
Rothe (1970) Sample: 174 consumer goods companies	• Sales volume • Product volume • Market share • Share of company's sales • Market share trend • % of actual/forecast sales volume • % of actual/projected production
Eckles (1971) Sample: 7 veterinary and 3 electrical manufacturing companies	• Profit margin • Past sales volume • Future sales volume • Inventory requirements • Competitive activity • Total generic demand
Pletcher (1973) Sample: 22 small home appliance manufacturers	• Profitability • Sales trend • Cost compared to competition • Unit sales • Gross margin trend • Dollar sales • Market growth rate • Market share
Hise and McGinnis (1975) Sample: 96 industrial companies from FORTUNE 500	• Future sales volume • Return on investment (ROI) • Past sales volume • Future sales potential • Market share trend • Executive time • Price trend • Operational problems • Competitive activities
Avlonitis and Hart (1985) Sample: 166 consumer and industrial companies	• Past sales volume • Profit margin/contribution • Price trends • Share of company's sales • Share versus resources utilized • Stock levels • Market share • Market growth rate • Service levels • Future service volume • Operational problems • Actual versus projected product loading • Product position on its life cycle curve • Customer acceptance • Activities of competitors
Avlonitis (1986) Sample: 114 engineering companies	• Profitability • Future sales volume • Past sales volume • Competitive activity • Operational problems (e.g., marketing, production, etc.) • Share of company's sales • Product's position on the PLC • Market growth rate • Market share

Crystal Pepsi: low profitability pulls it off the market

PepsiCo launched Crystal Pepsi in the USA in 1993 with a full-scale media campaign with Van Halen's hit song *Right now* as the background music theme. Pepsi Cola positioned this new cola as the 'clear alternative,' to normal dark-colored colas. Most clear sodas were lemon or lime flavoured, but this would supposedly retain the cola's flavour. This soft drink was a colourless soda that tasted like a cola.

Although initial sales were good, they fell, quickly considerably below targeted figures. As a result the product was no longer turning a good profit, so PepsiCo decided to withdraw it from the market.

Two additional criteria related to the product's sales trend, namely 'past sales volume' and 'future sales volume' were also rated as very important. Grouping these two criteria with the profitability criterion indicates that companies view financial data and the overall profitability as most important for the recognition of weak products. The next two criteria, namely 'competitive activities' and 'operational problems', which may be defined as moderately important, indicate a secondary consideration of the product's performance relative to competitive products and the product's compatibility with technical efficiency standards and the company's production and marketing operations.

Although 'market share' and 'market growth rate' are moderately important criteria for identifying weak consumer products, these two criteria along with the 'products' position on the PLC' criterion are used to a limited extent by industrial goods companies. However, these three criteria are very useful indicators of a product's performance. When they are jointly considered, they tend to reflect the total picture of the product's market situation and their use for the formulation of the company's product strategy in general and for the recognition of weak products in particular have been strongly emphasized in the normative literature (Kotler, 1965; Boston Consulting Group, 1972; Wind and Claycamp, 1976). However, the relatively low ranking of these criteria may be attributed to first, the lack of appreciation on behalf of management of the implications of these criteria upon the company's product planning and overall performance; secondly, the lack of marketing information, particularly in smaller companies which normally lack a marketing research unit; and thirdly, the extremely long life cycles of some of the product lines of industrial goods companies.

However, the identification of weak products is important not only for manufacturers but also for retail companies as well. This is because the finite shelf space in retail stores can accommodate only part of the wide and deep assortment of products of numerous suppliers-manufacturers, who are competing for as much retail space as possible. Despite the trend towards larger stores, space still remains a scarce and valuable resource for retailers (McGoldrick, 2002). It is common practice for a retail buyer to undertake periodic range reviews in order to make decisions on alterations to the width and depth of the product range, including product delisting (Biong, 1993; Davies, 1994; Davies and Treadgold, 1999). However, despite the significance of product delisting to retail companies, the empirical research on delisting decisions is indeed very limited (Davies, 1994; Davies and Treadgold, 1999).

Davies (1994) unveiled the following audit criteria used by retail buyers in order to red-flag candidates for delisting:

- sales volume too low;
- buyers' opinions of potential sales;

- change of retailer's strategy;
- price too high;
- gross and net margins too low;
- wrong price point;
- others' opinion of potential sales;
- growth margin too low;
- poor quality;
- poor delivery;
- price rise too high.

According to this study, the most important audit criterion that retailers use for identifying candidates for elimination is a too low sales volume, while other theoretically prominent reasons for delisting, such as poor delivery, poor quality and price rise (from the supplier) being too high, are not found to be important determinants of delisting decisions. 'Profitability' (either as gross or net margin) is rated as an audit criterion of only secondary importance in identifying candidates for delisting.

The audit criteria for identifying weak services

Service providers use similar criteria as industrial products' companies for recognizing candidates for elimination. Argouslidis and McLean (2004) found eight criteria for identifying weak financial services. In order of importance, these criteria are as follows:

- profitability;
- sales volume;
- market growth potential;
- customers' perceptions;
- activities of competitors;
- market share;
- position in the life cycle curve;
- operational problems.

It is obvious that the importance of 'profitability' and 'sales' as audit criteria in manufactured companies as well as retailing companies is also reported in the case of services, followed by 'market growth potential'. 'Customers' perceptions' and 'activities of competitors' which are considered as moderately important, while 'market share', 'position in the life cycle curve' and 'operational problems' are audit criteria with limited importance in identifying weak services.

'Profitability' is frequently cited as an audit criterion for the identification of candidates for elimination in the financial services industry. Measuring the profitability of financial services is not easy, if one considers the special nature of services in general and of financial services in particular. However, it must be noted that banks, building societies and insurance companies are not using a full cost method to calculate profitability. Instead, they use a system that monitors the net contribution of individual financial services. As such, financial institutions evaluate the profitability of an individual financial service by taking into account its variable costs, the risk level that it encompasses and the level of equity capital that it generates. Data on the profit performance are collected by internal profitability surveys or by some electronic databases. Despite the importance of profitability, not all financial services with an unsatisfactory profit performance are always red-flagged. Some large companies report that sometimes they faced the need to keep in the range unprofitable financial services, for example, as part of a full-line policy.

Table 9.2 Relative importance of audit criteria for recognizing weak services

	Mean*	Standard deviation
Past sales volume	4.27	0.93
Profit margins	4.06	0.98
Price evolution	3.44	1.10
Contribution to total company sales	3.49	1.05
Market share	3.56	1.20
Market growth rate	3.87	1.03
Competitive activities	3.78	1.00
Customers' reactions and comments	4.17	0.99
Position of service in the PLC	3.28	1.16
Future sales volume	3.98	0.87
Results of market research	3.30	1.21
Operational problems	3.51	1.16

*1: little or no importance, 5: extreme importance.

Source: Avlonitis et al. (2003)

'Sales volume' is the second most frequently identified audit criterion against which financial services are screened. As with profit-related information, the electronic databases of financial institutions make sales-related information readily available at any time, upon request. However regular sales volume reviews are conducted either quarterly or annually. In fact, it seems that only retail financial services are subject to regular sales volume analysis, while the sales performance of corporate financial services, which are usually custom-made, is of little or no importance.

'Market growth potential' and 'customers' perceptions' about a financial service are also extensively used as audit criteria for identifying weak financial services. In fact, larger financial institutions with a wider customer base use customer satisfaction surveys, customer indices and mystery shopping. On the other hand, smaller financial companies with a narrower customer base monitor customers' perceptions via less sophisticated ways, such as face-to-face informal discussion and deliberation.

In a recent study conducted by the authors of this book in various service industries in Greece (for example, banking, insurance, freight forwarding), it was found that there are three main audit criteria for identifying candidates for elimination, namely 'past sales volume', 'customers' reactions and comments', and 'profit margins' (see Table 9.2).

In general, 'sales', 'profits', 'customers' perceptions' as well as 'customers' reactions and comments' are considered as the most important audit criteria for identifying weak services, while the studies regarding the identification of weak products do not report any customer-related audit criterion. This finding can be easily attributed to the inseparability of production and consumption of services, as this service characteristic makes service providers more susceptible to customer judgements.

Internal and external influences on the identification of weak products

An attempt has been made by one of the authors of this book (Avlonitis, 1986) to uncover the impact that certain contextual organizational and environmental factors exert on the importance of the audit criteria used to identify weak products. In doing so, he first carried out a factor analysis to come up with a more manageable set of these criteria. From this analysis, three factors/dimensions emerged, namely:

- *Market trends*: this dimension is heavily loaded on three criteria, two of which, namely, 'market growth rate' and 'product's position on the PLC' reflect the product's market trends.
- *Market performance*: this dimension consists of criteria which involve the use of external data and require some form of marketing research and/or market intelligence studies. These criteria are: 'market share', 'future sales volume', 'competitive activity' and 'market growth rate'.
- *Financial performance*: this dimension comprises criteria which involve the use of internal data already available or easily obtainable through the company's accounting system, namely, 'past sales volume', 'profitability' and 'share of company' sales.

Further analysis revealed that the emphasis given in each of these dimensions is influenced by certain contextual organizational and environmental factors such as company size, product diversity, operations technology, market competition, and the degree of technological change. More specifically:

- The systematic analysis of market share, sales trends and competitive activities (namely, market performance) is usually conducted in the larger companies which tend to have formal marketing research departments and/or personnel responsible for the collection, analysis and interpretation of marketing information.
- The importance of the product's market performance, as a weak product identification factor, is also enhanced by product diversity. The product management system, which is usually used by companies producing a variety of products, may help to account for this finding. Indeed, one of the main responsibilities of product managers is to 'ensure adequate market information is available to effect, in conjunction with other departments, an objective assessment of the current product lines and the results of new product investigations'.
- There is a positive relationship between the market trends as a weak product identification factor and product-oriented technologies change. This relationship implies that, in the companies operating in an innovative environment, it is the anticipation of future trends and the planning of strategies to handle future problems (for example, development of new products) rather than the evaluation of the existing products' current problems that lead to the detection of weak products.
- The importance of the product's financial performance as a weak product identification factor is enhanced by market competition. One plausible explanation of this finding is that when a company is facing strenuous competition there is a need for internal control of operations and the use of such adaptive devices as internal audit and budgeting, so that management can adapt the company effectively to varying competitive pressures.

The lesson to be learnt from these results is that the audit criteria are not applied universally. Instead, companies seem to take a contingency approach and depending on the internal and external environment they use different criteria for identifying weak products.

Internal and external influences on the identification of weak services

In a service context, it has been also found that the importance attached to alternative audit criteria depends on the type of market in which the financial service is offered, business strategy, market orientation, competition, legislation, and rhythm of technological change (Argouslidis and McLean, 2004). More specifically:

1 'Sales volume' and 'activities of competitors' are significantly more important audit criteria for retail than corporate financial services. In contrast, 'profitability' seems to be a more important consideration for corporate than for retail financial services. These results may be attributed to the fact that retail officers tend to be preoccupied with sales maximization for retail services (such as current accounts), even when the latter are not profitable. By contrast, in corporate services where the delivery process is labour intensive and costly (Stevenson, 1989), it seems more difficult to ignore the cost and pursue sales maximization even in the short-term.

2 Financial institutions acting as 'fast imitators' value market share (as an audit criterion) significantly more than 'cost reducers', 'slow imitators' and 'technological innovators'. A plausible explanation of the latter relationship is that fundamentally 'technological innovators' are more concerned with market leadership, while 'fast imitators' focus on ways in which they can increase market share (Kotler, 2003). Further, 'slow imitators' tend to pay significantly less attention to the life cycle stage of their service than 'technological innovators', while the latter are less concerned with the operational problems of their services than 'cost reducers'.

3 Market orientation has the most the most profound impact on the importance of all audit criteria examined. Even the importance of relatively unimportant audit criteria like 'service's position on the life cycle curve' is enhanced by market orientation as well as by its components. Market orientation also has a positive impact on the relative importance of 'customers' perceptions'.

4 The legislative environment exerts a significant positive influence on the importance of 'market share' and 'sales volume' and a stronger positive impact on 'customers' perceptions'.

5 There is a positive relationship between the rhythm of technological change and the use of 'operational problems' as an audit criterion for identifying weak services in the portfolios of financial companies. Apparently, when more advanced technological solutions are available, financial institutions are more willing to confront the operational problems of their services. Similarly, there is a positive relationship between the rhythm of technological change and 'customers' perceptions'. This result finds support in the financial services' literature, which stresses the importance of financial institutions consulting their customers prior to introducing a kind of new technology in the delivery process of financial services (for example, Zeithaml and Gilly, 1987; Moutinho and Meidan, 1989). Finally, the rhythm of technological change is positively related to the audit criterion of 'activities of competitors'. This result shows that financial organizations realize that new technologies can help gaining competitive advantage (because of reduced processing time and less cost) and, therefore, they monitor how competitors are exploiting new technological solutions for enhancing their delivery and operating systems.

> Two UK-based insurance companies (one large- and one small-sized) had in their range a residential fire insurance policy. After an audit of their range, the large insurance company found that the market share of its product was the fifth highest in the market, which was considered low and the range management team decided to red flag it, with the decision to eliminate as an option. However, despite that the market share for the equivalent product of the small insurance company was the twelfth highest in the market, there was no intention whatsoever to consider it a candidate for elimination.

Clearly, the contingency approach that has been found in the identification of weak products, is also followed in the case of services. In other words, service providers tend to accommodate the audit criteria for identifying weak services on a number of internal and external conditions.

The weak product revitalization process

In the second stage of the revitalization/elimination process, management attempts to diagnose the causes for the unsatisfactory performance of the previously identified products and to generate alternative corrective or remedial actions that are able to restore the performance of these products.

The weak product revitalization decision differs from the traditional mature product strategies (for example, product modification, 'take-off' strategies and 'recycle' strategies, Bell, 1979) in that:

1 it is a defensive rather than an offensive strategy since its objective is not so much to send a product into a period of renewed growth by exploiting new opportunities, as to prevent a product's decline by restoring its performance to acceptable levels, and

2 it applies to products which exhibit unacceptable performance regardless of their position in the product life cycle (PLC).

Indeed, if we were to introduce into the discussion the BCG's market growth-market share matrix (see Chapter 4), then we would argue that the weak product revitalization decision applies equally well to 'problem children', and 'dogs', which are on the growth and mature/decline stages of their respective life cycles, respectively.

The nature of the weak product revitalization decision dictates that this particular decision should be treated explicitly together with the product elimination decision. Indeed, these two decisions represent the two key alternative courses of action a company can undertake in response to either current or projected unsatisfactory product performance. Also, both of these decisions require a routine performance evaluation of the product line, designed to identify products, which exhibit unacceptable performance ('weak' or 'problem' products) and which, unless they have a realistic chance of being restored to strength (weak product revitalization decision), they should be dropped (product elimination decision).

A detailed process for product revitalization has been proposed by one of the authors of this book (Avlonitis, 1985). This process is conceptualized as a multiple-stage sequential process as shown in Figure 9.2.

The process begins with a 'diagnostic' routine, which makes up the first stage. The overall intention of the 'diagnostic' routine is to define the causes of the product's unsatisfactory performance and generate alternative corrective actions, which are considered and evaluated by management at the second and third stages of the process, respectively. When management decides that a corrective action has a good possibility of making the product competitive again, then it proceeds to implement this particular action. If, on the other hand, management decides that no corrective action is feasible and/or judges that the product's situation does not justify further improvements and investment, then the next logical step is to undertake a detailed investigation to determine whether elimination is, indeed, indicated.

In the remainder of the chapter, we present this process in detail, based on empirical studies that are reported in the pertinent literature.

Diagnosis of weak industrial products

If a product's performance deviates from the established norms on the various performance measures used by the company, for example, profitability, sales volume, and so on, then some form of 'diagnosis' takes place.

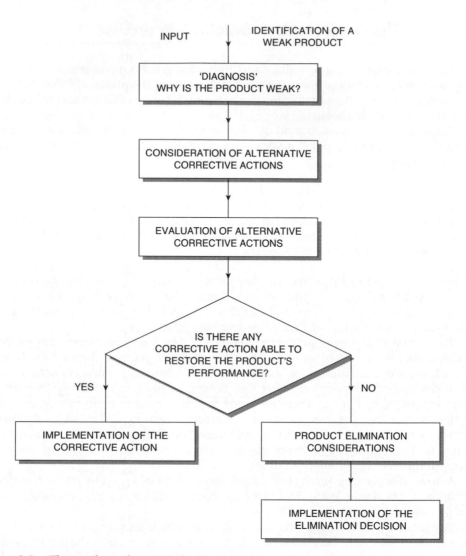

Figure 9.2 **The weak product revitalization process**
Source: Avlonitis (1985)

Three phases of a 'diagnostic' routine were identified by one of the authors of this book (Avlonitis, 1985) in a study of UK manufacturing companies:

Phase 1: The 'diagnosis' routine was generally started with a knowledge, based on management's experience and judgement, about the sources of deviation in the product's performance. Seven kinds of sources of deviation generally considered by management were identified, namely:

1 production methods;
2 product's cost structure;
3 product's design;
4 competitive activities;
5 customer requirements;
6 product's market price;
7 product's market share.

Taking into consideration the frequency of occurrence of each of these sources of deviation, Avlonitis (1985) concluded that management in industrial goods companies attempts to explain a product's weak performance by concentrating its attention more on internal and easily manipulated sources of deviation, for example, the product's cost and design, rather than on external and market-related ones, for example, competitors' policies, market trends, and so on. This behaviour can be explained on the following grounds: first, in most cases management recognized weak products on the basis of their financial performance and as a result the scope of its attention was limited to sources of deviation which tend to affect directly the product's profitability, namely, cost, design, and so on; secondly, the pressures on management to act quickly to bring the deviant product's performance to an acceptable or predicted level, tended to force it to jump to conclusions about sources of deviation which did not require a thorough investigation and considerable time and expense; finally, 'organizational learning', whereby the technically trained and oriented managements in industrial goods companies tend to 'diagnose' problems in terms specifically relevant to their specialization, may also help to explain this behaviour.

Phase 2: the identification of the sources of deviation is followed by an investigation within these sources to define the causes of deviation. This investigation is based on in-house studies which are usually conducted by the accounting and/or engineering departments and they aim at measuring the total costs associated with the product; analysing the product's design and production methods; and making recommendations regarding the feasibility of reducing the product's costs. In these meetings, the opinions of the sales force (sales representatives, sales engineers, product/marketing engineers) are sought regarding the weak performance of the product. These people, being in contact with the customers and occasionally with the competitors, are in a good position to collect significant bits of information.

Phase 3: the investigation into the sources of deviation is followed by the preparation of memos or reports stating the causes of the product's poor performance. These documents are generally studied during the 'general management' or 'product planning' meetings, where decisions regarding corrective actions are taken. However, it was found that a product's weak performance is less often the result of a single cause than the product of a variety of causes, which are frequently interrelated. In the study of Avlonitis (1985), a number of statements were made by respondents in explaining the unsatisfactory performance of specific products, namely:

- uncompetitive price;
- production problems (for example, inferior technology, not easy to assemble and so on);
- not mass produced-uneconomic batches;
- too costly to produce and market;
- high costs to manufacture;
- overengineered;
- competitors dominated the market;
- customer requirements not as expected;
- low selling price.

Diagnosis of weak services

In services, the only relevant study has been conducted by Argouslidis and McLean (2003) in the UK financial services industry. According to the results of the qualitative leg of their research, in the majority of the financial institutions examined, there was some kind of an analytical procedure which aimed at identifying the causes of a financial service's deviant performance. There was no blueprint to follow in order to find out why a financial service had a deviant performance. Instead, informal procedures were taking place between the functional areas that have red-flagged the service.

It must be noted though that the diagnostic procedure was not activated when the cause of the deviation of a financial service was very obvious from a problem situation triggering engagement into the service elimination decision-making process or from the regular review of the service range. For example, when a financial service was made illegal by a new regulation there was no need for financial institutions to engage in the diagnostic procedure.

> In 1999 the legislative authorities for the UK financial services sector dictated the withdrawal of a special financial product, namely the tax-exempt special savings accounts (TESSAs) and financial institutions had to comply. Because in this case no retention option was open to financial institutions, there was no engagement into the stage of revitalization.

The areas financial organizations are looking at in order to find the cause of deviation depend on the symptom. Thus, if poor profitability is the symptom, they check the cost structure of the financial service as well as the methods that they use to price it. If the symptom is poor sales, financial institutions tend to review their sales strategies, talk to the sales people, re-think their promotional strategies or check their service range for the identification of services that are cannibalizing the sales performance of the weak one.

Similarly, in case an operational problem is the symptom, financial institutions tend to review the service delivery process to identify what the problem is. Finally, if an unfavorable customer reaction is detected during the auditing process, financial organizations are getting in contact with customers, either through their customer-contact personnel or through an ad hoc piece of qualitative market research (for example, focus groups).

Alternative corrective actions for revitalizing weak products

Having established the dimensions and the causes of a product's weak performance, management then proceeds to consider corrective action, which, if brought about, could restore the competitive standing of the weak product.

In Table 9.3, we present the alternative corrective actions that have been identified in various studies from the early 1970s onwards. It becomes evident that these corrective actions focus either on changes in the marketing mix elements (for example, price, product), or the development of new markets. Below, we discuss these actions in detail.

Cost reductions/product modifications: one of the first steps in revitalizing a weak product is an active search for alternative means of reducing the product's cost. The studies conducted by the accounting and/or engineering departments during the 'diagnostic routine' (see Phase 2, p. 187) tend to reveal the ways by which the product's cost could be reduced including: redesigning/modifying the product; better buying of components and materials; and investing in capital equipment, tooling and plant. Product redesign (modification) aims either at reducing costs (thus allowing a greater flexibility in assigning a price to the product) by eliminating waste whatever its form through a value engineering exercise, or improving the product's quality, functional features or style, thus improving reliability and meeting customer requirements.

Price changes consideration: price changes are also considered as an alternative corrective action. The direction of such changes, however, (either upward or downward) tends

Table 9.3   **Alternative corrective actions for revitalizing weak products**

Study	Corrective actions
Eckles (1971) Sample: 7 veterinary and 3 electrical manufacturing companies	• Additional promotion • Product change • Package change • Price change • Cost analysis • New market development • Formula change
Hise and McGinnis (1975) Sample: 96 industrial companies from *Fortune* 500	• Product modifications • Increase in product's price • Increased sales force effort • Increased promotional expenditure • Decrease in product's price • Additional market research • Decreased promotional expenditure
Avlonitis (1986) Sample: 114 engineering companies	• Product modifications and improvement • Increase in the product's prices • Development of new markets • Increased effort by sales force • Increased promotional expenditure • Decrease in the product's price • Changed channels of distribution
Avlonitis and Hart (1985) Sample: 166 consumer and industrial companies	• Increase in effort by sales force • Cost reduction • Product modification/reformulation • Production efficiency improvements • Price decrease • Quality improvements • Sales promotion increase • Development of new markets • Product range reduction • Product range extension • Market concentration • Packaging changes • Distribution improvements • Product factoring/sourcing • Price increase • Print-media advertising increase • Change in channels of distribution • Warranty and guarantee extension

to be influenced by the company's pricing policy. Specifically, the possibility of increasing the price of a product as a form of corrective action is generally considered by those companies whose pricing policy is based on the objective of maintaining or increasing market share through a combination of cost and market oriented pricing, generally considering downward price changes as a form of corrective action. The same applies to the companies whose pricing policy is based upon the objective of meeting competition through a competitive oriented pricing approach.

Promotion changes consideration: changes in the product's promotion strategy provide another way for product rejuvenation. However, industrial companies do not use this corrective action extensively. This, of course, reflects the executives' attitudes towards promotion as well as their promotion policies. Promotion is not regarded as a significant element of their marketing strategy; heavy emphasis is placed on personal selling while sales promotion and print media advertising are used as supplementary activities. Here again, the emphasis that is placed on these supplementary activities appears to be dependent upon the nature of their products and markets.

Channel changes consideration: changes in the channels of distribution as a means of revitalizing a weak product is also found to have limited application in the industrial field. In particular, the companies which are involved in the manufacture and marketing of major capital equipment regard their channels of distribution as a totally inflexible factor in their marketing strategy. Only the companies, which manufacture accessory equipment and component parts and make use of one or two middlemen, evidence a definite willingness to adjust their channel policy to meet changes in their competitive environment and/or objectives.

Development of new markets: apart from the changes in the product's physical attributes and/or marketing strategy, the development of new markets is another additional method of revitalizing a weak product. Such an action is usually considered by companies whose kind of operations and market conditions provide very little scope for changes in the product's marketing strategy.

At this point, it must be noted that, apart from reviving a seriously declining offering, product rejuvenation may also be used to reintroduce an abandoned product, with or without product adjustments by marketing it to old or new users (Berenson and Morh-Jackson, 1994). Product abandonment can occur when the company lacks the necessary resources to support it, or diagnoses an unfavourable shift in market trends. Rejuvenation or reintroduction of an abandoned product has increased possibilities of success when it has nostalgic value to the target market, as it may evoke pleasant memories of the 'good old days'.

Cabbage Patch dolls: a success story of reviving an abandoned product

Cabbage Patch dolls had been a smash success in the USA for three years in the mid-1980s. More than 500,000 dolls were sold in 1984 and 1985. However, the dolls gradually lost market share and almost disappeared from the market. In the summer of 1989, Coleco Industries sold the production and marketing rights of Cabbage Patch dolls to the multinational toy manufacturer Hasbro Industries. The dolls were revived in the 1990s using heavy advertising and increasing shipments to big toy stores. Apparently, Hasbro extensively capitalized on the Cabbage Patch name.

Source: adapted from Berenson and Morh-Jackson (1994)

Alternative corrective actions for revitalizing weak services

As far as the corrective or remedial actions for weak services are concerned, a study by Argouslidis and McLean (2003) revealed that, if a problem arises, financial institutions follow corrective actions, when possible, in an informal manner though. Generally speaking, the alternative remedial actions for revitalizing a weak financial service resemble those for weak products, namely:

- price modifications;
- cost structure modifications;
- modifications/improvements in some of the service's attributes;
- increase the effort of sales force and customer contact personnel;
- modifications in the promotion/communications strategy;
- modifications in the service delivery process;
- modifications in the training of sales force and customer contact personnel.

The most important remedial action was found to be 'price modifications', followed by the related action 'cost structure modifications'. 'Modifications/improvements in some of the service's attributes' was reported as the third action in importance, while the fourth remedial action is 'increase in the effort of the sales force and customer contact personnel'. The remaining three actions that refer to modifications in the promotion/communications strategy, service delivery process and the training of sales force and customer contact personnel are used to a very limited extent.

The fact that 'price modifications' and 'cost modifications' are found as the most important revitalization actions reflects the importance of the pricing element of financial institutions' marketing mix, especially in the turbulent market conditions of the British financial services sector (Llewellyn and Drake, 1995; Meidan, 1996). Further, the relatively high importance of 'modifications/improvements in the attributes of a financial service' as a revitalisation action, clearly indicates that financial institutions are paying attention to the tangible component of their financial services. This marketing practice is in line with the suggested remedies to the intangibility of services in general and of financial services in particular (Shostack, 1982; Levitt, 1981; Ennew and Watkins, 1995).

It is also worth mentioning that 'increase the effort of the sales force and customer contact personnel' was found to be a moderately important remedial action, while the 'modifications in the training of sales force and customer contact personnel' do not seem to be an action that financial institutions use for reviving weak financial services. Apparently, when the cause of the deviant performance of a financial service is isolated to the front line personnel, financial institutions tend to have more confidence in the methods that they use to train their front line staff than in the way in which the latter conceive and use the acquired knowledge.

A study conducted by the authors of this book in various service industries in Greece, uncovered the most important corrective actions which are considered in rejuvenating weak services (Avlonitis et al., 2003). These actions focus, to a large degree, on the service's delivery process and comprise 'improvements in the delivery process' and 'improvements in customer service by front line personnel' and to a moderate degree on increases in the promotional efforts (particularly of the sales force) as well as 'cost reductions' and 'price modifications' (Table 9.4).

Apparently, while the general picture may show that the modifications in the delivery process and customer service is of paramount importance when attempting to remedy weak services in general, when financial services are examined, we see a limited use of corrective actions that refer to modifications in the service delivery process and the training of the sales force and customer personnel (Argouslidis and McLean, 2003).

Internal and external influences on the examination of alternative corrective actions for industrial products

The importance of alternative corrective actions for reviving weak industrial products is influenced by a number of factors relating to the internal and external environment of

Table 9.4   Relative importance of corrective actions for weak services

Corrective actions	Mean*	Standard deviation
Improvements in the delivery process	7.20	2.54
Cost reductions	5.59	3.08
Price modifications	5.59	3.03
Increase in the efforts of sales force	5.82	2.94
Increase in the promotional efforts	5.67	3.04
Intensified advertising	4.73	3.12
Market concentration	4.20	3.05
Development of new markets	4.92	2.97
Entering new channels of distribution (e.g. Internet)	4.08	3.16
Service customization to customer needs	5.47	2.85
Service standardization	5.59	2.66
Improvements in customer service by front line personnel	7.00	2.47

*1: not considered at all, 9: seriously considered.

Source: Avlonitis et al. (2003)

the company. In fact, one of the authors of this book has shown that the importance of alternative corrective actions for revitalizing weak B2B products is influenced by a number of contextual organizational and environmental factors such as company size, product diversity, operations technology, rhythm of technological change, and competitive conditions (Avlonitis, 1985). More analytically:

1   The larger companies attempt to revitalize weak products by 'increasing the efforts of the sales force' while 'decreasing the advertising budget' and by 'price reductions'. It appears that the larger companies, with greater financial resources, can sustain short-term losses that a reduction in the price of a weak product can bring about, and as a result they have a better chance to stimulate the demand for a weak product and/or to shake out weaker competitors.

2   Product diversity enhances the importance of the 'increased effort by the sales force' corrective action.

3   There is only an indication that 'price reductions' as a corrective action is more important for the companies employing primarily custom and small-batch product technologies than those employing large-batch and mass-production technologies.

4   Technological change has a largely negative impact on the importance of the various kinds of corrective action. It is easy to see the rationale for this finding. To the extent that technological change threatens a company with the obsolescence of its products, we should expect the company to seek to introduce new products into the market rather than to prolong the life of its existing products, which undergo a limited market life. Given finite resources of the company, those resources devoted to revitalize an ailing product are much less profitably invested than they might be, if available to produce, promote and distribute the product's next generation of design and applications.

5   Market competition has a positive impact on the importance of the various kinds of corrective action. It seems that to the extent that competition represents turbulence, risk and uncertainty, the company needs to by highly adaptive to be able to cope with the shifting 'arenas of battle' in the market place. The need to make creative and adaptive responses because of competition tends to push up the importance of a number of corrective actions and in particular 'price reductions' and 'development of new markets'. The emphasis placed on the first two corrective actions may be viewed as an attempt to strike a balance between selling price and promotion, both being constituent parts of sales promotion. In fact, a decision to reduce a product's price as an alternative to elimination presupposes a price-conscious market where there would be a less-than-normal beneficial reaction to promotion.

Internal and external influences on the examination of alternative corrective actions for services

In a study of financial institutions operating in UK, it has also been found that the importance of alternative remedial actions for weak financial services is affected by certain organizational and market conditions, namely method of delivery process, competition, rhythm of technological change, legislation and service diversity (Argouslidis and McLean, 2003). More specifically:

1 'Modifications/improvements in some of the service's attributes' is significantly more important remedial action for financial services which require customers to visit the financial institutions branch than for those that can be operated through alternative channels (see for example, phone banking or Internet banking). The rationale behind this finding can be found in the importance of physical evidence when customers visit the branch of a financial institution in order to use a financial service (Saunders and Watters, 1993; Ennew and Watkins, 1995). By contrast, customers using the telephone, the Internet or other means of electronic service delivery, tend to pay more attention to issues like less waiting time, convenience and simplicity during transactions with financial institutions and they are less concerned about the tangibles accompanying the financial service that they are using (for example, Birch and Young, 1997; Mols, 1999). Thus, the latter type of customers would not value so much (if they noticed them at all) remedial actions involving changes in the tangibles of financial services, such as a new cheque book.
2 Competition has a stronger influence on non-financial remedial actions. In particular, it is more strongly correlated with the remedial actions namely 'modifications in the promotions/communications strategy', 'increasing the effort of sales force and customer contact personnel' and 'modifications in the training of sales force and customer contact personnel'. A plausible explanation of this finding is that in a competitive market place, financial institutions must be flexible enough to react by emphasizing both financial efficiency and product/market strategies focused on customer care (Lewis 1995).
3 Even when the legislative environment is more intense and the technological changes in the market are more rapid the most important consideration is 'modifications in the promotions/communications strategy' in order to revitalize weak financial services.
4 Service diversity enhances the importance of 'cost structure modifications'.

Evaluation of alternative corrective actions

Having considered the means of revitalizing the performance of weak products and services, management then proceeds to determine whether a corrective action is feasible. The normative literature postulates that at this stage alternative corrective actions should be carefully and objectively evaluated and that their factual consequences should be explicitly determined by reference to choice criteria such as sales volume, market share, cash flow, return on investment (ROI), and so on, in order to select the most viable one (McSurely and Wilemon, 1973).

However, while companies seem to perceive certain criteria in evaluating corrective actions, for example, profitability, product quality/cost, total product investment, and so on, no explicit measures of consequences in terms of these criteria are attempted. In most cases management appeared to judge in some qualitative way the nature of consequences given the implementation of a particular corrective action. Only in a limited number of cases management has some more definitive approaches for predicting the outcome of a corrective action. Some of the more clearly defined approaches are those in which management is able to determine (through analysis of past sales and price data) the actual effects of various price changes on sales. Another clearly defined approach is the extrapolation of the management's past experience with the product's performance. This reliance on past experiences is evidenced by the following responses of two executives to a question about the factors that forced them to reject a particular corrective action (product modification).

> We had already spent enough money to keep the product going. We did not think that further improvements could have made the product competitive.
>
> The Engineering Executive of a large manufacturer of pumps

> Despite the engineering optimism that further cost savings could be achieved, we felt that it was not worth it, taking into consideration the product's past performance.
>
> The Marketing Director of a large manufacturer of boilers

In most companies, there exists a large reliance on judgement, discussion with other members of the company, and reliance on general past experience in selecting or rejecting a particular corrective action.

Selection/implementation of corrective action

Another interesting issue relating to product rejuvenation addresses which corrective actions are actually selected as well as when and how these actions are implemented.

Empirical evidence suggests that the weak product revitalization process in the industrial field is very much a hierarchical process (Avlonitis, 1985). In general, management begins its search for acceptable solutions to the product's problems in immediately accessible areas such as the product's cost and design; faced with repeated failures in search for an acceptable solution in familiar areas, management turns to less familiar areas, such as the product's marketing strategy, to consider feasible alternatives and select a course of corrective action. This became obvious by examining the corrective actions which were considered, evaluated and selected/rejected by management over a product's life cycle.

Indeed, the weak product revitalization process occurs at different points in time throughout the life of a product. The corrective actions actually selected and implemented by management in order to revitalize the products which had shown signs of weaknesses at an early stage of their respective life cycles include: product modifications, product improvement, price reduction, increased promotional expenditure, and changed channels of distribution.

Further trouble in the market place and/or failure of these corrective actions to provide a lasting recovery in the product's performance, required these products to undergo a further review. At this later stage, however, in which product elimination is considered as a real possibility, management attempts first, to challenge the appropriateness of the previously implemented corrective actions through a more intensive investigation and secondly, to determine the feasibility of corrective actions which had never been considered before. The corrective actions actually considered and evaluated by management at this stage include: price increases, product modifications, price reduction, product improvement, increased effort by the sales force, and increased promotional expenditure.

However, it should be stated here that not all of these corrective actions are particularly effective in making the product competitively healthy again. As the marketing director of a large manufacturer of boilers, who decided to increase the product's promotion, asserted, 'Well, promotion brought enquiries but not orders because of the price. Price was the real problem'. This is a fine point because it clearly indicates that a change in one element of the product's marketing programme (as a corrective action) should be compatible with the other elements in the programme; incompatibility can lead to waste of resources. In this case, the advertising outlays were wasted not because they were not productive as a communication exercise but because of the product's high price.

Summary

- The product revitalization/elimination decision-making process comprises four stages, namely the identification of candidates for elimination, the analysis and revitalization of weak products, the evaluation of weak products and the elimination decision-making, the implementation of the elimination decision.
- Two broad patterns of weak product identification activities exist, that is management-cycle activities, and product planning-cycle activities.
- An auditing mechanism exists with which most financial institutions periodically screen their range of financial services.
- The systematic audits are conducted annually.
- A number of alternative audit criteria have been identified, for example, profitability, sales volume, market share, operational problems, and so on.
- Profitability is extremely important in identifying weak products and services as candidates for the modification/elimination decision.
- The corrective actions for revitalizing weak products and services focus either on changes in the marketing mix elements (for example, price, product), or the development of new markets.
- The corrective action that stands out as being the most important for weak products is 'product modifications and improvement', for services in general 'improvements in the delivery process' and 'improvements in customer service by front line personnel', and for financial services in particular 'price modifications'.
- The importance of the audit criteria and corrective actions for weak products is influenced by company size, product diversity, operations technology, market competition, and the degree of technological change.
- The importance attached to alternative audit criteria and corrective actions for weak services depend on the type of market in which the financial service is offered, business strategy, market orientation, competition, legislation, and rhythm of technological change.

Questions

1   Describe the various product planning cycle activities that could be used by an electrical equipment company to identify candidates for elimination.
2   Think of a manufactured product and discuss the audit criteria that may be used to identify its problematic performance.
3   Explain the importance of modifications/improvements in the attributes of a financial service as a revitalization action.
4   Select a corrective action for a weak product and discuss how the size of the company and the intensity of competition may influence its relative importance.

References

Alexander, R. (1964) 'The death and burial of sick products', *Journal of Marketing*, 28: 1–7.

Argouslidis, P. and McLean, F. (2003) 'Service elimination decision-making: analysis of candidates for elimination and remedial actions', *Journal of Marketing Management*, 19: 307–344.

Argouslidis, P. and McLean F. (2004) 'Service elimination decision-making: the identification of financial services as candidates for elimination', *European Journal of Marketing*, 38 (11/12): 1355–81.

Avlonitis, G. (1985) 'Revitalizing weak industrial products', *Industrial Marketing Management*, 14: 93–105.

Avlonitis, G. (1986) 'The identification of weak industrial products', *European Journal of Marketing*, 20(10): 24–42.

Avlonitis, G. and Hart, S. (1985) 'Product elimination decision-making in British manufacturing industry: a conceptual framework and preliminary results', Research in Management Conference, Ashridge Management College, January.

Avlonitis, G., Gounaris, S. and Papastathopoulou, P. (2003) 'The identification of sick services', Working Paper, The Athens Laboratory of Research in Marketing (A.LA.R.M.) Athens University of Economics and Business.

Bell, M. (1979) *Marketing: Concepts and Strategy*, 3rd edition. Boston: Houghton Mifflin Company.

Berenson, C. and Morh-Jackson, I. (1994) 'Product rejuvenation: a less risky alternative to product innovation', *Business Horizons*, 37(6): 51–8.

Biong, H. (1993) 'Satisfaction and loyalty to suppliers within the grocery trade', *European Journal of Marketing*, 27(7): 21–38.

Birch, D. and Young, M.A. (1997) 'Financial services and the Internet – what does cyberspace mean for the financial services industry?', *Internet Research: Electronic Networking Applications and Policy*, 7(2): 120–8.

Boston Consulting Group (1972) *Perspectives on Experience*. Boston: Boston Consulting Group.

Davies, G. (1994) 'The delisting of products by retail buyers', *Journal of Marketing Management*, 10: 473–93.

Davies, G. and Treadgold, A. (1999) 'Buyer attitudes and the continuity of manufacturer/retail relationships', *Journal of Marketing Channels*, 7(1/2): 79–94.

Eckles, R.W. (1971) 'Product line deletion and simplification', *Business Horizons* 14: 71–7.

Ennew, C.T. and Watkins, T. (1995) 'The financial services marketing mix', in C. Ennew, T. Watkins, and M. Wright, *Marketing Financial Services*, 2nd edition. London: Butterworth Heinemann, pp. 86–95.

Hamelman, P.W. and Mazze, E.M. (1972) 'Improving product abandonment decisions', *Journal of Marketing*, 36: 20–6.

Hise, R.T. and McGinnis, M.A. (1975) 'Product elimination: practices, policies and ethics', *Business Horizons*, 18: 25–32.

Hurst, D. (1959) 'Criteria for evaluating products and product lines', Management Report No. 32, American Marketing Association: 52.

Kotler, P. (1965) 'Phasing out weak products', *Harvard Business Review*, 43: 107–18.

Kotler, P. (2003) *Marketing Management: Planning, Analysis, Control and Implementation*, 11th edition. Englewood Cliffs, NJ: Prentice Hall.

Levitt, T. (1981) 'Marketing intangible products and product intangibles', *Harvard Business Review:* 94–102.

Lewis, B.R. (1995) 'Customer care and service quality', in C. Ennew, T. Watkins, and M. Wright (eds), *Marketing Financial Services*, 2nd edition. London: Butterworth Heinemann, 193–211.

Llewellyn, D. and Drake, L. (1995) 'Pricing', in C. Ennew, T. Watkins, and M. Wright (eds), *Marketing Financial Services*, 2nd edition. London: Butterworth Heinemann, pp. 138–73.

McGoldrick, P.J. (2002) *Retail Marketing*, 2nd edition. London: McGraw-Hill.

McSurely, H.B. and Wilemon, D.L. (1973) 'A product evaluation, improvement and removal model', *Industrial Marketing Management*, 2: 319–32.

Meidan, A. (1996) *Marketing Financial Services*. London: Macmillan.

Mols, N.P. (1999) 'The Internet and the bank's distribution channel decisions', *The International Journal of Bank Marketing*, 17(6).

Moutinho, L. and Meidan, A. (1989) 'Bank customers' perceptions, innovations and new technology', *International Journal of Bank Marketing*, 7(2): 22–7.

Pletcher, B.A. (1973) 'The product elimination process in the small home appliance industry: an empirical study'. Unpublished DBA dissertation. Kent State University.

Rothe, J.T. (1970) 'The product elimination decision', *MSU Business Topics*, 18, Autumn: 45–52.

Saunders, J. and Watters, R. (1993) 'Branding Financial Services', *International Journal of Bank Marketing*, 11(6): 32–8.

Shostack, L.G. (1982) 'How to design a service', *European Journal of Marketing*, 16(1): 49–63.

Stevenson, B.D. (1989) *Marketing Financial Services to Corporate Clients*. Cambridge: Woodhead Faulkner.

Wind, Y. (1982) *Product Policy: Concepts, Methods and Strategy*. Reading, MA: Addison-Wesley.

Wind, Y. and Claycamp, H.J. (1976) 'Planning product line strategy: a matrix approach', *Journal of Marketing*, 40: 2–9.

Worthing, P.M. (1971) 'The assessment of product deletion decision indicators', in T.J. Scheiber and L.A. Madeo, *Fortran Applications in Business Administration*, Graduate School of Business Administration, University of Michigan.

Zeithaml, V.A and Gilly, M.C. (1987) 'Characteristics affecting the acceptance of retailing technologies: a comparison of elderly and non-elderly consumers', *Journal of Retail Banking*, 63(1): 49–68.

Further reading

Boatwright, P. and Nunes, J.C. (2001) 'Reducing assortment: an attribute-based approach'. *Journal of Marketing*, 50 (July), 50–63.

Putsis, W.P. Jr. and Bayus, B.L. (2001) 'An empirical analysis of firms' product line decisions', *Journal of Marketing Research* 38 (February): 110–18.

10 Evaluation of Weak Products/Services and Elimination Strategies

Introduction

In the previous chapter, we discussed the identification and revitalization of weak products and services, paying particular attention to the corrective actions that can be used to improve the competitiveness of a weak product/service. If management realizes that no corrective action is feasible for the identified weak product or service, then the managerial attention shifts from the product/service itself to the impact upon the entire company of eliminating it. Certain evaluation factors related to the product elimination decision are considered to determine whether it is in the best interests of the company to eliminate or retain the product/service.

In many instances, companies decide to eliminate certain products/services. For example, Procter & Gamble has eliminated one quarter of its entire product line by selling off marginal brands and reducing the varieties of other products (Narisetti, 1997). Similarly, IBM has slashed its number of product models more than twenty fold (Narisetti, 1998). Once the decision to eliminate a product/service has been taken, its departure should be systematically planned and coordinated. At this stage, management faces further strategic choices, which have to do with the speed with which the product/service is removed and the amount of support that it is to be given during the removal stage.

It should be stated, however, that the elimination strategy might have been largely determined at an earlier stage of the product elimination process, when management made a judgement on whether or not it could prolong the life of the product/service on the market by changing its design and/or its marketing mix.

In order to provide a complete presentation of the weak product/service evaluation, and the elimination strategies, in the present chapter, we address the following questions:

- What is the weak product/service evaluation process that leads to the elimination/retention decision?
- What are the evaluation factors considered by management in order to make the deletion/retention decision?
- What internal and external influences determine the evaluation factors deemed important by management during the weak product/service evaluation process?
- What alternative elimination strategies of products and services are open to management?

- What internal and external influences determine the importance of alternative elimination strategies of products and services?
- What factors tend to influence phase-out plans and timing?
- How is the elimination decision actually implemented?

The weak product evaluation process

With respect to the evaluation and decision-making stage of the product elimination process, the normative views vary in the degree to which this stage is structured. At the one extreme is a totally unstructured approach in which management examines each weak product separately on a number of key evaluation factors such as financial considerations, marketing factors, effect on the profitability and the sales of other products (Alexander, 1964; Browne and Kemp, 1976). Alternatively, this evaluation can incorporate a more structured approach based on compensatory decision rules. All relevant considerations are tabulated with numerical weights and ratings, which permit the computation of an 'index' number indicating the degree of product desirability (Berenson, 1963; Kotler, 1965; Worthing, 1971).

Despite the aforementioned normative literature, empirical evidence does not support the existence of a formalized procedure for evaluating weak products. An extensive investigation conducted by one of the authors of the present book in a sample of UK engineering companies, revealed a lack of formal evaluation (Avlonitis, 1984, 1993).

However, this is not to be thought of as being necessarily synonymous with lack of systematic thinking. The interviewed companies appeared to develop more-or-less clear perceptions of what factors need investigation in evaluating a weak product and in making the retention/elimination decision.

> Ensuring that the capacity released can be absorbed by either the replacement product or the remaining products is our primary consideration.
>
> The Sales Manager of a large manufacturer of automatic control systems
>
> Any product that has to be eliminated must be replaced from a financial point of view, or you must double the sales of what is left; if you knock a product you must know where to find money.
>
> The Marketing Director of a medium-sized manufacturer of compressors
>
> Finding an appropriate substitute for the customer is our main concern in deciding to drop a product.
>
> The Marketing Manager of a small manufacturer of electrical equipment

The financial and marketing implications of a product's removal tend to dominate the management's thinking, and, as a result, the involvement of the accounting and sales/marketing functions tend to occur most frequently at this stage of the product elimination process. Other determinant factors included customer relationships, the product's contribution to overheads, the product's contribution to the sales of other products in the range, the impact of the product's removal upon the company's 'full-line' policy.

However, in the study by Avlonitis (1984), it was found that the problem situation that triggers the elimination consideration initially is usually more influential towards forming management's decision rather than the evaluation process itself. This is particularly true when the company develops a new product to replace the one under evaluation. In fact, the intensity and nature of the weak product evaluation process was found to be dependent on whether or not a new product was available to replace the one under evaluation as well as on the importance of the role played by the product within the company's environment.

When a new product is planned to drive-out the one under evaluation, the management's primary concern is the identification and evaluation of the human, physical, and financial resources committed to it, in order to determine what and when released resources could be shifted to the production and marketing of the new (replacement) product. In addition, management also has to carefully consider the resistance that the sales force and the customers might put forth regarding the replacement of the existing product. In order to pre-empt the 'sales force resistance' some companies tend to keep the development of the replacement product secret. Attempts to pre-empt 'customer resistance' usually involve 'customer consultation' during development of the replacement product.

In those cases where the product of minor importance to the company's activities is to be dropped completely, the evaluation process is simple and straightforward and its impact upon the formation of the management's decision is generally of the secondary importance. The subjective opinions of the sales force regarding the possibility of residual customer demand and the marketing implications of the product's removal is generally sought, while a stock evaluation has to be conducted to assess the product's inventory, with the objective to clear it out before the product's elimination.

When evaluation involves products that account for a significant part of the company's resources and sales turnover (for example, 15–30 per cent) and play an important role within the company and vis-à-vis its users, the evaluation process requires intensive bargaining and persuasion among the departmental members of the company and between the company and its customers. In these cases, the effects of the product's elimination upon customer relationships and sales of other products in the range have to be carefully assessed. The ability of the other products to take its place has to be analysed and the future employment prospects of the people attached to the manufacture of the product have to be determined. The impact of the elimination upon the fixed and working capital invested has to be analysed and the company has to decide how previous profit levels could be maintained. This last issue is the most significant and contentious one and involves a budgeting routine. A budget, without the product under evaluation, has to be prepared to provide some guidelines as to how previous profit levels could be maintained. An increase in the sales of the company's other products may be required, and/or a drastic reduction in the amount of overheads must be thoroughly examined as they may encounter political impasses, which in turn could cause temporary delays.

It is clear from the foregoing discussion that the more important and contentious the outcome of the elimination decision on the company's overall activities, the more detailed the analysis of the impact of the product's removal on the company's performance.

Unilever is pruning its product portfolio

Unilever announced that it will pump an additional $1.6 billion into marketing its heavily pruned portfolio of 400 brands during the next five years. Last year, it spent $5.6 billion promoting 1,600 brands worldwide.

The company is undertaking a review of its brands that will leave it with three tiers of brands, for which it intends to marshal greater resources. All will be ranked No. 1 or No. 2 in their categories or markets.

Unilever last week said that the larger marketing budget will be funded partly by a broad new programme to streamline operations that should generate an expected annual savings of $1.6 billion by 2004. The programme includes layoffs of 25,000 workers over five years, or 10 per cent of Unilever's global work force.

Unilever has said it will have a top tier of around fifty international 'power' brands with the potential to cross both countries and product sectors, such as Calvin Klein fragrances, Dove soap and Lipton tea. Its second tier will be brands that share an international positioning but whose names may be different. The third grouping will incorporate 'local jewels' with strong market positions, good margins and robust growth.

The majority of Unilever products facing the axe are in food, a segment that accounts for 1,000 of the company's current brand total. In addition, laundry products, Unilever's biggest and oldest business, has 380 brand names that must be reduced to six or seven 'positionings' with several brands in each.

Source: Bidlake (2000)

Weak service evaluation process

The results of a recent study by Argouslidis (2003) in the UK financial services industry suggest that there are no differences as to the evaluation process between products and services. The large majority of the studied financial institutions conducted an evaluation in order to assess the effect that an elimination decision could have on various areas of the business. The broad objective of the evaluation stage is to make sure that the overall cost (not only in financial terms but also in terms of marketing and human resources) of withdrawing financial services is not greater than the cost of a retention decision.

This importance, notwithstanding, evaluation is not conducted unquestionably in all elimination cases. For example, when a new regulation forced financial institutions to comply by eliminating a financial service, there is no retention alternative and as a result there is no need for an evaluation of the impact of the elimination decision.

Moreover, even if there is a retention alternative, the evaluation process may be skipped because of the low importance of the candidate for elimination (as far as the service's contribution to the company's sales and profits), as management knows in advance that the impact of eliminating such a service on the company is minimal.

Evaluation factors for weak products

A number of studies which have been conducted in the USA and UK have uncovered the evaluation factors considered by companies in order to decide on the elimination or retention of a product. In the USA, the relevant studies have been undertaken by Rothe (1970), Eckles (1971) and Pletcher (1973), while in the UK by one of the authors of this book (Avlonitis, 1984, 1993). The evaluation factors that have been proposed by these researchers are presented in Table 10.1.

Table 10.1   **Weak product evaluation factors**

Study	Evaluation factors
Rothe (1970) Sample: 174 consumer goods companies	• Product profitability • Market position • Product investment • Product costs • Company alternatives
Eckles (1971) Sample: 7 veterinary and 3 electrical manufacturing companies	• Past costs • Future costs • Past profitability • Future profitability • Scope of line • Company new product research • Consumer satisfaction • Usage of product facilities • Production problems • Marketing problems
Pletcher (1973) Sample: 22 small home appliance manufacturers	• Profitability • Sales trend • Cost compared to competition • Unit sales • Gross margin trend • Dollar sales • Market growth rate • Market share • Price trend • Product effectiveness • Channel reactions • Service • Competitive action • Consumer awareness • Saturation level • Variable cost trend • Product line policy • Product interaction • Compatibility of distribution • Substitute products • Company image • New product potential • Organized intervention • Modification potential • Executive time • Emotional involvement
Avlonitis (1984) Sample: 114 engineering companies	• New product potential • Product's elimination effect on sales of other products • Product's elimination effect on customer relationships • Product's elimination effect on profitability of other products via production O/H allocation • Reallocation of capital and facilities to other opportunities • Product's elimination effect on 'full-line' policy • Release of executive time spent on the product • Existence of substitutes to satisfy the customer • Product's elimination effect on the profitability of other products via selling O/H allocation

(Continued)

Table 10.1 **(Continued)**

Study	Evaluation factors
	• Product's elimination effect on the fixed and working capital
	• Product's elimination effect on corporate image
	• Competitive moves in case the product is eliminated
	• Product's elimination effect on the profitability of other products via distribution O/H allocation
	• Product's elimination effect on employee relationships
	• Organized intervention (trade unions)
Avlonitis (1993) Sample: 166 consumer and industrial companies	• Product's market potential • Existence of substitutes to satisfy customer • Product's elimination effect on company sales volume • Availability of new product • Re-allocation of resources to other opportunities • Product's elimination effect (PEE) on customer/trade relations • PEE on sales and profits of other products • PEE on recovery of overheads • Product's contribution to profit centre • PEE on working capital (e.g. stock) • PEE on 'full-line' policy • PEE on company image • PEE on capacity utilization • Re-allocation of executive and selling time • PEE on employee relationships • Competitive reaction to elimination • Interchangeability (communization) of companies • PEE on fixed capital • PEE on distribution (e.g. loss of shelf space)

All in all, considerable emphasis is placed on the evaluation factors that are concerned with the financial and marketing implications of product's elimination (for example, in profitability, sales), reflecting the high product investment costs that companies generally incur and the importance of individual orders and/or customers in the industrial field, respectively.

Further, 'new product potential', 'product's market potential', 'availability of new product', 'existence of substitutes to satisfy customers' were found in the studies of Avlonitis among the most important evaluation factors. The emphasis placed upon these factors largely substantiates the argument put forward in the weak product evaluation process (see the weak product evaluation process, p. 199) that the intensity and nature of the evaluation process depends, among other things, on whether or not a new product is available to replace the one under evaluation. This finding also implies that the elimination decision is not independent of the new product decision in the companies manufacturing industrial products. One of the most frequently occurring problem situations leading to product elimination in the industrial field is the development of a new product.

Further, the evaluation factors that are concerned with the product elimination's effects upon corporate image, employee relationships, competitive moves and organized intervention are of low importance. One possible explanation for this result is that they tend to be product-specific, in that the emphasis placed upon them tends to vary with the importance of the product under evaluation, measured in terms of the percentage that it accounts for of the company's resources and sales. In fact, unless the product

Table 10.2   Factors for evaluating weak services and their dimensions

	Mean*	Standard deviation	First dimension: market considerations	Second dimension: efficient re-allocation of resources	Third dimension: no-drop cost
Market potential	7.39	2.37	0.556		
Reactions of competitors	4.40	2.92	0.768		
Impact on corporate image	5.44	2.98	0.719		
Impact on the relations with customers	6.21	2.76	0.651		
Existence of alternative services	6.47	2.82	0.490		
Utilization of sales force and executives	5.75	2.74		0.788	
Ability of redirecting resources to other activities	5.85	2.68		0.774	
Impact on total company sales	6.71	2.56		0.504	
Impact on the personnel's professional prospects	4.03	2.67		0.549	
Impact on sales and profitability of other services	6.05	2.89		0.474	
Negligible cost of sustaining the service	3.91	2.60			0.762
Limited demands in infrastructure for sustaining the service	3.65	2.52			0.767
Legal and contractual commitments	4.37	3.03			0.634

*1: not considered at all, 9: seriously considered.

Source: Avlonitis, et al. (2003)

under evaluation accounts for a considerable percentage and sales turnover, no appreciable impact on the corporate image, employee relationships, competitive moves, and organized intervention is usually anticipated as a result of product elimination.

Evaluation factors for weak services

In a study that has been conducted in various service sectors in Greece (namely, insurance, banking, advertising, professional services, freight forwarding, marine, telecommunications and hotels), the authors of this book examined the importance of thirteen evaluation factors of weak services that cannot be remedied (Avlonitis et al., 2003). The results of this study shows that these factors are comparable to the factors used for evaluating weak products. More specifically, 'market potential', 'impact on total company sales', 'impact on the relations with customers' and 'existence of alternative services' are the most important evaluation factors (Table 10.2).

By using factor analysis, these thirteen factors were grouped in three dimensions, namely:

Market consideration involves capturing factors such as the market potential, the reactions of competition, the impact on the company's image or the relations with the customers.

Efficient resources re-allocation incorporates factors such as the better utilization of sales force and executives, the impact on company's total sales or the profitability on other services offered by the company, and so on.

No-drop cost includes factors such as the cost for sustaining the service or the required infrastructure to sustain the service.

In another study that has been conducted in a sample of financial institutions (Argouslidis, 2003), nine evaluation factors were found. In order of importance, these factors are as follows:

- impact on the relationship with customers;
- impact on the corporate image;
- impact on the sales of other services (cross-selling);
- impact on the profitability of other services;
- impact upon full-line policy (namely, policy to offer a full range of services);
- extent to which a similar service exists in the market to satisfy the needs of customers;
- likelihood on an organized intervention (negative press releases, adverse governmental reaction);
- impact on human resources and employee relationships;
- benefits that competitors can develop as a result of the elimination of the service.

In this study, the financial institutions of the sample rated the impact on the relationship with customers as the single most important evaluation factor. This paramount attention upon the impact on customer relationships at this stage of the service elimination decision-making process, suggests that the studied British financial institutions recognize the need for customer care that presupposes the satisfaction of customers with the composition of a financial institution's service range (Lewis, 1995). A focus on the maximization of customer satisfaction is likely to result in aversion or procrastination from the part of management to make tough decisions (including elimination decisions), which could disturb the relationships between financial institutions and their customers (Stevenson, 1989).

> We have our student portfolio and every September we try to attract as many students as possible and sell them current accounts and give them overdrafts, which is a risky business and we don't make any money. Every September we know there will be a loss from the new business that we receive. But when they graduate and get a job, at least some of these students will be willing to have an account with us, because we have been their bank when they were studying. You see, we are in a relationship business that we cannot disturb without consequences.
>
> The Marketing Manager of a large bank

The second most important evaluation factor was the 'impact on corporate image'. As we discussed earlier, manufacturing companies do not consider this factor as important. By contrast, financial institutions seem to place considerable importance on the image implications of their elimination activities. The intangibility inherent in most financial services entails considerable uncertainties and risk to customers. Hence, having developed a good image in the eyes of the customer helps minimize the risk associated with the intangible nature and provides a reassuring feeling that the financial institution is serving them well.

Another two important evaluation factors refer to the impact upon the sales and the profitability of other financial services in the range. Although some financial services did not have a knock-on effect on the sales of other services in the range, some did. Interestingly if a candidate for elimination was a 'gateway' financial service (namely, a window to cross-sell other more profitable financial services), financial institutions would seriously consider avoiding elimination, even if the elimination candidate showed poor profitability. This is not to say that at this stage the studied companies had forgotten about their high preoccupation with profitability. By contrast, their motive behind this behaviour was a further increase in the corporate profitability.

> We are selling foreign exchange, so customers come to us before going abroad to buy foreign currency. But this service doesn't make us any money because today a large part of travellers use their credit cards abroad. But we haven't eliminated and we do not intend to eliminate this service because it gives us the opportunity to talk to travellers through our customer-contact personnel and sell them other more profitable services, such as travel insurance.
>
> The Marketing Manager of a medium-sized building society

Another evaluation criterion, which was used in a moderate extent though, is the assessment of the 'impact upon full-line policy' that existed within the company. Many financial institutions (mainly large) mentioned that they wanted to offer a full range of financial services, no matter if some of them were under-performing in terms of sales and profitability.

> In our general pensions portfolio we have some services that we offer only because we want to maintain a presence in the marketplace, as being known as a major player in the pensions market. If we pulled out, somebody may say you are not a major player any more.
>
> The Marketing Director of a large insurance company

Finally, it appears that when evaluating weak services, financial service providers did not pay particular attention to factors like the extent to which a similar service exists in the market to satisfy the needs of customers; likelihood of an organized intervention; impact on human resources and employee relationships; and benefits that competitors can develop as a result of the elimination of the service.

Internal and external influences in evaluating weak products

The factors that have been found as important for evaluating weak products do not apply to all types of companies and products. Instead, the importance of these factors is influenced by product, organizational and market variables.

In order to examine the internal and external influences posed on the evaluation factors, Avlonitis (1993) has first came up with a more manageable set of evaluation factors. More specifically, by factor analysing the nineteen evaluation factors shown in Table 10.1, six factors emerged that are indicative of the following six dimensions underlying the weak product evaluation process:

Implications for company resources (financial, physical and human) are composed of evaluation factors which reflect an assessment of the implication of a product's removal for the company's resources and is particularly heavily loaded on the capacity utilization issue.

Market reaction contains evaluation factors that are concerned with the company's image and the possible reactions of competitors and customers vis-à-vis a product's deletion.

Financial implications contain evaluation factors, which are clearly concerned with the financial implications of a product's elimination, and is particularly heavily loaded on the recovery of overheads issue, which represents a classical financial issue in the literature on product elimination. This factor is also concerned with the 'employment prospects of the workforce' and this may suggest that the analysis of an impending drop decision on the labour force may be based on the financial aspects of the possible redundancies involved.

New product potential portrays management's desire to consider the development of a new replacement product, which may involve some form of standardization of components and which will provide customers with a satisfactory alternative.

Managerial (alternative opportunities) considerations contain the two evaluation factors that are concerned with the exploration of the possibility of using the funds, transferable facilities and executive abilities, freed by eliminating the product in other ventures promising better returns.

Product range considerations are composed of evaluation factors which reflect an assessment of the product range implications of a product's removal. Basically, this factor suggests that considerations regarding the impact of a product's elimination on the company's 'full-range' policy and the sales and profits of the other products in the range, tend to incorporate estimates of the likely loss of distribution (shelf-space) that the deletion decision may bring about.

Next, Avlonitis (1993) related these six dimensions of evaluation factors with specific product-related variables (problem situations), organizational variables (size, operations technology, capacity utilization, formality, attitudes towards product elimination) and market variables (market competition, technological change, market diversity, and customer dependence). The following interesting results were revealed:

1   The evaluation dimension 'implications for corporate resources' is particularly important when companies are considering to drop a routine product in order to direct the released resources to other strategic ventures, have a positive attitudes and treat product elimination as a continuous managerial function, and are not dependent upon a small number of large customers.
2   'Market reactions' are particularly considered during the evaluation of weak products in companies that have high market diversity and face strong competition. By contrast, companies do not rely on this dimension when they evaluate products that are in the decline stage of their product life cycle or perform poorly in financial terms.
3   The weak product evaluation on the basis of 'financial implications' is followed for routine products which account for a large percentage of the company's resources and sales turnover and when companies consider dropping such products in order to make way for new strategic developments. Further, this evaluation dimension is particularly important when companies employ large batch and mass-production technologies for products that face intense market competition.
4   The emphasis placed on the 'new product potential' is particularly strong in companies that evaluate a routine product as part of a product variety reduction policy, experience a rapid technological change, and have developed formal product elimination programmes.
5   'The alternative opportunities considerations' is a particularly important evaluation factor when management is dealing with a product that places a burden on the company's resources and it considers its elimination in order to make way for alternative strategic developments. Further, this evaluation dimension is emphasized by management that has positive attitudes towards product elimination. This finding may be attributed to the fact that managers with such attitudes are particularly aware of high opportunity costs that a company may incur by failing to reallocate the resources (devoted to weak products) to more productive efforts.

6 Finally, the evaluation dimension 'product range policy considerations' is particularly considered by companies that experience strong competitive pressures and have high market diversity. Indeed, to remove a product from the range in such market conditions may jeopardize not only the 'full-range' policy which may be associated with the company's image and prestige but also the sales and profits of the other products in the range. Moreover, this evaluation dimension when management is considering the reduction of variety and has developed formal product elimination programmes.

The lesson to be learnt from these results is that, the evaluation criteria are not applicable to every occasion. Instead, companies seem to take a contingency approach and depending on the internal and external environment they use different criteria for evaluating weak products.

Internal and external influences in evaluating weak services

The influence of specific internal and external variables on the importance of various weak service evaluation factors has been confirmed by Argouslidis (2003). He examined a series of organizational and environmental contextual variables such as type of service delivery, business strategy, market orientation, competition, legislation and rhythm of technological change in the market, and their impact on the evaluation factors previously discussed (see evaluation factors for weak services p. 204). His analysis revealed the following:

1 The type of service delivery accounts for one significant difference with regards to the evaluation factor named 'impact on the sales of other services'. More specifically, when the financial institution and the customer transact at arm's length (for example, over the telephone, ATM or internet), the above evaluation factor is less important compared to when the customer physically visits the financial institution or when an employee of a financial institution visits the customer. An explanation of this result may be that the probability of a financial service acting as a gateway to selling other financial services is likely to be higher when a customer is directly influenced by the cross-selling skills of front-line staff during a face-to-face interaction, than when the customer and the financial institution transact at a distance (for example, when there is no physical contact between the two parts). The vital role of face-to-face interactions and of the physical environment during service encounters in general and financial service encounters in particular provides support to the above explanation (for example, Lewis, 1995).

2 As far as the impact of business strategy on the weak service evaluation factors, the following results were observed: first, the 'impact on the profitability of other services' is less important for 'slow imitators' than 'fast imitators' and 'technological innovators'. This contradicts the assertion that market followers give priority to profitability (Meidan, 1996). Secondly, 'slow imitators' are not as much concerned with the impact of the elimination decision on the corporate image, as are 'cost reducers' and 'fast imitators'. A rationale behind this finding is that customers would notice more easily the elimination of a financial service by a financial institution that provides it at the lowest cost and at the highest efficiency (ingredients of a cost leadership strategy) or from a financial institution that was among the first to introduce it in the market (fast imitation), than from a financial institution that provides the financial service in a me-too way (slow imitation). Further, 'technological innovators' are concerned significantly more about the benefits that competitors could develop as a result of the financial service's elimination, than 'cost reducers' and 'slow imitators'.

3   Furthermore, market orientation exerts a positive influence on evaluation factors that are market- and customer-related, for example, this variable impacts on the sales and profitability of other services, the relationship with customers, the corporate image, the full-line policy, and the benefits that competitors can develop as a result of the elimination of the service. These results prove that as financial institutions become more market-oriented, the evaluation of the impact of elimination decisions becomes more thorough (that is the number of evaluation factors increases).

4   The intensity of market competition increases the importance of all evaluation factors examined with the exception of 'impact on corporate image' and 'impact on human resources and employee relationships'. The most influence of market orientation is exerted to the evaluation factor 'extent to which a similar financial service exists in the market in order to satisfy the needs of customers'. This relationship reflects the paramount importance placed upon the impact of elimination decisions on the relationships with customers.

5   The legislative environment forces financial institutions to place more emphasis on the relationships with their customers as well as on the extent to which the latter can find a similar financial service in the market, prior to confirming an elimination decision. This implies that the legislative environment intervenes in order to find equilibrium between the attempt of British financial institutions not to favour their competitors on the one hand and the right of customers for continuity in the provision of eliminated-to-be financial services, on the other hand.

6   The rhythm of technological change facing companies enhances the relative importance of four evaluative criteria, namely 'impact on the relationship with customers', 'impact on corporate image', 'competitor's benefits', and 'extent to which a similar service exists in the market to satisfy the needs of customers'.

It is obvious that, the contingency approach that is used for the evaluation of weak products, is also followed in the case of services. In other words, service providers tend to accommodate the criteria for evaluating weak services on a number of internal and external conditions.

Alternative elimination strategies of weak products

Once the decision to eliminate a product has been taken, plans must be drawn for its 'burial' with the least disturbance to the other operations of the firm and to customer relations. A number of approaches to the implementation of the elimination decision have been proposed, and these can be grouped into two categories.

The first category includes those approaches that suggest alternative elimination strategies and the factors that management should take into account in formulating the implementation plans. The works of Alexander (1964) and Kotler (1965) fall into this category. Jointly considered, these works suggest three alternative elimination strategies, namely 'drop immediately', 'milk' (phase out slowly), and 'selling out' to another manufacturer, and six factors that influence the implementation plans, namely stocks on hand, status of replacement parts, holdover demand, effects on customers/distributors, salvage value of special machinery and equipment, and the time needed to shift over to a new product.

The second category includes those approaches, which suggest strategies that may assist management to first, make a profit out of a declining product and secondly, lessen the impact when the product is finally dropped. These strategies have been proposed by Talley (1964), Michael (1971) and Kotler (1978) and were presented in Chapter 3.

As it becomes apparent, the normative views suggest that there are two basic strategies, which a company may follow once a product has been scheduled for removal:

1 drop immediately and
2 phase out slowly

The first strategy ('drop immediately'), which implies that once the elimination decision has been made the manufacturing stops almost immediately was not found to be applicable in the industrial field (Avlonitis, 1983). By contrast, empirical evidence suggests that this strategy is used by consumer goods companies (Rothe, 1970; Eckles, 1971; Mitchell et al., 1996). In industrial goods companies, the implementation of the elimination decision involves the 'run down' of the product inventory by satisfying the customers' orders received up to the decision day and/or other contractual agreements: no one appreciates perfunctory treatment, including those on whom the company depends for sustenance. Thus, a modification of the 'drop immediately' strategy in the industrial field may be called 'phase out immediately.'

The 'phase out slowly' strategy is similar to the strategies proposed by Talley (1964), Michael (1971) and Kotler (1978) (see Chapter 3) and referred to as 'milk', 'run-out', 'harvest' or 'product petrification'. This strategy implies that specific changes in the product's marketing strategy are imposed (for example, reduction in marketing promotion, product formulation change, price changes) which capitalize upon the remaining strength of the product and any hard-core customer support. Many companies evidence a definite preference for the 'phase out slowly' elimination strategy. The main rationale behind the 'phase out slowly' preference in these companies is that it allows the companies to buy extra time until first, the replacement product which could utilize the same facilities as the eliminated product approaches readiness for launching; and secondly, the customer locates adequate substitutes. This is exemplified in the following statement:

> We usually phase out the product gradually and this policy gives us extra time to try to generate the alternatives, hold customer loyalty and carry out our long-term commitments. In fact, it appears that the 'phase out slowly' strategy gives scope for a planned phase-out, which can be intermeshed with the phase-in of new product.
>
> The General Manager of a medium-sized manufacturer of electrical equipment

However, only a limited number of companies seem to consider changes in the product's marketing strategy during the phase-out period. As part of such changes, they may raise the price of the product during the phase-out period and make some money out of it, knowing that this action would accelerate the rate of sales decline and the ultimate demise of the product.

It appears that the 'phase out slowly' strategy gives scope for a planned phase-out, which can be intermeshed with the phase-in of new product. In this case, the following alternative strategies can be used (Saunders and Jobber, 1994):

- *Butt-on*: a new product immediately replaces an old one (for example, Ford's replacement of its European models: from Cortina to Sierra to Mondeo).
- *Low season switch*: a product is switched with a new one while demand is low and consumers' attention is elsewhere (for example, many hotels renovate certain parts of their facilities during the autumn when they have fewer clients).
- *High season launch*: a product is replaced by a new one when demand is high. Although this can increase discontinuity problems in the distribution chain, it can also stimulate sales force and retailer effort (for example, Polaroid tends

to launch successive generations of its instant camera during the run up to Christmas).

- *Roll-in/roll-out*: the company drops the old product and launches the new product successively in various market segments (for example, Mercedes replaced series 190 by the C series in one country after the other).
- *Downgrading*: this is a variation on the roll-in/roll-out strategy where an old product is not replaced by a new one, but instead it is retained and it serves a distinct market segment. (for example, Rover did this when it decided to retain the Mini to serve the market for cheap basic cars after the development of Metro which was a more advanced model).
- *Splitting*: it resembles the roll-in/roll-out strategy for products that have specialized variations (for example, Ford and Rover used this strategy when retaining pick-up and van variations of their old vehicles after discontinuing the Cortina and Marina saloon versions).
- *Sharing*: this strategy occurs when one product changes radically, but parallel products retain major components (for example, GM's J-car replaced rear wheel drive family sedans, but GM's Opel Manta retained major components).
- *Sell off*: this strategy involves selling production licences to companies in other countries (for example, Fiat sold licenses and helped build factories in Russia for Lada and in Poland factories for Polski Fiat).
- *Specials/end of line kickers*: this strategy is used to stimulate demand in products being out (for example, Amstrad's MegaPC 386SX was heavily discounted and sold with many software programs before Christmas).
- *Teasing/leaking*: companies may use teaser campaigns or leaking news to the media about impending changes to a product. This can slow demand for the withdrawing product and stack up demand for the impending launch (for example, Gillette used this strategy before launching its Sensor Shaving System).
- *Fudging*: this strategy seeks to reduce discontinuity by overlapping and not broadcasting the relationship between the new product and the replaced one (for example, Casio continuously renews its huge range of calculators).

According to Saunders and Jobber (1994), the successful product replacement requires that the development and deletion activities are well coordinated, taking into account certain product-related and environmental conditions. For example, if the company aims at a fast market penetration with the new product, then the old product must be dropped immediately. However, if it aims at a gradual market penetration, then the old product must be phased out slowly, otherwise it may lose market share.

Besides the 'phase out immediately' and 'phase out slowly' strategies, two additional elimination strategies have been identified in the industrial market (Avlonitis, 1983):

- *Sell out* the product to another manufacturer. A variation of this strategy is to offer the discontinued product to another manufacturer through licensing arrangements. In this case, movable equipment, parts, and supplies are also sold to the licensee for a profit.
- *Drop the product from the standard range and reintroduce it as a 'special'*: the elimination of a product need not to be a final or lasting decision: the resources used are such that if some residual demand exists after the product's discontinuation, it can be manufactured and marketed again. Elimination in this case means that the product will no longer be manufactured as a standard, but will, if demanded by a customer, be produced as a 'special' charging a premium price. The existence of this kind of elimination strategy, which tends to reduce the gravity of the elimination decision, was indicated by the following kinds of response:

Our elimination decision is not lasting decision; the customer can still ask for the discontinued product provided that he is willing to pay a premium price to cover the additional costs involved in its production.

The Marketing Director of a small manufacturer of heavy machine tools

I have recently accepted, at a price of course, an order by a customer who wanted to replace an industrial valve which we discontinued ten years ago.

The General Manager of a large manufacturer of industrial valves

If we receive an order for the discontinued product which we cannot convert into an order for the new one, then we will manufacture it as a special and we shall charge a higher price.

The Marketing Director of a large manufacturer of boilers

This ability to reintroduce a product after its discontinuity forms a characteristic of the elimination decision, which is unique in the industrial field; it is hard to imagine the same process being followed in the mass-marketing of customer goods. However, it would be wrong to say that all industrial goods manufacturers can do this: their ability to carry out this form of elimination can be related to the resources used to manufacture the product. If the company employs custom and small-batch production technology (which is labour intensive, highly flexible and well suited to customized products) to manufacture a range of standard products to varying specifications, then the ability to change a product from a standard to a special is increased; but if the company employs large-batch and mass-production technology which is much less flexible than the unit and small-batch technology, requires a high volume of output in order to be economical, and involves expensive limited-purpose equipment which sometimes is used specifically for one product, then the cost of maintaining the equipment to produce small orders would be prohibitive.

In order to have a more complete picture of the alternative elimination strategies, which were actually implemented by industrial companies, Avlonitis (1983) reported their relative importance in terms of the frequency that each of them is used (Table 10.3).

The 'phase out slowly' strategy is the most frequently used, followed by 'drop from the standard range and reintroduce as a special', 'phase-out immediately', and 'sell out'.

In another study, Mitchell et al. (1996) examined the elimination process in a sample of 110 industrial and 75 consumer goods companies and concluded that the most frequently used strategy is 'phase out immediately' where pending orders are executed and stock is exhausted (in 63.2 per cent of the sampled companies). The same researchers also examined the 'drop immediately' strategy, and they made the distinction between the 'slow harvest' and the 'fast harvest'. In the former case, long-term investments are cut, followed by a gradual reduction in operating expenses (for example, marketing), while in the latter case, operating expenses are reduced immediately.

Alternative elimination strategies of weak services

In comparison to the other three stage of the elimination decision-making process, the implementation of the elimination decision is the most extensively researched area in the field of service deletion (Harness and Mackay, 1993, 1994, 1997; Harness et al., 1999; Argouslidis, 2004).

Harness and Mackay (1993) introduced the term 'partial elimination', whereby a financial service could experience some form of elimination but could still have its

Table 10.3   **Importance of alternative elimination strategies**

	Mean*	Standard deviation
Phase out immediately	25	26
Phase out slowly	39	26
Sell out	6	10
Drop the product from the standard range and re-introduce it as a 'special'	30	21

*Using the 100-point constant sum measurement technique, respondents distributed 100 points between the alternative elimination strategies that best reflect their relative importance in terms of the frequency that they are used to.

Source: adapted from Avlonitis (1983)

existence and entity in the service range of financial institutions. In an attempt to examine empirically this issue, Harness and Mackay (1997) conducted a study in the UK financial services industry and identified the following six alternative elimination strategies (in order of use):

1 Make a service a closed issue. This strategy can be operationalized in three ways:

- Service is withdrawn from new customers and existing customers are unaffected.
- Service is withdrawn from new customers; existing customers cannot add further funds or purchase additional units.
- Keep the service open for specific customer segments, but closed for other customer segments.

2 Withdraw features: the service is retained, but with fewer features.
3 Multi-service amalgamation: the old service is eliminated and is replaced by a new service which is an amalgamation of other financial services.
4 Drop a service, keeping its name, change the nature and function of the service.
5 Elimination of customer: the service is not available any more to unprofitable customers.
6 Core service elimination: the service is dropped immediately from the company's service range.

A more recent study conducted by Argouslidis (2004) also in the UK financial services market revealed the following ten elimination strategies (in order of use):

- Eliminate the service to new customers, leaving the existing customers unaffected.
- Eliminate the service to new customers; existing ones cannot purchase additional units.
- Drop immediately (namely, the service is completely eliminated and has no further existence or entity in the company).
- Service simplification (elimination of some features of a financial service).
- Phase out slowly.
- Service merging (elimination of two or more financial services as individual offerings and creation of a new amalgamated financial service).
- Eliminate the service from some segments and keep it open for other segments.
- Eliminate the service, keep its name and introduce a new service with the same name but of different nature and function.
- Eliminate and sell out.
- Drop from standard range and offer it only as a special.

This study confirmed that the most frequently used strategy is to eliminate a financial service to new potential customers, while leaving its existing users unconditionally unaffected by the elimination decision. This finding is consistent with the general observation that the diligent maintenance of good relationships with the existing customers is of momentous significance to financial institutions (Shultz and Prince, 1994).

Drop immediately was the second most frequently used strategy, resulting in a full elimination of financial services, since the latter had no further existence in the range of financial institutions. This finding is in contrast with Harness and Mackey (1997) who argued that the full and immediate withdrawal of financial services from the market is impossible.

The fact that the 'drop immediately' strategy is the second most frequent strategies for eliminating financial services, which it has no application to the manufactured goods industry (Avlonitis, 1983), can be attributed to the perishability characteristic of services: this strategy fails to assist manufacturers in running down the inventory of finished or of semi-finished units of the to-be-eliminated product. However, when legal, market or other circumstances dictate the immediate elimination of a financial service, financial institutions can drop it immediately since they have no concerns about running down inventories or completing a semi-finished production batch.

The third most frequently used strategy was the withdrawal of a financial service for new potential customers, while its existing users could continue using it but could not purchase additional units of it. In other words, the existing customers/users of a financial service, which is no longer on offer to new potential customers, could still enjoy its benefits but could not renew it after a specific date of termination.

> When the UK treasury abolished the tax-relief on certain mortgage endowments, these products instantly become less advantageous to existing holders and to financial institutions offering them. As many financial institutions kicked off the withdrawal of such products, the legislative authorities dictated that the elimination decision could be implemented only if there was a more advantageous replacement mortgage endowment, to which existing holders could be migrated.

Extending the investigation of service elimination strategies in various service industries (namely, insurance, banking, advertising, professional services, freight forwarding, marine, telecommunications and lodging), the authors of this book examined the use of nine alternative elimination strategies in a sample of 164 service companies. These strategies and their frequency of use are presented in Table 10.4. The most frequently used elimination strategy is 'phase out immediately – eliminate service for new customers, provision for existing customers', followed by 'drop immediately' and 'service merging'. These results are similar to those found in the UK financial services industry (Argouslidis, 2004). Thus, we may conclude that the most frequently elimination strategies of weak services transcend service sectors.

Internal and external influences on alternative elimination strategies of weak products

The relative importance of the aforementioned elimination strategies used by industrial goods companies was found by Avlonitis (1986) to vary depending on the company's size, product diversity as well as the rhythm of technological change that it experiences. More specifically, it was found that:

1   The importance of the 'drop from the standard range and reintroduce as a special' strategy is decreased by size. Apparently, the smaller companies, being more flexible, can accommodate, much more easily than the larger companies, the residual demand that may exist for a product after its discontinuance.

Table 10.4   **Alternative service elimination strategies**

	Percentage of use
Phase out immediately – eliminate service for new customers, provision for existing customers	30.9%
Drop immediately	20.7%
Service merging	15.1%
Eliminate additional service features offered with the core service (service simplification)	11.1%
Offer the service to a limited number of customers under specific conditions (tailor made services)	10.4%
Cut down service support expenses, phase out the service slowly	7.1%
Implement marketing strategies (e.g. pricing) directing customers to another service	2.2%
Sell out (sell service rights to another company)	1.3%
Eliminate service, but use its brand name in another service	1.2%

Source: Avlonitis et al. (2003)

2 Technological change is significantly and positively related with the 'phase out slowly' strategy. Indeed, to the extent that the companies operating in an innovative environment tend to treat the product elimination process as an integral part of their new product development process, we should expect these companies to use the 'phase out slowly' strategy. This particular strategy enables management to expedite the timely development of the new (replacement) product and gives scope for the planned phase out of the existing (obsolete) product, which can be intermeshed with the phase in of the new replacement product.

3 Product diversity exerts a moderate positive effect on the importance of the 'phase out slowly' strategy and a negative effect on the importance of the 'selling out' strategy. One plausible explanation of the positive relationship between product diversity and the 'phase out slowly' strategy is that the larger the number of products manufactured and marketed by a company, the higher the percentage of tie-in sales attributable to the product being dropped and, consequently, the more desirable the strategy that gives the customer time to make whatever adjustments required and helps to minimize resistance to elimination.

Internal and external influences on alternative elimination strategies of weak services

As in the case of manufactured products, certain variables of the internal and external environment of the company influence the importance of the alternative elimination strategies of weak services as well. In an attempt to shed more light in this area, Argouslidis (2004) analysed the ten elimination strategies he had identified (see Alternative elimination strategies of weak services, p. 212). From this analysis, four underlying dimensions of elimination strategies were revealed, namely:

- *Pseudo elimination strategies*: this dimension involves strategies that lead to a partial service elimination, like 'eliminate the service from some segments, keep it open for other segments', 'service merging', 'eliminate the service, keep its name and introduce a new service with the same name but of different nature and function', 'service simplification', and 'phase out slowly'.

- *Relationship elimination strategies*: this dimension refers to strategies like 'eliminate the service to new customers, leaving the existing customers unaffected', and 'eliminate the service to new customers, existing ones cannot purchase additional units'.
- *Sell out strategy*
- *Drop strategies*: this dimension encompasses the full elimination strategies like 'drop immediately' and 'drop from standard range and offer it only as a special'.

Then, Argouslidis (2004) related these four underlying elimination strategies to a number of organizational and environmental variables, namely company size, market orientation, market competition, rhythm of technological change and legislation. This analysis led to the following results:

1   The greater the degree of a financial institution's market orientation, the more applicable is the use of elimination strategies that leave the existing customer base unaffected (conditionally or not) by the elimination of a financial service.
2   The higher the degree of a financial institution's market orientation, the lower the use of an elimination strategy that results in an immediate and complete elimination of a financial service, like 'drop immediately' and 'drop from standard range and offer it only as a special'.
3   The more intense the market competition, the higher the use of an elimination strategy that results in an immediate and complete elimination of a financial service. Under harsh competitive circumstances a financial institution is keen to proceed with an immediate withdrawal of a financial service in order to free resources and reallocate them to services that exhibit a competitive advantage.
4   As the austerity of the legislative environment increases, financial institutions avoid implementing drop strategies, while they tend to implement elimination strategies that leave existing users unaffected. This is an illustration of the concern of the legislative authorities of the British financial services sector for the right of customers to enjoy as an uninterrupted as possible provision of the financial services that they have chosen (Harrison, 2000).
5   The larger a financial institution, the higher its propensity for ceasing to offer a financial service and for ceding its production and selling rights to another financial institution.
6   The greater the technological change, the less important are strategies like 'eliminate the service to new customers, leaving the existing customers unaffected', and 'eliminate the service to new customers, existing ones cannot purchase additional units'. This relationship clearly shows that, as the rhythm of technological change accelerates the obsolescence of certain financial services, even the existing customer base of the to-be-eliminated financial service have to be migrated to the more technologically advanced one.
7   Finally, the rhythm of technological change has a notable negative effect on the general applicability of the sell-out elimination strategy. Apparently, in a highly innovative technological environment, financial institutions are less keen to acquire a technologically obsolete service, which has been deleted by their competitors.

Factors influencing phase out plans and timing

Apart from the elimination strategies that are open to management, and which we discussed in the preceding sections, another important issue pertaining to the implementation of the elimination decision refers to the factors that influence the phase out plans and the timing of the product elimination.

One of the authors of this book has uncovered six factors that influence the phase-out plans and the timing in the industrial field (Avlonitis 1983), namely:

The problem situation that evoked the elimination decision

One basic factor that influences the phase-out strategy and timing is the problem situation that initiated the product's elimination in the first place. If the rationale behind the elimination of a product is either the decline in its market potential or a variety reduction policy developed by the company, then it is generally phased out immediately. If, on the other hand the rationale behind elimination of a product is the development of a new and improved one, then the 'phase out slowly' strategy is generally preferred. When a product is dropped because of its poor financial commercial, and/or technical performance, then either of these two alternative elimination strategies may be used.

Market trends/holdover demands

The problem of anticipating future orders and holdover demand is found to be an important factor in the determination of the date at which elimination is scheduled. This factor is found to be of primary importance to the companies operating in oligopsonistic or monopsonistic markets. These companies tend to postpone elimination for some months in order to produce a certain amount of the discontinued product, which is likely to be demanded by their important and loyal customers. Also, the study of the market demand leads companies to select the 'phase out slowly' strategy in eliminating their products. Faced with declining product sales and a holdover demand by a loyal customer group, these companies phase the product out slowly and make some money out of it by raising its price.

However, in cases where a replacement exists in the development stage or is ready for market introduction, the influence of the market trends/holdover demand factor in determining the elimination date is generally of secondary importance. In these cases, the elimination date is generally planned to coincide with the date at which the replacement product is scheduled for introduction; the holdover demand for the old product could be met by the replacement product, following a policy of changing the orders received and accepted for the old product into orders for the new replacement product.

Stock on hand

In general, the primary task of companies in implementing the elimination decision is to use up the product's inventory before the product could cease to be produced. As such, before the establishment of the elimination date, the companies tend to conduct an inventory audit for the product: its raw materials, supplies and components. During this audit, particular emphasis is given to the high-value materials and components. In auditing the inventory level of the product, the companies also consider vendor commitments and the time when the last shipment of materials and components which could not be cancelled or employed elsewhere are due to be received. The extent to which the product's inventory both in house and in vendors is greater than, equal to or less than what is required to produce the amount of the product for which the company's management has been committed, largely determines the phase-out timing.

Status of replacement parts

Many companies consider the problem of maintaining components and parts for future service and replacement demands to be an important factor that influences the phase-out plans and timing. Some companies even tend to ask their major customers how many replacement parts they would require when they phase out a product; the customers' spare-parts requirements are then incorporated into final build before the product's withdrawal. Still others may postpone elimination for a period of time in order to make sure that they have available replacement parts to meet the customers' future spare-parts requirements.

Effect on customers

The importance of the individual orders in the industrial field necessitates the consideration of customer goodwill in determining not only whether a product is to be eliminated but also the manner of its elimination. Minimizing losses while retaining the goodwill of customers appeared to be the two basic but at the same time, conflicting objectives of the sample interview companies in planning the timing of the phase-out. The emphasis placed on each of these objectives was found to be dependent on three factors: first, the position of the company in the market; secondly, the cost (losses) entailed by delaying the elimination; and thirdly, the importance of the users of the eliminated product to the company.

In cases where the eliminated product is one of the many other products that the company sells to individual customers in highly competitive markets, it is desirable to notify the customers, particularly the major ones, and phase out the product slowly while educating them about the replacement product. When the deleting company is monopolistic with respect to the other products used by its customers, then it is desirable to phase out the product immediately, using up the stock of materials, components, and supplies.

However, little concern about the cost engendered by the loss of goodwill – as well as a strong preference for the 'phase out immediately' strategy – is observed in a case involving an unprofitable product whose elimination is surrounded by strong sentiments. In these instances, an immediate phase out is much easier to administer than a slow phase out. They failed to indicate, however, whether the benefits of the 'phase out immediately' strategy had been to protect customer goodwill.

Finally, in cases where the product that is to be eliminated is one of many other products that the company sells to original equipment manufacturers (OEMs), it is usually desirable to notify the customers far enough in advance before the actual elimination to allow not only for purchase of sufficient quantities to minimize inconvenience, but also for sales/customer liaison concerning the change to another (replacement) product.

Replacement product development

Another major factor affecting the productivity of resources employed and influencing the timing of the phase out is found to be availability of replacement products in research and development or otherwise planned for introduction. More specifically, the scheduled launch date of the replacement product tends to determine not only the time at which the eliminated product could cease to be produced, but also the timing of certain important implementation tasks such as 'when to cancel or not place more orders on vendors', and 'when to notify the salesmen and customers'. Synchronization of the elimination of the old product with the introduction of the replacement product is found to be the basic aim of most of the sample companies. In most cases, however, this cannot be achieved. One of the most common ways of approximating this ideal situation is to postpone the elimination for certain period of time while continuing to manufacture and market of the old product. This practice, however, may be proved to be very costly indeed.

> Sometimes the replacement is so slow in development and production that we have to make an extra batch of the old model at a considerable cost, as many items are obsolete and the stock has been run down.
>
> The Sales Manager of a large manufacturer of automatic controls

> When the company experiences problems in launching the replacement product, the old product's range is simplified by cutting down the number of frame sizes offered, in order to minimize losses.
>
> The Executive Engineer of a manufacturer of boilers

Product-elimination implementation system

Regardless of the elimination strategy that will be ultimately selected and the timing for its implementation, product elimination is a complex process that may last from two months to over three years (Avlonitis, 1983). Consequently, it is important for the company to establish a systematic deletion implementation system, which will clearly define all the relevant tasks, their sequence of execution and the people in charge.

One of the authors of this book has developed an empirically based product elimination implementation model to provide some guidance in this area (Avlonitis, 1983). This system is graphically represented as a sequential flow diagram (Figure 10.1) and is described below.

The implementation process usually starts with the determination of the marketing programme before the product is completely discontinued. This marketing programme will serve to meet the demand for which the company's management has already been committed, such as order backlogs or completion of certain contracts. It will also serve to satisfy first, the anticipated demand up to the desired withdrawal date, which may coincide with the date, at which the replacement product is scheduled for introduction; secondly, the future contingency demand, namely, the unforeseen amount which is likely to be demanded in the future by very strongly loyal customers; and thirdly, the customers' future spare-parts requirements. The marketing department is normally involved in this task and it may or not consult the sales force and the customers. Having determined the marketing programme, an inventory and capital plant facilities audit is then conducted. The inventory audit consists of two phases that can be carried out at the same time. The first phase of this audit is to determine whether the product's finished stock and work in progress is greater than, equal to, or less than that required to fulfil the marketing programme. The purpose of this phase of the inventory audit is to suggest to management whether to stop production immediately or to produce an additional batch so that the sum of the product's inventory on hand and the additional batch will equal the marketing programme. If the finished stock and work in progress checked up by the stock control and production personnel is equal to, or greater than, what is required to fulfil the marketing program, then the production department is instructed to stop manufacturing the product immediately. On the other hand, if the inventory on hand is less than what is required, then the production department is ordered to produce an additional batch of the product.

The second phase of the inventory audit is to ascertain whether the product's inventory of raw materials, components, and supplies both in house and in vendors is greater than, equal to, or less than what is required to fulfil the marketing programme. The tendency observed is to instruct the stock controller to provide details of the stockholding of the product's raw materials, components and supplies. Few companies, however, make use of the standards department: when management decides to investigate and, subsequently, to eliminate a product, the standards draftsman compiles a product breakdown and sends copies of the parts to production control. On receipt of the product breakdown form, the stock controller supplies standards with details on the parts breakdown form of the value and quantity of the stockholding of each part. If the materials and components level in house and with vendors is less than the amount required, then the material procurement department is instructed to purchase amount X, so that the X + inventory on hand equals the requirements for the marketing programme. If, on the other hand, the materials and components level is greater than what is needed to fulfil the marketing programme, then the material procurement department is ordered to stop purchasing materials and components and to save the surplus for future replacements (spare-parts).

Only a few companies, however, report that they conduct a capital plant facilities audit at this stage of the process. This audit is carried out by the chief tooling engineer and the chief production engineer who provide information with respect to the equipment (tooling, plant) necessary to complete the marketing programme and the book and scrap value of redundant equipment. This practice gives management time to locate a buyer for the redundant equipment before the actual withdrawal date. In this way, if a used market exists for this equipment, then a better price can be obtained.

Taking into consideration the outcome of the inventory and capital plant facilities audit, the time that the last shipments of raw materials and components required for the production of the final batch of the eliminated product will be received, and the daily production rate, the production and material procurement managers estimate the time required to produce the final batch. At this stage, management is in a position to determine the date at which the elimination of the product can be scheduled; this date coincides with the date at which the final build is completed.

During the production for the final batch and the 'run-down' of the product's inventory of materials, components and supplies, management instructs the stock controllers to ensure the obsolescent parts are carefully controlled to minimize the cost of eliminating the product from the range. At the time when the final build is completed and before the issue of a final note (for example, circular, memorandum) declaring the product obsolete (withdrawn), management asks three important questions:

1   Is there an adequate substitute for the product?
2   Is the replacement product ready for introduction?
3   Is there any residual demand that needs to be accommodated?

If the answer to the first and second questions is 'yes', and to the third question is 'no', then management proceeds immediately with the declaration of obsolescence (withdrawal). If, on the other hand, the answer to the first and/or second question is 'no', and to the third question is 'yes', then management postpones the elimination date for some period of time until the replacement product approaches readiness for launching and/or the customer locates an adequate substitute and/or the residual demand is satisfied. Meanwhile, the production and material procurement departments are notified of the postponement decision and ordered to build an extra batch of the old product:

Having adjusted the marketing programme and the final elimination date on the basis of these considerations, management proceeds then to declare the product obsolete (withdrawn) and to circulate the sales force, distributors, and customers as appropriate with the decisions reached, stating in particular the following:

1   The product is now obsolete (withdrawn).
2   A specific spare-parts policy is to be applied.
3   All orders and inquiries are to be referred to production control before accepting or quoting.

The third statement, observed only in a few companies, is of prime importance because it ensures than no orders are received from the market without the knowledge of the production control personnel who are most knowledgeable with respect to the product's remaining finished and partly finished stocks. Put in another way, it ensures that management does not accept an order when the materials and components required for its completion are not available.

After the issue of obsolescence (withdrawal) circular the customers' orders are phased out. At the same time, the spare-parts policy for the product comes into effect and the product data and facilities are withdrawn and eliminated, respectively. The standards draftsman compiles two lists of the product's parts: one includes the parts that will be offered as spares and is forwarded to the marketing department; the other includes the parts to be scrapped and is forwarded to the stock controller, who ensures that the parts required under the spare parts programme are maintained and those not required are eliminated. The standards draftsman also first, withdraws all drawings, time-study records, and inventory cards related to the product and its component parts; secondly, returns to file drawings of parts common to other products; thirdly, marks appropriate drawings 'for spares only' and returns them to file. The chief production engineer, the chief tooling engineer, and the quality control manager dispose of the manufacturing, tooling, and quality-control facilities – unless, of course, they required for future spare-parts capabilities or parts still required elsewhere.

Once these tasks have been executed, the product's 'burial' has been completed. Evidence from the study shows that the duration of a product's 'burial' can vary from two months to two and a half years. Customer opposition, changes in demand from the planned phase-out rate, supply/manufacture problems on the replacement product, and attempts to synchronize the elimination of the product with the introduction of the replacement product are usually responsible for delays in a product's 'burial'.

However, the empirical model described in this chapter provides a framework that successfully integrates fundamental tasks of the implementation process. These tasks involve several segments of the organization (the marketing department, the production department, the materials procurement department, and so on), which must not only take an active part, but also cooperate very closely with each other if the implementation process is to be executed smoothly and economically. The fact that the empirical model incorporates very fundamental considerations actually detected in this diverse sample of engineering companies renders it more flexible and applicable to diverse companies and products. Moreover, given the fact that the greatest problems experienced by companies with respect to product elimination are involved in the implementation stage, the model may serve to point out to managers the most important factors that must be taken into account and allow them to systematize the thoughts and procedures in implementing the elimination decision and phasing out a product.

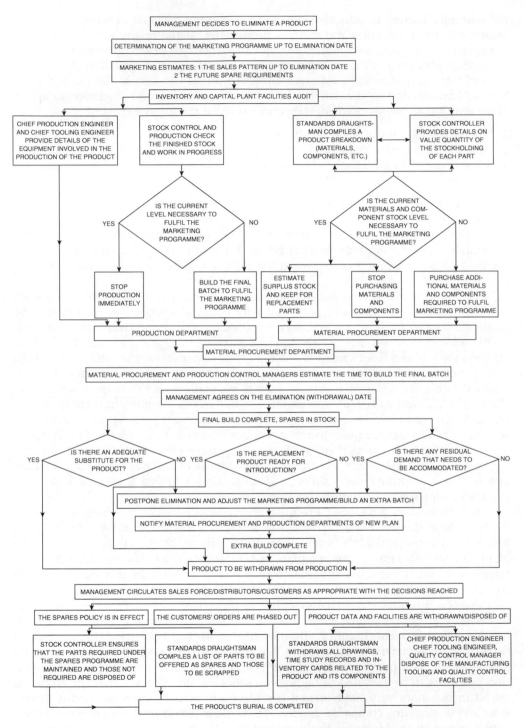

Figure 10.1 **A sequential flow diagram for the implementation of the product-elimination decision**

Source: Avlonitis (1983)

Summary

- If management realizes that no corrective action is feasible for the identified weak product or service, then the managerial attention shifts from the product/service itself to the impact upon the entire company of eliminating it.
- Certain evaluation factors related to the product elimination decision are considered to determine whether it is in the best interests of the company to eliminate or retain the product/service.
- There are no differences as to the evaluation process between products and services. Empirical evidence supports the existence of an informal procedure for evaluating weak products and services.
- The financial and marketing implications of product's elimination (for example, in profitability, sales) as well as 'new product potential' and 'product's market potential' are among the most important evaluation factors of weak products.
- 'Market potential', 'impact on total company sales', 'impact on the relations with customers' and 'existence of alternative services' are the most important evaluation factors of weak services in general, while 'impact on the relationship with customers', 'impact on the corporate image', and 'impact on the sales of other services (cross-selling)' are the most important evaluation factors for financial services.
- The 'phase out slowly' strategy is the most frequently used strategy for eliminating industrial products, followed by 'drop from the standard range and reintroduce as a special', 'phase-out immediately', and 'sell out'.
- The most frequently used strategy of a financial service is to eliminate a financial service to new potential customers, while leaving its existing users unconditionally unaffected by the elimination decision. Other frequently used strategies include 'drop immediately', and 'withdrawal of a financial service for new potential customers, while its existing users could continue using it but could not purchase additional units of it'.
- The importance of certain evaluation factors and elimination strategies is influenced by product, organizational and market variables, like for instance, company size, market competition and rhythm of technological change in the market.
- Six factors influence the phase-out plans and timing in the industrial field, namely: first, the problem situation that evoked the elimination decision, secondly, market trends/holdover demands, thirdly, stock in hand, fourthly, status of replacement parts, fifthly, effect on customers, and sixthly, replacement product development.

Questions

1. Select a fast moving consumer product and discuss the most important evaluation factors that need to be considered before management decides to drop it.
2. Which evaluation factor of weak services can the type of service delivery process influence and how?
3. Discuss the organizational and environmental conditions that may influence the selection of the elimination strategy of an electrical generator for industrial use.
4. Identify two factors that an insurance company should take into consideration for deciding the phase-out plan and timing of a life insurance scheme?

References

Alexander, R.S. (1964) 'The death and burial of sick products', *Journal of Marketing*, 28: 1–7.
Argouslidis, P. (2003) 'Factors to consider prior to eliminating a financial service: empirical evidence from the British financial services sector', Working Paper, Athens University of Economics and Business.
Argouslidis, P. (2004) 'An empirical investigation into the alternative strategies to implement the elimination of financial services', *Journal of World Business*, 39(4).
Avlonitis, G. (1983) 'The product elimination decision and strategies', *Industrial Marketing Management*, 11: 31–43.
Avlonitis, G. (1984) 'Industrial product elimination: major factors to consider', *Industrial Marketing Management*, 13: 77–85.
Avlonitis, G. (1986) 'The management of the product elimination function: theoretical and empirical analysis', in A.G. Woodside (ed.), *Advances in Business Marketing*, Vol. 1. Greenwich, CT: JAI Press.
Avlonitis, G. (1993) 'Project dropstrat: what factors do managers consider in deciding whether to drop a project?' *European Journal of Marketing*, 27(4): 35–7.
Avlonitis, G., Gounaris, S. and Papastathopoulou, P. (2003) 'Service elimination decision-making: major factors to consider', Working Paper, The Athens Laboratory of Research in Marketing (A.LA.R.M.) Athens University of Economics and Business.
Berenson, C. (1963) 'Pruning the product line', *Business Horizons*, 6: 63–70.
Bidlake, S. (2000) 'Unilever's linear lineup to get $1.6 bn', *Advertising Age*, 71(9).
Browne, W.G. and Kemp, P.S. (1976) 'A three stage product review process', *Industrial Marketing Management*, 5: 333–42.
Eckles, W.R. (1971) 'Product line deletion and simplification', *Business Horizons*, 14: 71–4.
Harness, D.R. and Mackay, S. (1993) 'Service product elimination: a conceptual view', MEG Conference Proceedings, Loughborough University Business School, pp. 462–71.
Harness, D.R. and Mackay, S. (1994) 'Product elimination strategies of the financial services sector'. in J. Bell, S. Brown and D. Carson (eds), *Marketing: Unity in Diversity*. Proceedings of the Marketing Education Group Conference, Coleraine.
Harness, D.R., and Mackay, S. (1997) 'Product deletion: a financial services perspective', *International Journal of Bank Marketing*, 15(1): 4–12.
Harness, D.R., Marr, E.N. and Harness, T. (1999) 'A comparison of elimination strategies for physical goods and financial service products', Academy of Marketing Conference, Stirling University, July.
Harrison, T. (2000) *Financial Services Marketing*. London: Prentice Hall.
Kotler, P. (1965) 'Phasing out weak products', *Harvard Business Review*, 43: 107–18.
Kotler, P. (1978) 'Harvesting weak products', *Business Horizons*, 21: 15–22.
Lewis, B.R. (1995) 'Customer care and service quality', in Christine Ennew, T. Watkins and M. Wright (eds), *Marketing Financial Services*, 2nd edition. London: Butterworth Heinemann, pp. 193–211.
Meidan, A. (1996) *Marketing Financial Services*, London: Macmillan.
Michael, G.C. (1971) 'Product petrification: "a new stage in life cycle theory"', *California Management Review*, 9: 88–91.
Mitchell, A., Taylor, D. and Tanyel, F. (1996) 'Product elimination decision-making: after-the-fact', *Journal of International Management and Marketing Research*, 21(2): 59–66
Narisetti, R. (1997) 'P&G, seeing shoppers were being confused, overhauls marketing', *Wall Street Journal*, (January 15), A1, A8.
Narisetti, R. (1998) 'How IBM turned around its ailing PC division', *Wall Street Journal*, (March 12), B1, B6.
Pletcher, B.A. (1973) 'The product elimination process in the small home appliance industry: an empirical study'. Unpublished DBA Dissertation. Kent State University.
Rothe, J.T. (1970) 'The product elimination decision', *MSU Business Topics*, 18: 45–52.
Saunders, J. and Jobber, D. (1994) 'Product replacement: strategies for simultaneous product deletion and launch', *Journal of Product Innovation Management*, 11: 433–50.
Stevenson, B.D. (1989) *Marketing Financial Services to Corporate Clients*. Cambridge: Woodhead Faulkner.
Shultz, C.J. and Prince, R.A. (1994) 'Selling financial services to the affluent', *International Journal of Bank Marketing*, 12(3): 9–16.

Talley, W.J., Jr. (1964) 'Profiting from the declining product', *Business Horizons*, 7: 77–84.

Worthing, P.M. (1971) 'The assessment of product deletion decision indicators', in T.J. Scheiber and L.A. Madeo (eds), *Fortran Applications in Business Administration*. Graduate School of Business Administration, University of Michigan.

Further reading

Harness, D. and Marr, N. (2001) 'Strategies for eliminating a financial services product', *Journal of Product and Brand Management*, 10(7): 423–38.

Kent, R.A. and Argouslidis, P.C. (2005) 'Shaping business decisions using fuzzy-set analysis service elimination decisions', *Journal of Marketing Management*, 21(5–6): 641–58.

11 Organizational Arrangements for Developing, Managing and Eliminating Products and Services

Introduction

As part of product/service management, decisions must made regarding the organizational arrangements of developing, managing and eliminating products/services. These arrangements include the structure and formality of relevant activities and the functional units to be involved.

In this chapter, we address the following questions:

1 What are the alternative organizational structures that can be used for developing, managing and eliminating products/services?
2 What is the degree of formality of new product/service development and product/service elimination processes?
3 Which functional units participate in the development, management and elimination of products/services?

Alternative organizational structures for developing new products and services

Organizational structure refers to the design of roles and administrative mechanisms to control and integrate work activities and resource flows (Olson et al., 1995). In this respect, the organizational structures, which can be used for developing new products/services can be classified on the basis of:

- The degree of autonomy of different functional areas.
- The type of coordination between functional units.
- The degree of exclusive orientation towards the new product/service project (namely, projectization).

In the following sections, we will present each of these three classifications separately.

Classification of new product/service organizational structures based on the degree of autonomy of different functional areas

Depending on the degree of autonomy of different functional areas, there are two broad categories of structures when organizing for new product development (Booz et al., 1982), namely:

1 Free-standing or autonomous units
2 Functionally based units

Free-standing or autonomous units

These units act independently from the traditional functional units of the company (for example, marketing, production). These units serve the following purposes:

- Top management is not actively involved in the development of new products/services.
- New product/service development process becomes more efficient as well-trained and competent executives work closely together.
- Innovation becomes a full-time concern and primary goal.
- New product development activities are separated by those activities that refer to existing products and services.

The autonomous or free-standing units can take one of the following forms (Sands, 1983):

- New product department
- Task force
- Venture team (or unit)

New-product department   It is a full-time permanent unit operating on the same level as other functions, such as marketing, production, finance, and so on and research evidence shows that it is one of the most commonly used in industry (Mahajan and Wind, 1992). This department can be staffed with functional specialists or entirely with new product specialists. The department head typically has substantial authority to oversee the complete development function from idea generation to commercialization and relatively easy access to top management. However, generalizing about the department's form is difficult because of the diversity of the personnel included, functions served and reporting relationships. New product departments are appropriate for companies that face a continuous demand for new products, particularly new product lines and highly innovative products.

Task force   It can be viewed as a temporary new product department, which is formed for the purpose of coordinating and managing the development of an assigned new product. Task forces draw specialized personnel from functional departments either on a full-time or part-time basis for the duration of the project and are well-suited to companies whose new product needs are sporadic and tend to involve significant departures from existing products. When the development task is completed, the structure is dismantled.

Venture team The most autonomous form of new product organization is the venture team which evolved during the 1960s. This unit is located at the corporate level and consists of specialists with freedom to develop a new product or business, which is beyond the product/market expertise of the company. Like the task force, its members can belong to the company's personnel. But unlike the task force, its members may also be recruited from outside the company, while the internal members divorce themselves from their original duties and work full-time on the development project.

Functionally based units

In order to develop new products, many companies use organizational units that are part of existing functions, for example, marketing, finance. We distinguish between the following alternative functionally based units (Sands, 1983):

- new product committee;
- integrative new product organization;
- product management system.

New product committee A new product committee consists of representatives from marketing, production, engineering, finance and other functional areas. New product ideas that originate anywhere in the organization are examined, evaluated, funded for development, or cancelled by this committee. Basically, this committee coordinates all phases of the development process and works well if the projects are close to current operations involving the present line of products, for example, improvement/revision to products, repositioning, cost reductions.

There are two types of new product committees:

- An ad hoc new product committee is a high-level management committee, existing at the corporate or SBU levels. Under this structural approach, committee members are put together and work from idea generation till product launch. After the development task has ended, the committee is disbanded.
- A permanent new product committee is a standing structure at the corporate and/or SBU organizational levels. The committee's members are responsible for reviewing and approving (or rejecting) new product programmes.

Integrative new product organization The integrative new product organization falls into the following two structural groups:

1 Vice president (VP) of innovation, is a position located at the same level as corporate planning, corporate finance and so on, and is the direct link between top management and product-planning activities at the SBU level. The Vice President of innovation is assigned to control, monitor and advise the product planners in every phase of the development process.
2 The modular approach which has been proposed by Benson and Chasin (1976) includes: a core component in the form of a new product development department; an executive approval and review committee in which the Vice President of innovation is also a member; an ad hoc component including task forces and venture teams; a liaison committee; and a new-brand manager. Another modular approach suggested in the literature consists of staff specialists, a new product review group and venture teams (Midgley, 1977).

Product management system   According to this organizational structure, product managers are given new product development responsibilities in addition to responsibility for existing products. Product managers initiate, plan and coordinate the new product development process for a product line or brand. Like the new product committee, this approach appears to be effective when new products are line extensions or minor modifications of existing products for familiar markets.

Classification of new product/service organizational structures based on the type of coordination between functional units

Another categorization of organizational structures for developing new products/ services can be made on the basis of the coordination mechanisms used for inter-functional interactions.

In late 1970s, Galbraith and Nathanson (1978) and Mintzberg (1979) identified five sets of structural mechanisms that organizations use to coordinate activities including the new product development process. These include:

- Bureaucratic control/hierarchical directives – it is the most formalized and central-ized, and at the same time, the least participative form of structure where npd activ-ities rely on standard operating procedures coordinated by the general manager.
- Individual liaisons – individuals from different functional departments communicate directly to one another during npd process, but such 'liaisons' have no formal authority to make decisions aimed at resolving inter-functional conflicts.
- Temporary task force – it is a more participatory and less formalized mechanism than the previous two, where individuals from various departments constitute a working group within the context of a specific project.
- Integrating managers – individuals are assigned to coordinate various functional departments but typically do not have any formal authority to impose decisions to those departments.
- Matrix structures – activities are structured by products, markets or functions.

In these structural mechanisms, Olson et al. (1995) have added two newer structural forms, namely:

- Design teams – these are an alternative structural form, where a number of functional specialists are brought together to work on the development of a new product, while having considerable authority in choosing their own leaders, or managing the process themselves.
- Design centres – these are like the design teams, but reflect a more permanent organiza-tional arrangement, where the members of the centre are involved in multiple develop-ment projects over time.

Classification of new product/service organizational structures based on the degree of exclusive orientation towards the new product/service project

New product/service organizational structures can also be based on the extent to which participants see themselves as independent from the new product project or committed to it. On the basis of this criterion, five new product development (npd) structures have been identified by Larson and Gobeli (1985, 1988), ranging from functional (lowest degree of projectization), to project team (highest degree of projectization). In between these two extremes lie three different types of matrix structures (namely, functional, balanced, project). More specifically:

- *Functional*: the new product project is divided into segments and assigned to relevant functional areas and/or groups within functional areas. The project is coordinated by functional and upper levels of management.
- *Functional matrix*: a project manager with limited authority is designated to coordinate the new product project across different functional areas and/or groups. The functional managers retain responsibility and authority for their specific segments of the project.
- *Balanced matrix*: a project manager is assigned to oversee the project and shares the responsibility and authority for completing the project with the functional managers. Project and functional managers jointly direct many workflow segments and jointly approve many decisions.
- *Project matrix*: a project manager is assigned to oversee the project and has primary responsibility and authority for completing the project. Functional managers assign personnel as needed and provide technical expertise.
- *Project team*: a project manager is put in charge of a project team composed of a core group of personnel from several functional areas and/or groups, assigned on a full-time basis. The functional managers have no formal involvement.

How Toyota organizes for product development

For about forty years, the Japanese car manufacturer Toyota had been using the balanced matrix structure for new product development. More specifically, each new product was developed by a development team. The members of this team came from various functions like design engineering, marketing, manufacturing engineering, and retained their position and responsibility within their functional unit while in the team. Every new product development project was headed by a product manager. This position was first established in the mid-1950s and named *shusa*, while in 1989 it was renamed as chief engineer. For example, Kenya Nakamura was the first shusa of the 1955 Crown model. The project manager had complete responsibility for the new product project and the authority to make all the necessary decisions (for example, engineering, manufacturing, product concept creation). In fact, the *shusa* was a respected leader who set the strategic direction of the new vehicle, recruited and motivated the team, secured resources and removed impediments. On the other hand, the functional managers were responsible for the training, guidance and overall assistance of the 'developers'.

However, in early 1990s, the chief engineer system, was considered inappropriate, as each project was too independent and therefore serious marketing problems had occurred like, product cannibalization. Further, production costs remained high, as there was a tendency that each project overly developed proprietary components. Therefore, Toyota needed to increase commonalty of components and technologies among multiple new projects. Clearly, multiple related projects needed more coordination. Hence, in 1992, the Japanese automobile manufacturer Toyota underwent an extensive change in its product development organization in order to strengthen the integration mechanisms for engineers in different functions and thus, create a well-integrated new product, as well as to facilitate coordination among different projects, so that technologies and components can be effectively transferred and shared. In this context, Toyota divided all its new product development projects in to three development centres.

Centre 1 is responsible for rear-wheel-drive platforms and vehicles, Centre 2 for front-wheel-drive platforms and vehicles, Centre 3 for utility vehicle/van platforms and vehicles. Each centre has approximately 1,500 employees and works on about five different new development projects at the same time. In 1993, Toyota created Centre 4 that develops components and systems for all vehicles.

Source: Nobeoka (1995)

In order to understand better the differences between these five npd structures, Crawford (1997) summarizes their operating characteristics in terms of:

- decision of power leader.
- independence of group from departments.
- percentage of time spent on one project by member.
- importance of project(s).
- degree of risk of project(s) to firm.
- disruptiveness of project(s).
- degree of uncertainty in most decisions.
- ability of team to go against company policies.

In the 'functional' structure, these characteristics are found to a minimum degree. As we move along the spectrum of structures these characteristics are found to an increasing degree, whereas the 'project team' (or 'venture') structure incorporates these characteristics to a maximum degree.

Formality of new product development process

The extent to which a new product development process is formal or not is another critical issue that a company must decide upon when designing its new product development activities.

The formality of the new product development process can be conceptualized in accordance with the structuring of activities dimension of the organizational structure, which comprises the following characteristics (Pugh et al., 1963; Hage and Aiken, 1970):

- *Specialization*: the degree of division of labour achieved internally in terms of functions and roles.
- *Formalization*: the extent to which rules, procedures, and structures are written down for defining roles and for passing information.
- *Standardization*: the degree to which roles are defined for carrying out tasks in a certain way.
- *Centralization*: the degree of dispersal of power by the chief executive office.
- *Stratification*: the degree that status differentials are adhered to in the execution of tasks.

In fact, these characteristics have been defined as 'hidden' or 'infra'-structures (Khandwalla, 1977; Mintzberg, 1979) as opposed to the 'super'-structures such as new product committees or venture teams, which have been discussed in the previous section.

A number of authors in organizational theory postulate that in innovative, fast-changing environments successful companies tend to have less formalized, organic structures and processes (Burns and Stalker, 1961; Child, 1975; Orrock and Weick, 1990). In innovation literature, it is also stated that when a product concept is fairly unfamiliar, more organic mechanisms produce better performance outcomes (Olson et al., 1995). Further, there are arguments suggesting that the initiation of an innovation process (namely, idea generation, screening, business analysis and marketing strategy) is facilitated through a loose structuring of activities, whereas a change into more tight, mechanistic structures is probably most appropriate during the implementation phase (namely, development, testing, launching) (Zaltman et al., 1973; Baldridge and Burnham, 1975; Dewar and Duncan, 1977; Cummings and O'Connell, 1978; Johne, 1984; Hise et al., 1989).

An interesting study regarding the informal organizational structures of developing new products as well as the appropriate conditions for their implementation has been conducted by Johne (1984). The researcher compared the organizational characteristics of eight active and eight less active product innovator companies. These characteristics included specialization, formalization, standardization, centralization and stratification. Recognizing the existence of a two-stage product innovation process (Zaltman et al., 1973; Rogers, 1982), the analyses were conducted separately for the initiation and implementation phases of product innovation.

According to the study's findings, in the *initiation* of product innovation, it was found that active product innovator companies use rather informal or loose structures. On the other hand, less active product innovators establish much more tight structural mechanisms. More specifically, in active product innovators there is high role specialization that is accompanied by medium functional specialization. Typically, the marketing and engineering functions intimately engage in the initiation phase. Less active product innovators witness low levels of specialization and sometimes the task of generating new product ideas is assigned solely to the production function. Both formalization and stratification were low for active and high for less active product innovator companies. Standardization was measured in two ways. First, consistency in control was medium for active product innovators and high for less active ones. Second, frequency of reviews scored low for both types of companies. Finally, centralization is medium priority in active product innovators, but high in less active product innovators.

In the *implementation* phase, active product innovator companies turn into more tight structures for organizing development activities, characterized by high levels of specialization, formalization, standardization, centralization, and stratification. As far as less active product innovators are concerned, they make a so-called 'dysfunctional' shift in their operating structures. Specifically, less active product innovator companies have high and medium centralization and stratification, respectively. Functional specialization is low, whereas role specialization is medium. Formalization is low in terms of written guidance, but medium in terms of written communication.

Formality of new service development process

In a sample of nine commercial banks the in UK, Johne and Harborne (1985) found that both active and less active product innovators have a loose structuring of the development tasks during initiation. However, as they move to the implementation phase, active product innovators witness a shift in their structure, towards a tighter one, while less active product innovators do not seem to change tighter structures.

In a recent study conducted by the authors of this book of the Greek financial services market, it was found that the new service development process is characterized by the following three unique structural dimensions (Avlonitis and Papastathopoulou, 2000):

- *Assignment of responsibilities*, which refers to the existence of clearly identified responsibilities between functional units.
- *Documentation*, which refers to the existence of a typical/formalized process with activities depicted in a written form.
- *Systematic behaviour*, which describes the existence of specific criteria and objectives for selecting new product ideas and monitoring the development process.

This study revealed that the more formally organized the development process of new retail financial services, the more complete is their development process. Given the importance of a complete new service development (nsd) process for reaching high new service performance (for example, Edgett, 1996), financial companies should seriously consider establishing more standardized procedures for initiating and monitoring the development process of their new offerings. What is more, while systematic behaviour is essential for extensively executing all nsd stages, as we move from the initiation to the implementation of the innovation process, assigning responsibilities is also important, suggesting that nsd managers should 'shift their operating structures' from a loose towards a tighter form. This is probably so because the first two stages (namely, initiation) include activities that are performed particularly by the marketing function (Davison, et al., 1989), while the proceeding three stages (namely, implementation) are more cross-functional.

Another interesting finding of this study is that successful new retail financial services are characterized by higher levels of nsd process formality. This result may be attributed to the intangible nature of new services in general. As such, their success in the market place requires a development process that is based on a well-defined set of criteria, objectives and procedures, not necessarily in writing, in an attempt to tightly control the development process and to facilitate the evaluation of its progress.

Functional involvement in new product development process

Another important issue pertaining to the organization for new product development has to do with the functions that will be engaged in every stage of the new product development process, and further, with the way that these functions could be effectively integrated. During the last decade, an increasing number of researchers have been preoccupied with this issue.

In *Best Practices Study* of the Product Development and Management Association, it was found that there are three primary functional areas which are involved in the development of new products, that is marketing (in 82 per cent of companies), R&D (69.3 per cent) and engineering (57.1 per cent) (Page, 1993). The remaining functional areas of manufacturing, new products, sales, and finance were involved in npd in less than half of the companies.

The importance of cross-functional cooperation and coordination between the three aforementioned functions and especially between marketing and R&D has been extensively reported in the literature (Gupta et al., 1986; Gupta and Wilemon, 1988; Hise et al., 1990; Moenaert and Souder, 1990a, b; Rochford and Rudelius, 1992; Moenaert et al., 1994; Song et al., 1998). This stems from the importance of the information exchange between these functions in an attempt to reduce the uncertainty inherent in new product development in relation to identification of customer needs, technology, competition and necessary resources.

Gupta et al. (1985) developed an analytical model for studying the R&D-marketing interface in the product innovation process. More specifically, marketing cooperates with R&D in:

- setting new product goals and priorities;
- preparing R&D's budget proposals;
- establishing product development schedules;
- generating new product ideas;
- screening new product ideas;
- finding commercial applications of R&D's new product ideas/technologies.

Recognizing the need for different information in the various stages of the new product development process, Song et al. (1998) examined which is the most productive joint involvement of marketing, R&D and production by stage, which managers can use as a road map. The following joint functional involvement by stage may be *productive*:

- in market opportunity analysis: R&D and marketing;
- in planning: R&D and manufacturing – manufacturing and marketing;
- in development: R&D and manufacturing – R&D and marketing;
- in pre-testing: R&D and marketing – manufacturing and marketing;
- in launch: R&D and manufacturing.

By contrast, the following joint functional involvement by stage may be *counterproductive*:

- in market opportunity analysis: R&D and manufacturing;
- in planning: none;
- in development: manufacturing and marketing – all three functions;
- in pre-testing: all three functions;
- in launch: manufacturing and marketing.

Cross-functional development at BMW

Once a year, a dozen of BMW employees go to the company's R&D facilities in Palo Alto, California and form teams of three employees that work together for ninety days to identify, explore, and develop new automotive innovations. These development teams are cross-functional and involve people from various specializations (for example, marketer, engineer, strategist, and so on). Every team builds a working prototype and if it passes the rigorous testing process, it goes to the company's headquarters in Munich, Germany for further evaluation, development, and final commercialization.

In a similar study, Olson et al. (2001) found that:

- The level of cooperation between marketing and R&D is greater during the early stages of the development process (namely, idea generation, concept testing and business assessment) than the later stages (namely, prototype development, product testing and commercialization).
- The level of cooperation between marketing and operations, and R&D and operations increases as the development process proceeds from the early to its later stages.

- The level of cooperation between marketing and operations, and R&D and operations is positively related to the development of successful innovative products.
- The level of cooperation between marketing and operations in the early stages is positively related to the development of successful non-innovative products, but also the development of unsuccessful innovative products.

Given the importance of cross-functional cooperation, Souder (1988) has suggested that managers could pursue the integration of R&D and marketing by:

- making personnel aware of the fact that interface problems are inevitable;
- making personnel sensitive to the characteristics of disharmony;
- giving equal praise to both functions;
- reinforcing the desire of personnel for R&D and marketing cooperation;
- using teams of R&D and marketing as often as possible;
- solving personality clashes soon enough;
- avoiding contentment.

All in all, in order to increase the effectiveness cross-functional teams, Donnellon (1993) has suggested the following:

- communicating the priority of strategic goals to teams;
- changing the role of functional managers from controllers to suppliers of resources;
- making teams accountable for their performance;
- suspending individual performance reviews;
- investing resources;
- giving professionals autonomy to choose team assignments;
- balancing leadership with membership;
- giving teams access to senior managers;
- training everyone for membership.

Nokia 6650 mobile phone: cross-functional cooperation

The Finnish company Nokia, known for its continuous innovation, has recently entered the 3G mobile phone market with its Nokia 6650 model. The model is designed for recyclability. On the basis of a material content survey, at the end of the product's life cycle, the different components of the phone can be traced and handled in the appropriate way. This environmentally sound mobile phone was developed by a cross-functional team comprising R&D, operations, marketing, sales, logistics and environmental experts. External suppliers, recycling service providers and an accessory team were also involved in the development process.

Functional involvement in new service development process

The 'key' functions regarding new service development are marketing, sales (as the latter is frequently separated from marketing in the organizational chart), EDP (also called IT or Systems) and operations.

Whereas the role of marketing and sales is largely the same between goods and service companies, operations is comparable to the production function in manufactured goods and is responsible for blueprinting the service delivery and executing all the necessary back-office activities, while the EDP/systems function is analogous to the R&D function in manufactured goods and is responsible for designing the electronic systems that would allow the seamless delivery of the new service.

The involvement of various functions when developing new services has also been investigated, to a lesser extent, though compared to the development of new products. Scheuing and Johnson (1989) were among the first who examined this topic. These researchers explored how five functions (namely, marketing, operations, product management, training and systems) share responsibility for key steps in the development of new financial products, namely concept development, service development and testing, process/system development and testing, marketing programme development and testing, training programme development and testing. They conclude that marketing plays a major role in most activities of the process (particularly marketing programme development and testing, and concept development), whereas the role of technical/operations functions, particularly systems is limited to the actual development stage.

In the insurance sector, a study by Johne (1993) revealed that marketing and underwriting (a function responsible for measuring the financial risks of insurance services) cooperated closely throughout the innovation process, from the initial activities of identifying new product opportunities up to the launch. However, despite the significant position of the underwriting function, marketing is increasingly influencing product development, while in several sampled companies actuaries involved in such activities were given the title of 'marketing actuary' because of their promotion related responsibilities at the late stages of the process.

The dominant role of marketing in all stages of new service development has also been confirmed in both innovative and non-innovative services in a study by Papastathopoulou et al. (2004). However, the involvement of the other functions differs by stage. For example, operations seems to take an active part during the actual development of the new service, when the delivery process is designed, while sales are considerably involved during the final stage of launching irrespective of the degree of innovativeness of the new service.

The importance of cross-functional cooperation for achieving increased performance has been revealed in a study conducted by de Brentani (1995). On the basis of seventeen factors relating to the nature of the service, product-market characteristics, project synergy and new service development proficiency, the researcher clustered 276 new B2B services into five new service 'scenarios'. The most successful scenario included 'customized expert services', which based their development partly on the excellent communication among functional areas such as marketing, IT, process design and service delivery.

Organizational arrangements for managing existing products and services

The management of existing products and services is one of the most critical marketing tasks. Therefore, the organizational structures for managing products and services that are included in the company's product portfolio may be described in the context of the organizational structure of the marketing function. This structure depends on the organizational structure of the company. The most common organizational structures are as follows:

- functionally-focused structure;
- market-focused structure;
- product-focused structure.

Table 11.1 Comparing the involvement of marketing, sales, EDP and operations in five stages of the development process between 'me-too' and new-to-the-market retail financial services

		Marketing	Sales	EDP/Systems	Operations
Idea generation and screening	'Me-too'	3.48*	2.52	1.42	2.40
	New-to-the-market	3.80	2.54	1.58	2.32
Business analysis and	'Me-too'	3.40	1.87	1.29	2.20
marketing strategy	New-to-the-market	4.06	1.64	1.48	2.22
Technical development	'Me-too'	3.20	1.40	2.87	3.18
	New-to-the-market	3.63	1.80	3.38	3.47
Testing	'Me-too'	3.40	2.73	3.00	2.81
	New-to-the-market	2.97	2.70	3.13	2.53
Launching	'Me-too'	3.40	3.60	1.52	2.26
	New-to-the-market	4.08	3.84	1.62	2.21

*Figures depict mean involvement of each function to each stage. Involvement was measured using a 1–5 scale (where 1: none, 5: very high).

Source: Papastathopoulou et al. (2004)

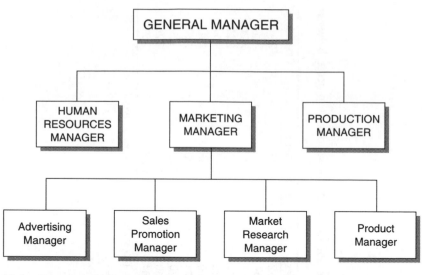

Figure 11.1   **Functionally-focused structure**

Another organizational arrangement that has recently been adopted by many consumer goods companies operating in the grocery industry is known as category management. We will now present each of these structures separately.

Functionally-focused structure

When the company has a functionally-focused structure, for every function there is a different department (or division), as it is shown in Figure 11.1. As we can see, the basic organizational functions of human resources, marketing, and production, have been organized in separate departments. Every department has a Manager who is accountable to the General Manager.

Market-focused structure

In a market-focused structure (Figure 11.2), the Marketing Director (or Manager) assigns marketing activities by market segment. In this respect, the manager who is responsible for each market segment is responsible for all the marketing activities (including product management) relating to the company's products in this segment.

This particular structure is most suitable when there are significant differences in the characteristics of the various markets served by the company (for example, customers' buying behaviour, intensity of competition, type of customer – B2B or B2C), which require a different marketing approach.

Product-focused structure

When a product management system is set (Figure 11.3), marketing activities are undertaken by product/brand managers, and at a higher level by group product/brand managers.

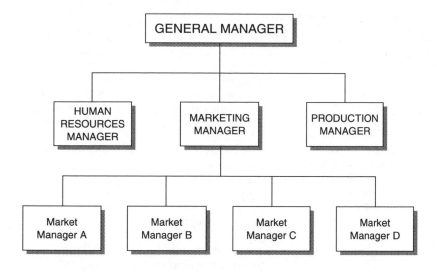

Figure 11.2 **Market-focused structure**

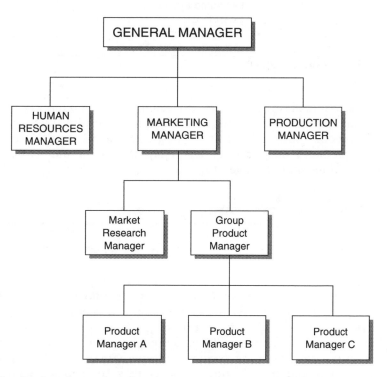

Figure 11.3 **Product-focused structure**

This structure is very common in multinational companies. In fact, the first company that adopted this structure was Procter & Gamble back in 1931 for its soap brand 'Camay'.

The responsibilities of the product/brand manager cover the whole spectrum of marketing activities, product development activities (for example, market research, concept

Table 11.2 **Product manager's duties**

Day-to-day duties	Short-term duties	Long-term duties
• Maintain a product fact book • Motivate the sales force and distributors • Collect marketing information referring to competitive activities and best practices, market trends, and customer behaviour • Act as a liaison between sales, manufacturing, R&D, and other functional areas • Control the budget and achieve marketing goals	• Participate in marketing plan and forecast development • Work with advertising departments/agencies to implement promotional strategies • Organize trade shows/conventions • Initiate regulatory acceptance • Participate in new product development teams • Predict and manage competitors' actions • Modify product and/or reduce costs to increase value • Recommend line extensions • Participate in product elimination decisions	• Design the product's marketing strategy • Identify new product opportunities • Examine and implement product changes, enhancements and introduction

Source: adapted from Gorchels (2000)

development), activities during production (for example, design of packaging, supply of raw materials) and promotional activities (for example, advertising, public relations).

In her recent book entitled *The Product Manager's Handbook*, Linda Gorchels (2000) postulates that product managers have day-to-day, short-term and long-term duties. These duties are summarized in Table 11.2.

Category management

One recent development in the grocery industry is ECR (effective consumer response), defined as a strategy in which retailers and suppliers are working closely together to bring better value to the grocery consumer. By jointly focusing on the efficiency of the total grocery supply system, rather than the efficiency of individual components, they are reducing total system costs, inventories, and physical assets, while improving the consumer's choice of high quality, fresh grocery products. The ultimate goal of ECR is to develop a responsive, consumer-driven system, in which retailers and suppliers work together as business allies to maximize consumer satisfaction and minimize cost. Accurate information and high quality products flow through a paperless system between manufacturing line and check-out counter with minimum degradation or interruption both within and between trading partners.

The ECR initiative started in the USA. In mid-1992 grocery industry leaders created a joint-industry task force, the Efficient Consumer Response Working Group, which was charged with examining the supply chain and its trade practices to identify potential opportunities for changes in practices or in technology that would make the supply chain more competitive.

In 1994 the ECR Europe was formed to provide European consumers with the best possible value, service and variety of products through collaborative action to improve the supply chain. Among the companies participating in ECR Europe are, from the industry side, Behlen, Coca-Cola, Mars, Procter & Gamble, Nestlé and, from the trade side, Albert Heijn, Tesco, KG Dorthmund. More than twenty countries have already established their own ECR boards and formal organizations including Italy, Germany, Spain, Greece, Denmark, the Netherlands and the UK.

There are four areas in which ECR participants have been working closely together. These areas represent major ECR strategies and include:

1 *Efficient store assortments*: which address the optimum use of store and shelf space, the critical interface between the supply chain and the consumer.
2 *Efficient replenishment*: which links the consumer, retail store and the supplier into a synchronized system.
3 *Efficient promotion*: which refocuses suppliers' promotion activities from selling to the retailer and towards selling through to the consumer.
4 *Efficient product introduction*: which addresses the processes of developing and introducing new products.

However, the realization of these strategies requires the adoption of the category management (CM) concept. CM is a critical component of an overall ECR strategy. Indeed, ECR is focused on the development of internal CM capabilities and selective joint efforts between trading partners to enhance the efficiency and effectiveness of product introductions, assortment planning and promotions. At the heart of CM are fundamental shifts in the way retailers and manufacturers manage their product portfolio with an increased emphasis on category-based thinking.

The general themes of CM are:

- A shift in focus away from buying to selling products that provide value to consumers.
- The use of categories or strategic business units to achieve company objectives and satisfy consumer needs. It is definitely a move away from micromanaging of the brand on stock keeping unit (SKU) level to managing a category of products that consumers perceive to meet their needs.
- The reliance on strategic partnership between retailers and suppliers to optimize consumer value while meeting trading partners' company objectives. CM is the framework for linking retail and supplier processes to focus on selling to consumers.
- A change in organizational structure, responsibilities and reward systems from a traditional departmental to an integrated process structure. For retailers this may mean the merging of buying, merchandizing, pricing, promotion and inventory management departments into one CM function responsible for sales and profits. For suppliers this may also mean new job titles and revised job descriptions during the move from brand management to category management and from the traditional salesperson to advanced salesperson, category sales manager, trusted advisor and finally to strategic alliance partner.
- CM is a fact based discipline relying on information technology and scan data to support product decision-making and business processes.

The implications of CM for product decision-making are far reaching. When it comes to store assortment optimization, the CM concept focuses on:

- understanding the role of the category within the retailer or manufacturer's portfolio;
- ensuring that the assortment reflects the retailer and manufacturer strategy;
- eliminating poorly performing SKUs;
- improving the shelf presentation of each category.

While retailers and manufacturers can do much to optimize their assortment alone, true assortment optimization often requires a free flow of information between trading partners.

With respect to product introductions, the CM focuses on:

1 the need for manufacturers, retailers and partnerships to develop an improved understanding of consumer needs and desires to avoid launch failures;
2 ways of eliminating complexity and reducing time/costs associated with new product introduction.

It is true, however, that product introduction optimization is the most difficult ECR strategy to be implemented due to:

1 difficulty of assessing product success ahead of launching;
2 traditional friction between trading partners;
3 the fear of branded launches being copied into private label;
4 chronic lack of trust.

Organizational arrangements for eliminating products and services

Apart from organizing for developing or/and managing products and services, a company should decide upon the organizational arrangements for eliminating products and services which do not meet their objectives.

The organizational issues relating to product/service elimination refer to both the involvement of various functions in the process and the formality of the elimination process.

Formality of product elimination process

Apart from the modes of organization for product elimination, another important organizational characteristic is the formality of the product elimination process.

One of the authors of this book has shown that the formality of the product elimination process is composed from the following dominant structural characteristics (Avlonitis, 1985):

- *Assignment of responsibilities* – the presence and/or degree of defined and specialized roles and assigned responsibilities regarding product elimination decision making.
- *Documentation* – the extent and intensity of formal paperwork pertaining to product elimination.
- *Systematic behaviour* – the degree to which regular systematic procedures and rules govern the product elimination activities.

According to the same study, the degree of formality that characterizes a product elimination process depends on specific organizational variables, namely company size, product diversity, and organizational technology. More specifically:

- Bigger companies tend to have more formal product elimination processes, particularly as far as the 'assignment of responsibilities' component is concerned.
- The higher the number of products in the company's product mix, the more formal is the product elimination process.

- Mass output technology orientation is positively related to the formality of the product elimination process.

In addition, formality raises the importance of a large number of decision variables that bear on each specific stage of the product elimination process (namely, identification, revitalization, evaluation of weak products, implementation of the product elimination decision). More specifically:

With respect to the *identification* of the weak products stage, formality enhances the importance of audit criteria that can assist companies to identify products that are on the decline of their growth curve (market growth rate, product's position on the life cycle curve), and products that are maturing or growing (past sales volume, future sales volume), but fall below the operating standards of the company (market share).

When we move to the *revitalization* stage, it seems that formality tends to enhance the importance of alternative corrective actions that involve changes in the company's selling function (for example, increased effort by the sales force, increased promotional expenditures, and so on).

Regarding the *evaluation* of weak products, formality appears to exert a strong effect on evaluation factors that are crucial for the retention/elimination decision. These factors reflect a concern for the reallocation of resources to other opportunities and the marketing (full line policy), social (employee relationships), and ethical (existence of a substitute product) implications of a product's elimination.

Finally, as far as the *implementation* of the product elimination decision is concerned, in formal processes the 'phase out slowly' (run out and so on) strategy is usually preferred to a 'selling out' strategy. As a consequence, it is hardly surprising to find that formality has a significant positive impact on the importance of those factors which tend to determine the most opportune time of a product's withdrawal, namely stock on hand, status of replacement parts, and effect on middlemen/customers.

Formality of service elimination process

The three dimensions that have been found to characterize the formality of the product elimination process (namely, assignment of responsibilities, documentation, systematic behaviour), also characterize the formality of the service elimination process (Gounaris et al., 2002).

Further, formality influences the content of the service elimination process. More specifically:

Formality and particularly the systematic behaviour component enhance the importance of audit criteria that can assist companies to detect 'weak' services, such as market share, sales, competitors' reactions, and operational problems. However, documentation exerts a proportionately lesser influence, while the existence of assigned responsibilities during the elimination process is not related to the level of importance of such audit criteria.

When we move to the evaluation stage, the picture is more or less the same. Again, formality tends to have a positive and significant impact on evaluation factors that are crucial for the retention/elimination decision (for example, impact on business partners, dealing with excess manpower and delivery points, reactions from company executives). However, the role of systematic behaviour and documentation is less influential during this stage, while assignment of responsibilities exerts no actual effect on the evaluation factors.

Finally, regarding the implementation of the service elimination decision, in more formal elimination processes, the elimination strategies 'service simplification' and 'implement marketing strategies (for example, pricing) directing customers to another service' are preferred.

It is worth mentioning that the existence of more tight procedures during the initiation and evaluation stages has a positive effect on the importance of audit criteria. This may be attributed to the intangible nature of service offerings. As such, services require a detection procedure that is based on a well-defined set of criteria and objectives, not necessarily in writing, in an attempt to tightly control the intangibility inherent and to further facilitate the evaluation of its progress.

Functional involvement in product elimination process

For better understanding of what functions participate in the product elimination process, we will examine their involvement in three stages, namely: detection of weak products, collection, analysis and interpretation of information, and decision making. The participants in the first two stages have an advisory role, while they play a decision-making role in the third stage.

According to the results of one of the authors of this book (Avlonitis, 1985), the marketing function assumes a highly significant portion of the advisory role, followed by finance, engineering and purchasing. As far as the locus of decision making is concerned, the elimination decision is very much a committee decision. The results of this study are summarized in Table 11.3.

The same study has shown that the participation of various functions in product elimination varies with the company's certain idiosyncratic conditions including size, product diversity, operations technology and competitive environment.

More specifically, as size increases, the participation of finance in the advisory role to initiate the elimination decision decreases. Moreover, as the number of products manufactured and marketed by a company (or product diversity) increases, the participation of finance in the initiation of the decision decreases, while the participation of engineering in the same role increases. Further, as the number of products manufactured and marketed (namely, product diversity) by a company increases, the participation of production in the information-handling activities also increases. What is more, as the operations technology advances from custom and small batch to large batch and mass production, the participation of the production function in the information-handling activities increases. Finally, as the degree of market competition experienced by the company increases, the participation of finance in the initiation of the decision also increases.

Functional involvement in service elimination process

The involvement or participation of various functions in the service elimination process has been examined by the authors of this book in a sample of service providers operating in Greece (Papastathopoulou et al., 2001). The organizational participants that lead the service elimination activities are shown in Table 11.4.

As in the case of manufactured products, marketing plays a dominant role in the detection of weak services, as well as the collection and analysis of information, followed by general management and finance. With respect to service elimination decision, this is usually made by general management, while the implementation of this decision is mainly assigned to sales and marketing.

In another study in a sample of financial companies in UK, Argouslidis (2001) found that marketing participates more than any other function or committee in the detection

Table 11.3 Organizational participants in product elimination activities (n = 24)

Advisory role				Decision-making role	
Detection of weak products		Collection and analysis and interpretation of information		Locus of product elimination decision-making	
Function or committee/group	No. of companies	Function or committee/group	No. of companies	Committee/group	No. of companies
Marketing	+++	Marketing	+++	Managing Director/Management group	++
Finance	++	Finance	++	Board of Directors/consensus group	+
Engineering	+	Engineering	+	General Manager/parent group board	+
Production	+	Production	++	Ad hoc elimination committee	+
Purchasing	+	Purchasing	–	Product planning committee(s)	++
Committee/group					
Ad hoc elimination committee	++	Ad hoc elimination committee	+		
		Product planning committee	++		

* +++: 11–15 companies, ++: 6–10 companies, +: 5 or less companies.

Source: adapted from Avlonitis (1985)

Table 11.4   Organizational participants leading the service elimination activities

	Detection of weak services	Collection and analysis of information	Service elimination decision-making	Implementation of service elimination decision
Marketing	31.3%	36.2%	8%	22.7%
Finance	18.4%	16%	5.5%	7.4%
Sales	19%	25.2%	6.7%	16%
Operations	5.5%	8.6%	2.5%	14.7%
General management	22.1%	6.7%	74.2%	28.2%
Executive committee	4.9%	3.7%	4.3%	3.1%

Source: Papastathopoulou et al. (2001)

Table 11.5   Organizational participants leading the elimination activities of financial services

	Detection of weak services	Collection and analysis of information	Service elimination decision making
Manager responsible for elimination	14.7%	11.1%	5.5%
Marketing	33.9%	25%	7.3%
Sales	4.6%	3.7%	1.8%
Financial/actuarial	21.1%	42.6%	1.8%
Management committee	10.1%	5.6%	30.9%
Managing director	4.6%	1.9%	5.5%

Source: adapted from Argouslidis (2001)

of weak services. During the collection and analysis of information, the financial/actuarial function has the highest participation, while a management committee, composed by managers from various functions is mainly responsible for the elimination decision (Table 11.5).

Summary

- The organizational structures set for developing new products/services can be classified on the basis of the degree of autonomy of different functional areas, the type of coordination between functional units, and the degree of exclusive orientation towards the new product/service project.
- Depending on the degree of autonomy of different functional areas, two alternative structures can be set, namely free-standing or autonomous units (namely, new product department, task force, venture team or unit), and functionally based units (namely, new product committee, integrative new-product organization, and product management system).
- Depending on the type of coordination between functional units, structures include bureaucratic control/hierarchical directives, individual liaisons, temporary task forces, integrating managers, matrix structures, design teams, design centres.

- Based on the degree of exclusive orientation towards the new product/service project, structures can be functional, functional matrix, balanced matrix, project matrix, and project team.
- The formality of the new product development process is characterized by specialization, formalization, standardization, centralization, stratification.
- The initiation of an innovation process is facilitated through a loose structuring of activities, whereas a change into tighter, mechanistic structures is considered most appropriate during the implementation phase.
- Successful new retail financial services tend to be positively influenced by higher levels of nsd process formality.
- Cross-functional cooperation and coordination is critical during new product development because of the importance of exchanging information between functions to reduce the uncertainty inherent in innovation activities.
- The effectiveness of the joint involvement of various functions differs by npd process stage.
- Marketing has a leading role in new product/service development.
- The marketing function can be organized in the context of first, a functionally-focused organizational structure, secondly, a market-focused organizational structure, or thirdly, a product-focused organizational structure.
- Category management is another organizational mode that has been recently adopted by retailers.
- The formality of the product as well as elimination process is composed by assignment of responsibilities, documentation and systematic behaviour.
- The degree of formality that characterizes a product elimination process depends on company size, product diversity, and organizational technology.
- The marketing function assumes a highly significant portion of the advisory role in the product elimination process, followed by finance, engineering and purchasing, whereas the elimination decision is very much a committee decision.
- Marketing plays a dominant role in the detection of weak services, as well as the collection and analysis of information, followed by general management and finance.
- General management makes the service elimination decision, while the implementation of this decision is mainly assigned to sales and marketing.

Questions

1 Present the characteristics of the balanced matrix structure that are related to the independence of the npd group from the operational departments of the company and the degree of risk of the npd project to the company.
2 Discuss the appropriate informal or 'hidden' organizational structures for developing innovative financial services.
3 Provide a discussion of the role of the main functions of a manufacturing company vs. a service company in the various stages of the development process.
4 Discuss the advantages of category management for retailers and consumer goods companies.

References

Argouslidis, P. (2001) 'The service elimination process: an empirical investigation into the British financial services sector', Unpublished Ph.D. thesis, University of Stirling.

Avlonitis G. (1985) 'Advisors and decision – makers in product eliminations', *Industrial Marketing Management*, 14: 17–26.

Avlonitis, G. and Papastathopoulou, P. (2000) 'Effective development of new retail financial services: does formality matter?', 29th European Marketing Academy Conference, Erasmus University, Rotterdam, The Netherlands.

Baldridge, J.V. and Burnham, R.A. (1975) 'Organisational innovation: individual, organisational and environmental impacts', *Administrative Science Quarterly* 20: 165–76.

Benson, G. and Chasin, J. (1976) *The Structure of New Product Organisation*. New York: AMACOM.

Booz, Allen and Hamilton (1982) *New Products Management for the 1980s*. New York: Booz, Allen and Hamilton, Inc.

Burns, T. and Stalker, G (1961) *The Management of Innovation*. London: Tavistock.

Child, J. (1975) 'Managerial and organisational factors associated with company performance: part 2', *Journal of Management Studies*, 12: 12–27.

Crawford, M. (1997) *New Products Management*. Homewood, IL: Richard D. Irwin, Inc.

Cummings, L.L. and O'Connell, M.J. (1978) 'Organisational innovation: A model and needed research', *Journal of Business Research* 6: 33–50.

Davison, H., Watkins, T. and Wright, M. (1989) 'Developing new personal financial products – some evidence on the role of market research', *International Journal of Bank Marketing*, 7(1): 8–15.

de Brentani, U. (1995) 'New industrial service development: scenarios for success and failure', *Journal of Business Research*, 32: 93–103.

Dewar, R.D. and Duncan, R.B. (1977) 'Implications for organisational design of structural alteration as a consequence of growth and innovation', *Organisation and Administrative Sciences*, 8: 203–222.

Donnellon, A. (1993) 'Cross-functional teams in product development: accommodation of the structure to the process', *Journal of Product Innovation Management*, 10: 377–92.

Edgett, S. (1996) 'The new product development process for commercial financial services', *Industrial Marketing Management*, 25: 507–15.

Galbraith, J. and Nathanson, D. (1978) *Strategy Implementation: The Role of Structure and Process*. St. Paul, MN: West Publishing Company.

Gorchels, L. (2000) *The Product Manager's Handbook*, 2nd edition. Chicago, IL: NTC Business Books.

Gounaris, S., Papastathopoulou, P., Avlonitis, G. and Argouslidis, P. (2002) 'An exploratory investigation of the effect of formality on the content of the service elimination process', 31st European Marketing Academy Conference, University of the Minho, Braga, Portugal.

Gupta, A. and Wilemon, D. (1988) 'Why R&D resists using marketing information', *Research-Technology Management*, 31(6): 36–41.

Gupta, A., Raj, S. and Wilemon, D. (1985) 'R&D and marketing dialogue in high-tech firms', *Industrial Marketing Management*, 14: 289–300.

Gupta, A., Raj, S. and Wilemon, D. (1986) 'A model for studying R&D-Marketing interface in the product innovation process', *Journal of Marketing*, 50: 7–17.

Hage, J. and Aiken, M. (1970) *Social Change in Complex Organisations*. New York: Random House.

Hise, R., O'Neal, L., McNeal, J. and Parasuraman, A. (1989) 'The effect of product design activities on commercial success levels of new industrial products', *Journal of Product Innovation Management*, 6: 43–50.

Hise, R., O'Neal, L., Parasuraman, A. and McNeal, J. (1990) 'Marketing/R&D interaction in new product development: implications for new product success rates', *Journal of Product Innovation Management*, 7: 142–55.

Johne, A. (1984) 'How experienced product innovators organise', *Journal of Product Innovation Management*, 4: 210–223.

Johne, A. (1993) 'Insurance product development: managing the changes', *International Journal of Bank Marketing*, 11(3): 5–14.

Johne, A. and Harborne, P. (1985) 'How large commercial banks manage product innovation', *International Journal of Bank Marketing*, 3(1): 54–72.

Kwandwalla, P. (1977) *The Design of Organisation*. New York: Harcourt, Brace, Jovanovich.

Larson, E. and Gobeli, D. (1985) 'Project management structures: is there a common language?', *Project Management Journal*, 16(2): 40–4.

Larson, E. and Gobeli, D. (1988) 'Organising for product development projects', *Journal of Product Innovation Management*, 5: 180–90.

Mahajan, V. and Wind, J. (1992) 'New product models: practice, shortcomings and desired improvement', *Journal of Product Innovation Management*, 9: 128–39.

Midgley, D. (1977) *Innovation and New Product Marketing*. London: Croom Helm.

Mintzberg, H. (1979) *The Structuring of Organisations*. Englewood Cliffs, NJ: Prentice-Hall.

Moenaert, R. and Souder, W. (1990a) 'An information transfer model for integrating marketing and R&D personnel in new product development project', *Journal of Product Innovation Management*, 7: 91–107.

Moenaert, R. and Souder W. (1990b) 'An analysis of the use of extra-functional information by R&D and marketing personnel: review and model', *Journal of Product Innovation Management*, 7: 213–39.

Moenaert, R., Souder, W., De Meyer, A. and Deschoolmeester, D. (1994) 'R&D – marketing integration mechanisms, communication flows, and innovation success', *Journal of Product Innovation Management*, 11: 31–45.

Nobeoka, K. (1995) 'Reorganizing for multi-project management: Toyota's new structure of product development centers', Research Institute for Economics and Business Administration, Kobe University.

Olson, E., Walker, O. and Ruekert, R. (1995) 'Organising for effective new product development: the moderating role of product innovativeness', *Journal of Marketing*, 59: 48–62.

Olson, E., Walker, O., Ruekert, R. and Bonner, J. (2001) 'Patterns of cooperation during new product development among marketing, operations and R&D: Implications for project performance', *Journal of Product Innovation Management*, 18: 258–71.

Orrock, J. and Weick, K. (1990) 'Loosely coupled systems: a reconceptualization', *Academy of Management Review*, 15: 203–23.

Page, A. (1993) 'Assessing new product development practices and performance: Establishing crucial norms', *Journal of Product Innovation Management*, 10: 273–90.

Papastathopoulou, P., Avlonitis, G. and Gounaris, S. (2001) 'Functional involvement during service elimination', Working Paper, Athens University of Economics and Business.

Papastathopoulou, P., Gounaris, S. and Avlonitis, G. (2004) 'Successful new-to-the-market vs. "me-too" retail financial services: the influential role of marketing, sales, E.D.P. and operations', Working Paper, Athens University of Economics and Business.

Pugh, D., Hickson, D., Hinings, C., MacDonald, K., Turner, C. and Lupton, T. (1963) 'A conceptual schema of organisation analysis', *Administrative Science Quarterly*, 8: 289–315.

Rochford, L. and Rudelius, W. (1992) 'How involving more functional areas within a firm affects the new product process', *Journal of Product Innovation Management* 9: 287–99.

Rogers, E. (1983) *Diffusion of Innovations*. New York: The Free Press.

Sands, S. (1983) 'Problems of organising for effective new-product development', *European Journal of Marketing*, 17(4): 18–33.

Scheuing, E. and Johnson, E. (1989) 'New product development and management in financial institutions', *International Journal of Bank Marketing*, 7(2): 17–21.

Song, M., Thieme, J. and Xie, J. (1998) 'The impact of cross-functional joint-involvement across development stages: an exploratory study', *Journal of Product Innovation Management*, 15: 289–303.

Souder, W. (1988) 'Managing relations between R&D and marketing in new product development projects', *Journal of Product Innovation Management*, 5: 6–19.

Zaltman, G., Duncan, R. and Holbek, J. (1973) *Innovations and Organizations*. New York: John Wiley & Sons.

Further reading

Bernasco, W., de Weerd-Nederhof, P., Tillema, H. and Boer, H. (1999) 'Balanced matrix structure and new product development process at Texas Instruments Materials and Controls Division', *R&D Management*, 29(2): 121–31.

Sethi, R., Smith, D. and Park, W. (2001), 'Cross-functional development teams, creativity and the innovativeness of new consumer products', *Journal of Marketing Research*, 38 (February).

Appendix 1   New Product Budget[1]

The present appendix describes the theoretical background regarding the process of developing a budget for a new product. A real-life example is also provided.

Theoretical background

The time period covered by a new product budget is usually twelve months, or an accounting period, depending on the policy followed by the company. In addition, this budget can be developed into a monthly, quarterly, semi-annual or other frequency that is considered to be appropriate by the company. The time period on which the budget analysis will be based depends on the existing control procedures regarding its implementation, namely, the comparison of the budgeted with the actual figures in order to calculate the variances, justify them and make the right decisions and necessary corrective actions.

The development of a new product budget is called master budget. A number of separate budgets compose the master budget of the new product (Figure 1). These budgets are developed either sequentially or in parallel.

The basic elements of the separate budgets are briefly presented below.

Sales budget

The sales budget forms the basis of the master budget. In this sense, the accuracy of the sales budget is extremely important for developing the master budget. Specifically, an over-estimation of demand may lead to the creation of undesired inventories and an unnecessary commitment of resources, which could possibly be used more efficiently in other company products. On the other hand, an under-estimation of demand may not allow the company to satisfy its customers' needs and, thus, lose profits and market share.

Sales forecasting can be done in different ways depending on the policy that each company follows. The basic methods of sales forecasting are as follows: subjective/qualitative methods, for example, estimations of sales directors and sales persons, analysis of customers' intentions and objective/quantitative, for example, market testing. In either method, a series of internal and external factors must be taken into account. The main internal factors are: sales of previous versions of the product or similar products of the previous year, production capability of the company, marketing and sales promotion strategies, product seasonality, expected life cycle of the product, and so on. The main external factors that may be considered are: competitive and substitute products, economic conditions and negotiating power of company's customers, general economic conditions, general trends in the manufacturing industry and governmental policies.

In order to develop the sales budget, the pricing policy for the new product must also be considered. Thus, decisions about the sales price, the discount policy, the special

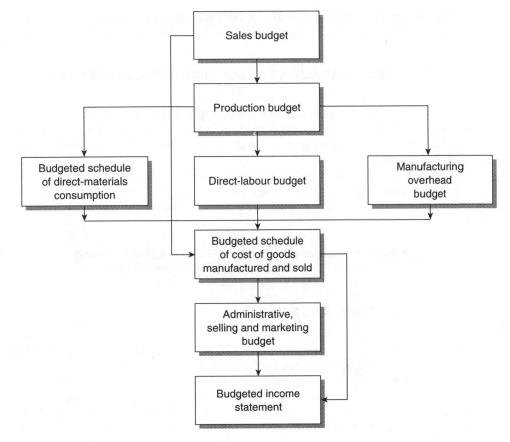

Figure 1   **New product budget development**

offers of the product, are important parameters in developing the sales budget. Sales are budgeted as follows:

sales budget (in €) = sales budget (in units) × sales price per unit

Production budget

The production budget is based on the sales budget after making the necessary adjustments in the level of the desired ending inventories of finished goods. Specifically, by taking into account: the inventory of finished goods at the beginning of the month, the expected sales during the month, and the desired inventory at the end of the month, the quantities that must be produced on a monthly basis can then be calculated. The level of inventories retained is relevant to the policy followed by the company and is affected, among others, by the vulnerability of the product, the speed of its technological obsolescence and the warehousing costs. Production can be budgeted as follows:

production budget (units) = sales budget (units) + desired ending inventory (units)
– beginning inventory (units)

Based on the production budget, a company can develop the budgets for direct materials, direct labour and manufacturing overheads, as is presented further down in this chapter.

Budgeted schedule of direct-materials consumption

Direct materials are all the raw materials that are incorporated into the product and they constitute an important part of the total cost of the materials that will be consumed for its production. Direct materials are part of the direct cost because they are directly associated with the product.

The scheduled budget of direct material consumption is referred to the quantity and the cost of direct materials that are necessary for producing the required product units according to the production budget. The direct materials consumption is budgeted as follows:

budget of direct-materials consumption = required direct materials (units)
× direct materials cost per unit

Direct labour budget

Direct labour is the labour offered by those who are directly involved in the processing of direct materials that are incorporated into the product, and it constitutes an important part of the cost of the total labour that will be required for its production. Direct labour is part of the direct cost because it is directly associated with the product. Direct labour may be required during the whole range of processing activities that take place from the original shaping to the final production of the product. Finally, the cost per direct labour hour in each department, namely, the hourly labour cost per department varies according to the remuneration policy of the company. Hence, direct labour is budgeted as follows:

direct labour budget = production units
× hours of direct labour per unit
× hourly labour cost

Manufacturing overhead budget

Manufacturing overheads are the indirect costs that are incurred in the context of a production process of a company and must be allocated to all of the products produced. Examples of such expenditure are: indirect or other materials, indirect labour, various operational expenses (rent, energy, insurance, depreciation, utilities), and so on. The calculation of manufacturing overheads that should be allocated to the new product should incorporate not only the manufacturing overheads that are directly associated with the new product, but also the manufacturing overheads that concern the total production of the new product (or part of it). It should be noted that manufacturing overheads that should be associated with the new product will be calculated by multiplying an allocation rate of manufacturing overheads determined by the company with the base used for the allocation (for example direct labour hours, number of machine hours, number of product units, and so on). Thus, manufacturing overheads can be budgeted as follows:

$$\begin{aligned} \text{manufacturing overhead budget} = {} &\text{manufacturing overheads directly associated} \\ &\text{with the new product} \\ &+ (\text{allocation rate} \times \text{allocation base}) \end{aligned}$$

On the basis of the information provided from the budgets of direct-material consumption, direct labour and manufacturing overheads, the budgeted production cost per unit can then be calculated.

Budgeted schedule of cost of goods manufactured and sold

The cost of goods manufactured during a period involves the cost of the products that were finished during this period and it is calculated as the sum of direct materials consumed, direct labour and manufacturing overheads.

The cost of goods sold during a time period refers to the cost of the products that were sold during this period and it is the sum of the value of the beginning inventory of finished goods and the cost of manufactured goods minus the value of ending inventory of finished products. The valuation of inventories is based on the method used by the company namely LIFO (last in, first out), FIFO (first in, first out) or weighed average method.[2]

Administrative expense budget

The general administrative expenses are the expenses created in the general context of a company's administration. Examples of such expenses are the expenses of supporting departments such as the accounting department, the human resource management department, the legal services, but also the General Manager's salary, rent, electricity and so on. In most cases there are no direct administrative expenses related to a new product. Usually the budgeted administration expenses that are associated with the new product are calculated by multiplying the budgeted sales value of the new product with a predetermined rate.

Selling and marketing expenses budget

The selling and marketing expenses are the expenses created in order to promote sales and deliver the products to the customer. Examples of such expenses are advertising costs, the salaries of the Sales and Marketing Managers, the salaries and commissions of sales staff, the expenses of participating in trade shows, the storage expenses of finished products, the transportation expenses of finished products, the market research expenses, the promotion expenses, and so on.

The budgeted selling and marketing expenses of the new product are direct and indirect. The direct selling and marketing expenses of the new product concern the special promotion activities for the new product (free samples, advertisements), listing fees, and so on, and, therefore should be allocated only to this product. The indirect selling and marketing expenses refer to the expenses that are associated with the new product, for example the proportion of sales staff salaries and those of their managers, their travelling expenses, the cost of participating in exhibitions, and so on. However, a portion of them should be allocated to the new product as well. The budgeted selling and marketing expenses that are associated with the new product are calculated by multiplying the budgeted sales value of the new product with a predetermined rate.

Budgeted income statement

The budgeted income statement is based on the previous budgets. This statement presents the budgeted gross income (profit or loss) of the new product as well as the operating income (profit or loss) of the new product.

Sensitivity analysis and scenario planning

Given the complexities and uncertainties of the business world, unexpected changes usually occur. In this sense, companies need to examine their forecasts and assumptions on a regular basis. To do this, sensitivity analysis and scenario planning are often performed.

In sensitivity analysis one or more parameters that participate in the budget development are changed. The parameters that are proved to have a considerable impact on the profitability and the viability of the new product are identified and carefully monitored.

In scenario planning, companies prepare different combinations of a number of parameters. Usually, companies determine the pessimistic, the normal and the optimistic scenario and estimate their outcomes by assessing both the financial and the non-financial results from the introduction of the new product in the market.

A real-life example of a new product budget

The new product development department of Razors' Manufacture S.A.[3] is currently assessing the possibility of launching a new modern razor for women into the market. This razor, which will guarantee soft skin, will have an anatomic shape and will be available in pleasant colours. In addition, it will be sold with a modern case, which will make the product a nice bath accessory. The product will be introduced to the market in two variants. The first one will be the razor device with the blade (henceforward razor), while the second one will be the shaving cartridge consisting of four blades (henceforward blades).

Financial data of the product

1   The expected sales mixture and pricing policy for the first year of the product's introduction to the market organized in quartiles have been determined as follows:

		Quartiles	
Pieces	Q1	Q2	Q3
Razors (units)	4	2	1
Blades (units)	1	2	3

Price in €	Quartiles		
	Q1	Q2	Q3
Razors	€5.9	€6.5	€6.5
Blades	€3.9	€3.5	€3

2 The expected demand, based on a marketing research that has been previously conducted and costed at €44,645, showed that 6,000 razors, with conservative estimates, could be sold during the first month of introduction with a monthly rise of 5 per cent.
3 The company has as a policy of producing each month only as many product units as to cover the monthly demand plus 5 per cent of the expected sales of the next month.
4 The technical descriptions of the products regarding direct materials and direct labour, are presented below:

Cost data	Razor	Blades
Direct materials		
Plastic (grams)	12	
Cost per kilogram (€)	50	
Blade/piece (€)	0.35	0.35
Case/piece (€)	0.2	0.1
Direct labour		
Cost/hour (mean value in €)	25	25
Processing time for the razor (min)	4	0
Processing time for the blade (min)	0.5	2

The company allocates manufacturing overheads using as an allocation base the expected number of the products to be produced on a yearly basis.
5 The annual manufacturing overheads regarding the two products are:

Manufacturing overhead budget	
Indirect materials	10% of direct materials' value
Managers' salaries	Two managers, one for each shift with a total monthly cost of €2,500
Machine depreciation	For the production of the new products a new machine will be bought. Its value will be €80,000 and its useful life 5 years (depreciation rate 20%). The machine will be paid in 5 monthly equal instalments
Maintenance expenses	Expected to be 10% of the machine's acquisition cost value (annually)
Machine set-up expenses	Expected to be 5% of the machine's acquisition cost value (annually)
Electricity, telephone expenses, etc.	Expected to be 10% of other overheads

6 The annual selling and marketing expenses regarding the two products have been budgeted as follows:

Budgeted selling and marketing expenses	
Advertising	1% of the monthly sales value
Sales persons' salaries	Five sales persons will spend 5% of their time in the promotion of the product. Each of them will have a monthly salary of €2,000.
Sales persons' commissions	The sales persons will receive 0.05% of the sales as a commission.
Distribution expenses	Have been budgeted to be €0.10 per item of product.
Market research	It was decided to allocate the cost of market research in each product unit based on the budgeted sales of the first year.
Listing fees	The listing fees have been estimated to be €3,000.

7 The administration expenses are expected to mount to 8 per cent of the sales value.

Based on the above data, the following budgets for the first year of the new product introduction can be developed both on a *monthly* and a *yearly basis*:

- sales budget in units of each product;
- sales budget in values;
- production budget in units of each product;
- budgeted schedule of cost of goods manufactured per product unit;
- budgeted schedule of selling, marketing and administration expenses;
- budgeted income statements.

It is noted that, in the following exhibits the *grey* parts refer to the basic assumptions that have been made during the budget development of the new product, while the *white* parts provide the results of the computations based on these assumptions. In changing these assumptions, the results will change as well. The analysis that follows can be undertaken using any spreadsheet software package.

Data

Pieces/Case

	Razor	Blades
Razor + blade (base)	1	1
Blades	0	4

	January	February	March	April	May	June	July	August	September	October	November	December
Razor + blade (Base)	4	4	4	4	2	2	2	2	1	1	1	1
Blades	1	1	1	1	2	2	2	2	3	3	3	3
Total pieces	5	5	5	5	4	4	4	4	4	4	4	4
Analogy blades/razor	0.25	0.25	0.25	0.25	1	1	1	1	3	3	3	3

Rise per month	5%
Beginning pieces of razor	6,000

Pricing policy	January	February	March	April	May	June	July	August	September	October	November	December	Mean value
Razor + blades (base)	5.9	5.9	5.9	5.9	6.5	6.5	6.5	6.5	6.5	6.5	6.5	6.5	6.34
Blades	3.9	3.9	3.9	3.9	3.5	3.5	3.5	3.5	3	3	3	3	3.14

Sales budget

Sales budget break down	January	February	March	April	May	June	July	August	September	October	November	December	Total
Razor + blade (base)	6,000	6,300	6,615	6,946	7,293	7,658	8,041	8,443	8,865	9,308	9,773	10,262	95,504
Blades	1,500	1,575	1,654	1,737	7,293	7,658	8,041	8,443	26,595	27,924	29,319	30,786	152,525

Sales budget (values – €)	January	February	March	April	May	June	July	August	September	October	November	December	Total
Razor + blade (base)	35,400	37,170	39,029	40,981	47,405	49,777	52,267	54,880	57,623	60,502	63,525	66,703	605,259
Blades	5,850	6,143	6,451	6,774	25,526	26,803	28,144	29,551	79,785	83,772	87,957	92,358	479,112
Total	41,250	43,313	45,479	47,756	72,930	76,580	80,410	84,430	137,408	144,274	151,482	159,061	1,084,371

Production budget

5% of the next month's sales

Break down of production budget

	January	February	March	April	May	June	July	August	September	October	November	December	Total
Sales	6,000	6,300	6,615	6,946	7,293	7,658	8,041	8,443	8,865	9,308	9,773	10,262	95,504
+ Desired ending inventory	315	331	347	365	383	402	422	443	465	489	513	513	
= Available for sale	6,315	6,631	6,962	7,311	7,676	8,060	8,463	8,886	9,330	9,797	10,286	10,775	
− Available beginning inventory	0	315	331	347	365	383	402	422	443	465	489	513	
= Required production in units	6,315	6,316	6,631	6,964	7,311	7,677	8,061	8,464	8,887	9,332	9,797	10,262	96,017

Break down of production budget (blades)

	January	February	March	April	May	June	July	August	September	October	November	December	Total
Sales	1,500	1,575	1,654	1,737	7,293	7,658	8,041	8,443	26,595	27,924	29,319	30,786	152,525
+ Desired ending inventory	79	83	87	365	383	402	422	1,330	1,396	1,466	1,539	1,539	
= Available for sale	1,579	1,658	1,741	2,102	7,676	8,060	8,463	9,773	27,991	29,390	30,858	32,325	
− Available beginning inventory	0	79	83	87	365	383	402	422	1,330	1,396	1,466	1,539	
= Required production in units	1,579	1,579	1,658	2,015	7,311	7,677	8,061	9,351	26,661	27,994	29,392	30,786	154,064

Budgeted schedule of cost of goods manufactured

Production costs	Product Razor + Blades	Blades
Direct materials		
Plastic (grams)	12	
Cost per kilogram (€)	50	
Plastic value per product unit	€0.60	
	(12 × 50/1,000)	
Blade/piece (€)	0.35	0.35
Case/piece (€)	0.20	0.10
Direct materials per unit (€)	€1.15	€1.50
	(0.60 + 0.35 + 0.20)	[(0.35 × 4) + 0.10]
Direct labour		
Cost per hour (mean) in €	25	25
Processing time (min)/razor	4	0
Processing time (min)/blade	0.50	2
Direct labour per unit	€1.88	€0.83
	(25/60 × 4 + 25/60 × 0.50)	(25/60 × 2 × 4)
Manufacturing overhead*	€0.58	€0.58
Total production cost	€3.61	€2.91
	(1.15 + 1.88 + 0.58)	(1.50 + 0.83 + 0.58)

*Manufacturing Overhead Budget

	Amounts in €	Calculations
Indirect materials	34,152	11,042 (96,017 × 1.15 × 10%) + 23,110 (154,064 × 1.5 × 10%)
Managers' salaries	70,000	(2 managers (shifts) × 2,500 × 14)
Machine depreciation	16,000	80,000 × 20%
Maintenance expenses	8,000	10% × 80,000
Machine set-up expenses	4,000	5% × 80,000
Electricity, telephone expenses, etc.	13,215	10% × 132,152
Total overheads	145,366,72	

Allocation of overheads based on breakdown of the products

Number of products	250,081	(96,017 razors + 154,064 blades)
Overhead/unit	0.58	(145,366,72/250,081) = €0.58/piece

Finally, in order to assess whether the new product is efficient in financial terms under alternative conditions, the company prepared three scenarios: the optimistic, the normal, and the pessimistic making different assumptions regarding the sales price of the products, the number of units sold with which the budget will begin and the rate of sales variation. These assumptions are the following:

Parameter	Optimistic scenario	Normal scenario	Pessimistic scenario
Price	Increase 10% compared with the normal scenario	See 'Financial data of the product', point 1, p. 254	Reduction 5% compared with the normal scenario
Beginning sales quantity	Increase 10% compared with the normal scenario	6,000 units (see point 2)	Reduction 2% compared with the normal scenario
Monthly sales variation	Increase 8%	Increase 5%	Increase 2%

The results of the three scenarios in terms of operating income are the following:

	Optimistic scenario	Normal scenario	Pessimistic scenario
Sales	€,1,608,490	€,1,084,371	€ 882,684
Cost of goods sold	1,034,844	788,617	688,729
Gross profit	573,646	295,754	193,955
Selling expenses	104,686	90,832	84,613
Administration expenses	128,679	86,750	70,615
Operating income	€ 340,280	€ 118,172	€ 38,727

From the above analysis, it is obvious that in case the pessimistic scenario is verified, the sales as well as the profitability of the new product will certainly be lower in comparison to the figures of the normal scenario by 18.63 per cent and 67.23 per cent, respectively. On the other hand, in case the optimistic scenario comes true then sales and operating income will be increased by 48.33 per cent and 187.95 per cent respectively in relation to the normal scenario. It has to be noted, though, that under any scenario the new product seems to be a profit-making project.

Notes

1 This appendix was prepared by Dr Sandra Cohen, Lecturer in Accounting at the Athens University of Economics and Business, under the guidance of Professor George J. Avlonitis.
2 For a discussion on these methods, see any basic accounting textbook.
3 The name of the company is disguised for confidentiality reasons.

Further reading

Drury, C. (2004) *Management and Cost Accounting*, 6th edition. London: Thomson Learning.
Hilton, R., Maher, M. and Selto, F. (2002) *Cost Management: Strategies for Business Decisions*, International edition, 2nd edition. New York: McGraw Hill.
Horngren, C.T., Foster, G. and Datar, S. (2003) *Cost Accounting: A Managerial Emphasis*, 11th edition. Englewood Cliffs, NJ: Prentice Hall International Editions.
Schmidt, R. and Wright, H. (1996) *Financial Aspects of Marketing*. Basingstoke: Macmillan Business Press.

Index